Palgrave Socio-Legal Studies

The Palgrave Socio-Legal Studies series is a developing series of monographs and textbooks featuring cutting edge work which, in the best tradition of socio-legal studies, reach out to a wide international audience.

Sharon Cowan · Simon Halliday
Editors

Socio-Legal Generation

Essays in Honour of Michael Adler

palgrave
macmillan

Editors
Sharon Cowan
School of Law
University of Edinburgh
Edinburgh, UK

Simon Halliday
Law School
University of Strathclyde
Glasgow, UK

ISSN 2947-9274 ISSN 2947-9282 (electronic)
Palgrave Socio-Legal Studies
ISBN 978-3-031-67243-9 ISBN 978-3-031-67244-6 (eBook)
https://doi.org/10.1007/978-3-031-67244-6

Cover illustration: imageBROKER/Peter Fischer/Gettyimages

This Palgrave Macmillan imprint is published by the registered company Springer Nature Switzerland AG
The registered company address is: Gewerbestrasse 11, 6330 Cham, Switzerland

Contents

Notes on Contributors

T. T. Arvind is a professor at the University of York. His research draws on frameworks from across the social sciences to develop new ways of understanding the relationship between law, individuals and governing bodies, particularly in the context of commercial societies.

Dave Cowan is the Journal of Law and Society Professor of Socio-Legal Studies at Cardiff University. He specialises in housing and socio-legal studies.

Sharon Cowan is the professor of Feminist and Queer Legal Studies at the University of Edinburgh School of Law. She researches in the fields of law, gender and sexuality, criminal law and asylum law.

Shelley Eder is a lecturer in Law at the Charles Darwin University, Australia. She is currently undertaking PhD research into correctional institutions and has practised as a community lawyer, mostly in the area of social security law.

Jackie Gulland is a senior lecturer in Social Work at the University of Edinburgh. Her research concerns social security and social care, with a particular focus on gender, disability, ageing and care.

Simon Halliday is a professor of Socio-Legal Studies at the University of Strathclyde. His research examines law in everyday life, with a particular focus on administrative justice.

Paul W. Fay Henman is Professor of Digital Sociology and Social Policy at The University of Queensland and a Chief Investigator of the Australian

Research Council Centre of Excellence for Automated Decision Making and Society. He researches the use of automation and Artificial Intelligence in government.

Robert A. Kagan is Emeritus Professor of Political Science and Law, University of California, Berkeley. His scholarship has included works on comparative legal institutions and on regulatory decision-making, enforcement and compliance.

Gráinne McKeever is a professor of Law and Social Justice at Ulster University School of Law. She researches in the fields of social security and access to justice.

Linda Mulcahy is the statutory chair of Socio-Legal Studies at the University of Oxford. Her research focuses on the dynamics of disputes, user experiences of the legal system, human-led design and qualitative methodology.

Jonathan Simon is the Lance Robbins Professor of Criminal Justice Law at the University of California, Berkeley. His scholarship concerns the role of crime and criminal justice in governing contemporary societies, risk and the law, and the history of the interdisciplinary study of law.

Sara Stendahl is Professor in Public Law at The Department of Law, The School of Business, Economics and Law, Gothenburg University, Sweden. Her main fields of research are social security law, social welfare law and law and social justice.

Lindsay Stirton is a professor of Public Law at the University of Sussex. He has researched widely in the fields of public law and regulation and the history of public law and public administration.

Sally Wheeler is Vice-Chancellor of Birkbeck, University of London. She is a socio-legal scholar working on company and contract law.

List of Figures

1

Introduction

Simon Halliday and Sharon Cowan

Introduction

The history of socio-legal studies in the UK is now well known (Thomas 1997; Wheeler 2020). Beginning in the early 1970s, the movement grew to a point where, by 2004, roughly half of legal academics were describing themselves as 'socio-legal' (Cownie 2004). Writing in 2023, that proportion has likely increased, with a number of UK universities offering masters programmes in socio-legal studies.

The growth of socio-legal studies has been associated with post-1960s developments in legal education (Twining 1993), as well as strategic funding initiatives, such as the creation of the Centre for Socio-Legal Studies at Oxford University (Harris 1983). Such attempts to understand and explain the general trajectory of socio-legal studies with the UK, including periods of ebb and flow (Adler and Simon 2014), are both important and persuasive. However, by virtue of the scale at which the enquiry takes place, the efforts of key individuals in championing the growth of socio-legal studies are

S. Halliday
Professor of Socio-Legal Studies, University of Strathclyde, Glasgow, UK
e-mail: simon.halliday@strath.ac.uk

S. Cowan (✉)
Professor of Feminist and Queer Legal Studies, School of Law, University of Edinburgh, Edinburgh, UK
e-mail: s.cowan@ed.ac.uk

S. Cowan and S. Halliday (eds.), *Socio-Legal Generation*, Palgrave Socio-Legal Studies,
https://doi.org/10.1007/978-3-031-67244-6_1

inevitably (and understandably) overlooked in favour of a focus on broader institutional forces.

Yet, if we were to 'zoom in' and conduct a more micro-level analysis of the success of socio-legal studies in the UK, we would discover the role that individual scholars have played. As Thomas observes in his history of the socio-legal movement (Thomas 1997), there was a first generation of socio-legal scholars who recognised the value and potential of a social scientific approach to the study of law and legal phenomena, and whose sustained and collective efforts helped the discipline to flourish.

This collection of essays acknowledges and celebrates the contributions of one member of that first generation of scholars, Michael Adler. Throughout his career, Mike Adler championed the importance of socio-legal studies. Through both his teaching and research, he pushed forward the socio-legal agenda, particularly within Scotland, where he spent his career. He led by example, demonstrating through his own research the necessity of understanding law in its social contexts, and the importance of interdisciplinarity. Through his teaching, he encouraged and trained others to do likewise.

In this introductory essay, we offer a bird's-eye view of Mike's contributions to the success of socio-legal studies as an intellectual movement in the UK. We focus, first, on his teaching, before going on to examine some of the key themes and questions that animated his own research, situating them in relation to the essays that populate the remainder of this collection of essays, and focusing throughout on the depth and breadth of Mike's influence on the development of the field of socio-legal studies.

Mike Adler's Teaching of Socio-Legal Studies

This part of the introduction offers a sense of Mike's pedagogical influence over the years, and his academic collegiality and friendship. Both of the co-authors met Mike in the 1990s as a result of Mike having been the external examiner for Simon's PhD, one of the many doctoral students that Mike has supervised, mentored or examined in his long career. If we fast forward nine years to 2008–2009, Sharon was convening an interdisciplinary masters level research training course with Mike in the School of Social Policy, University of Edinburgh, called 'Key Issues in Law and Society Research'. Such experiences of being pedagogically alongside Mike have influenced both of these co-authors in profound ways.

Mike's approach to examining and teaching has always been Freirean in its resistance to the 'banking' model of learning, where the teacher holds the knowledge that is deposited into students as passive learners, rather than students and teachers constructing knowledge together through curious engagement with the world (Friere 1970). Instead, for Friere, the teacher is a 'catalyst, or animator' creating space for students to "become creative subjects of the learning process rather than passive objects" (Calder 2012; 223). Mike is one such 'animator'—his pedagogical practice is that as a teacher he learns as much from the students, regardless of their status, as they do from him. This speaks to his own openness to and excitement for critical knowledge production, and in part this is due to his lifetime commitment to academic knowledge as a tool for activism and social change, as explored in Mulcahy's chapter in this collection (Chapter 2).

Being present in this pedagogical space with Mike is a little unpredictable; when he suddenly seizes upon an idea that pleases him, his body and mind engage, literally as well as metaphorically, in a little dance of delight at its expression. When this happens, he speaks loudly, quickly and effusively, sometimes waving his arms around to embrace the moment of shared inspiration. In these moments, his enthusiasm for this Freirean co-learning approach is tangible and contagious—not only in his impassioned intellectual interactions with students and co-teachers alike, but in the way he literally *leans in* to the educational process. And it is this curiosity about people and their ideas that bring his classroom to life, allowing his students to feel listened to and valued, and confidently able to bring those ideas to fruition. In generating this kind of open, creative kind of environment for students and co-teachers, Mike's classroom is a challenging and dynamic, transformative space for learning.

Importantly, and unsurprisingly, Mike's teaching has been interdisciplinary, too. This reminds us that what might seem to be neat compartments or silos, within university studies and beyond, have more porous parameters than we might think—not only conceptually, but also in practice when defining and addressing problems of social justice and inequity that need to be solved. Along the way, Mike collaborated and conversed with those he learned from, bringing their insights into co-taught interdisciplinary classrooms. In so doing, Mike has often pointed to the work of influential legal and criminological scholars and interlocutors, for example, in law and legal theory—such as Neil MacCormick (e.g., MacCormick 1994), in legal pluralism—such as Anne Griffiths (e.g., Griffiths 2002), in constitutional law—such as Tony Bradley (e.g., Adler and Bradley 1975) and criminology/criminal justice—such as David Garland (e.g., Garland 2016). But Mike has also always been keen to promote the work of emerging scholars in empirical legal studies. This includes the work of some of the authors in this edited collection, as well as that of others whose work he has admired or with whom he has collaborated.

The present co-authors, who both come from a background of legal training, have enjoyed many conversations and learning moments with Mike, where he seems to know more about the law than either of us. The literature and language of social justice, as conceptualised in the world of social welfare and administrative policy that Mike inhabits, have also left deep impressions on us both, as teachers and academics. Presenting reflexive opportunities to encounter interdisciplinarity in teaching and writing about social justice is one of the many gifts that Mike has bequeathed to law and policymakers, students, teachers and academic colleagues across the UK and beyond.

Mike Adler's Research Within Socio-Legal Studies

As Linda Mulcahy notes in her short biography of Mike (Chapter 2 in this collection), he has been one of the most influential people of his generation—the first generation of UK socio-legal scholars—in the development of the discipline. Unusually, given the fact that socio-legal studies have mainly been a feature of law schools in the UK, Mike spent his career within the discipline of social policy. A key and enduring concern of his research career was social security. Yet, given that social security benefits are always creatures of statute, that the implementation processes in the street-level agencies of the welfare state are subject to the governance of administrative law, and that social security claimants are frequently afforded (on paper, at least) mechanisms of legal redress, Mike was unavoidably drawn to law; and, as Mulcahy notes, Mike collaborated with legal scholars from the outset. To some degree, this was as a result of his early friendships with some of the members of Edinburgh University School of Law, and the influence of his first wife Ruth, who had been a legal theory PhD student at the University of Edinburgh. But given his position as a social scientist studying a feature of social policy that is saturated with legalities, Mike was, we might say, 'naturally' socio-legal and interdisciplinary, as well as markedly collaborative. Whereas many legal scholars have been drawn to the social sciences because of a frustration with the limits of purely doctrinal or legal-philosophical scholarship (e.g., Bradney 1998; Cotterrell 2002), Mike, as a social scientist, was drawn to law because of the necessity of socio-legal enquiry for the broader understanding of social policy and social justice.

Whilst Mike's research career maintained its focus on social security policy and administration, his work touched on and developed a number of key themes and questions that have been of wider significance in the development of socio-legal studies. As Paul Henman notes in his chapter in this volume (Chapter 3), Mike has been concerned from the very earliest stages of his career with what Charles Epp later described as the challenge of 'making rights real' (Epp 2009). The three decades following the Second World War—the 'Golden Age' of the welfare state (Esping-Andersen 1996)—witnessed a growth of rights of entitlement in social security. Yet rights on paper are only worthwhile if taken up and exercised by those they target. And as various studies across disciplines and jurisdictions have demonstrated, there is much that can stand in the way of the exercise of legal rights by those who hold them (e.g., Bumiller 1988; Cowan and Halliday 2003; Brodkin and Majmundar 2010; Roman 2016). This was the challenge examined in some of Mike's early work with his colleague, Du Feu, where the UK government in the 1970s was attempting to increase the take-up of means-tested social security benefits through the use of a computerised information system. The purpose of the assistive technology was to inform would-be claimants about their entitlements. Yet, it had little effect on take-up rates. Adler and Du Feu point to the complexity of people's interactions with welfare systems and welfare bureaucracies: the challenge of 'making rights real' frequently cannot be solved by a simple solution of information provision.

It is noteworthy that Mike was exploring the significance of information technology for social security administration in the mid-1970s—an issue that has now become particularly prominent in the current age of 'the digital welfare state' (van Zoonen 2020; Kersing et al. 2022; Halliday et al. 2024). In his chapter, Henman uses Adler and Du Feu's work as a springboard for exploring the ethical use of artificial intelligence in contemporary government. He also draws on Mike's later contributions to our understanding of administrative justice to advance a 'Just AI' agenda, arguing that the various rationales for deploying and evaluating algorithms/AI within governmental operations map onto the legitimating goals of Adler's models of administrative justice. More broadly, however, Henman argues that AI fairness is not an attribute of its algorithmic design. Rather, developers and deployers of AI must give greater attention to the social and organisational context of their use. And for that, Henman suggests, a 'socio-technical' view of fairness is required: AI starts with society, not the technology, he argues. And in this conviction, we can see the traces of the work Mike conducted almost 50 years ago.

Dave Cowan and Sally Wheeler in their chapter (Chapter 4) review a collection of essays that emerged from a series of seminars convened by Mike and his colleague Stuart Asquith in the late 1970s. The book, published in 1981, explored the issue of discretion in relation to the workings of the welfare state (Adler and Asquith 1981). The question of discretion's relationship to law became a central and enduring one in the development of socio-legal studies from the 1970s onwards. The programme of work pursued, for example, at the Centre for Socio-Legal Studies at Oxford University during the 1980s and beyond—particularly in relation to the development and operations of the regulatory state—did much to deepen our understanding of the uses of discretion by the officers and agencies of the welfare state, and their significance for law in society. Keith Hawkins' collection of essays captured the socio-legal importance and complexity of the law-discretion nexus particularly well, it is suggested (Hawkins 1992). Yet, as Cowan and Wheeler note, Mike's earlier collection of essays co-produced with Asquith was the pathbreaker in the socio-legal exploration of discretion. Moreover, as they put it, "the assembled cast of scholars now reads as an assembly of the founding parents of socio-legal studies".

Cowan and Wheeler draw our attention to the themes which Mike and Stuart Asquith focused on, particularly around the relationship between discretion, law and power. Their analysis centred on power differentials in the encounter between social security claimants and welfare bureaucrats and pointed to the importance of interrogating the relationship between structure and agency. Cowan and Wheeler reflect on how these early insights have become central to much later socio-legal analysis, illustrating their continuing relevance to their own work: on the regulation of housing standards in the private rented sector; and on the disqualification of directors of failed companies under the Company Directors Disqualification Act 1986. As they note, Mike's early analysis suggested key themes for socio-legal analysis that have become standard and have ongoing significance: the micro-physics of power; how discretion apparently written into legislation comes to be used against the interests of the poor; and how professional and lay knowledges combine with unequal outcomes.

Shelley Eder in her chapter (Chapter 5) focuses on a monograph Mike published in 1994 with Brian Longhurst, which focuses at length on questions of the legitimacy of prisons—both substantively in terms of the appropriate ends to be pursued through imprisonment, and procedurally in terms of the ways in which a prison might be run in pursuit of those ends. The question of the legitimacy of power, pioneered in Weber's work (Weber 1978), has become one of criminology's enduring concerns. Most famously, perhaps, the work of Tom Tyler around courts and policing (e.g., Tyler 2006) has examined the relationship between the procedural justice of citizens' encounters with legal institutions or legal officials and their assessments of the legitimacy of law. The procedural justice and legitimacy research agenda, whilst focusing largely on policing, has also been extended to prisons (Sparks and Bottoms 1995). Yet, Mike and Brian Longhurst's earlier insight, reading across from the socio-legal administrative justice literature, was that procedural justice should be framed in plural terms. Drawing on the work of the US legal scholar, Jerry Mashaw (1983), this enabled them to posit three competitive 'models' of procedural justice, or, as they put it, three 'means discourses' as regards the administration of the prison.

As Eder notes in her chapter, Adler and Longhurst's work significantly enhanced our understanding of the internal dynamics of the penal institution: "part of the book's appeal is that it turns the lens of administrative justice to the field of penology, and by doing so lays the groundwork for a reframing of penal power in terms of the institutional forces on which it rests". Eder uses their study as a stimulus to extend that enquiry deeper into the everyday dynamics of the work of prison officers. In a highly innovative way, Eder proposes the use of peer-to-peer discussions in an online forum to interrogate the extent to which, and the ways in which, the ideal–typical 'ends' and 'means' discourses posited by Mike and Brian Longhurst are reflected in the routines of prison officers and their recurring interactions with inmates. Her argument is that the question of how power is understood and legitimated by prison officers is central to our understanding of carceral authority. And through the exploration of prison officers' perspectives, we may develop and extend the work of Mike and Brian Longhurst, she suggests, allowing for the inclusion of more informally generated legitimacy narratives.

The influence of Jerry Mashaw's work on Mike's research, noted above, is taken forward in Chapter 6 by Arvind, Halliday and Stirton. As they note, Mike has made a major contribution to administrative justice theory by interpreting and extending Mashaw's pioneering typology of 'bureaucratic justice' (Mashaw 1983). At the heart of Mashaw's analysis of bureaucratic justice was the conviction that procedural legitimacy is contested and should be thought of in plural terms. Mike extended that line of thought, recognising that Mashaw was writing in the early 1980s, before neoliberalism had gained its full strength. Consequently, twenty years later, he re-interpreted Mashaw's work for the age of New Public Management (Hood 1991), acknowledging that legitimacy narratives rooted in the logic of the market were now firmly embedded in the world of public administration, and to be taken seriously in its study.

Yet, whilst Mike's 2003 article (Adler 2003) has been very influential, it has not been without its critics. Arvind et al. push back at the critics somewhat, offering a more constructive way of reading his article. They emphasise that Mike implicitly invites the administrative justice scholar to think about 'administrative justice systems', and not merely administrative decision-making processes. In bringing modes of redress into his typology of administrative justice, Mike reminds us that there is more to administrative justice than the initial decision a citizen receives about their entitlements, needs or obligations: there is also the possibility of redress. In combination, we might frame them as two elements of larger administrative justice systems. In this vein, Arvind et al. reinterpret Mike's work through the lens of 'grid-group cultural theory' (Douglas 1982), an analytical framework that proposes a set of four basic 'thought styles' that underpin cultural phenomena. This re-reading of Mike's work suggests that his extension of Mashaw's work can itself be extended. Arvind et al. identify two thought styles that have been under-played in Mike's work, but which merit serious consideration: first, because one of the thought styles seems already to be evident in strands of public law thinking outwith the narrower confines of administrative justice scholarship; second, because we might expect to see growing evidence of the other thought style around administrative justice in the contemporary world. In such thinking, there may be an emphasis on the conferral of unchecked power and the importance of 'getting things done' under a rubric of protecting the interests of 'the real people'. With some hesitation—and perhaps trepidation—Arvind et al. warn that narratives of administrative justice may soon require updating for an age of populism.

The theme of populism and its significance for the stability of administrative states of the sort analysed by Adler and others is taken forward by Bob Kagan in Chapter 7. Kagan notes that, within much administrative justice literature, the stability and public-regarding posture of the administrative state as a whole is taken for granted. Our discussions of models of administrative justice, and our explorations hitherto of the dynamics that affect the fairness of bureaucratic decision-making, rest on an unchallenged sense that the administrative state and its tradition of impartial public administration for the promotion of general welfare is a stable and permanent feature of society. Yet, there are now good reasons, Kagan suggests, for questioning that quiet confidence. Perhaps, he counsels, we should take seriously the possibility that the administrative state is at some risk. Using recent American experience as a case study in the politics of the administrative state, Kagan focuses on President Donald Trump's stated intent to 'deconstruct' the federal regulatory state. He examines the features of the US political system that renders it vulnerable to efforts to weaken it, as well as recent political and legal developments that have intensified the threat of such weakening. He also considers the significant institutional and cultural sources of resistance to such a threat.

The creation of a simultaneously populist and plutocratic anti-statist Republican party in the United States, together with a federal judiciary staffed with many ideologically sympathetic judges, certainly threatens the American administrative-regulatory state that has characterised American governance in the last 70 years, Kagan suggests. Yet, at the same time, there is an enduring pro-government strain in American political culture, he observes, rooted in the technologically and organisationally sophisticated nature of advanced societies: where governments have the capacity to devise and implement programmes to prevent serious risks of harm, a cultural expectation of doing so follows. And whilst Kagan acknowledges the risks of predicting the future, he ultimately places his bet on the survival of the administrative state: "conservative backlashes against the administrative-regulatory state may recur as well, but … it is more likely that they will merely delay the further expansion of the administrative-regulatory state than deconstruct it".

As Mike progressed through his career, like many socio-legal scholars he became increasingly preoccupied with the effects of neoliberalism for society and the role played by law within neoliberalism (e.g., Collier 2014; Barlow et al. 2017; Valenzuela and Cordero 2023). Adler viewed policies of welfare conditionality as an expression of neoliberalism within the social security field. Neoliberalism tends towards an association of welfare needs with social deviance, at least in relation to mainstream unemployment (Garland 2016). It is a cultural narrative that stresses individual responsibility more than collective solidarity, whereby poverty is better explained by reference to agency as opposed to structure. The consequences, according to Mike, could be seen in punitive policies of the sanctioning of welfare claimants where they failed to comply with various conditions of social security entitlement. He subjected these welfare practices to a powerful critique in his 2018 monograph, *Cruel, Inhuman or Degrading Treatment? Benefit Sanctions in the UK* (Adler 2018).

Gráinne McKeever picks up this theme in her chapter in this volume (Chapter 8). Yet she also connects it to a parallel challenge for social security policy, one that has been an enduring concern for Mike throughout his career: the barriers welfare claimants face in challenging decisions they feel are wrong. In connecting the problems of a neoliberal narrative around welfare conditionality with access to justice failures as regards rights of redress, McKeever highlights the considerable risks of administrative *in*justice that remain for social security claimants. She also recognises and stresses the importance of Mike's contributions to this challenge. The response, she suggests, consistent with aspects of Mike's work too, may revolve around fundamental social rights: core rights that reflect a Marshallian vision of social citizenship (Marshall & Bottomore 1992).

In Chapter 9 in this volume, Sara Stendahl continues this theme of human rights and access to social entitlements, focusing in particular on the historical and contemporary regulation of street begging in Sweden. Again, building on Mike's analysis of punitive welfare sanctions (Adler 2018), and the link between extreme inequality and the erosion of solidarity, Stendahl examines both the normative clash of values and the scramble for political power manifested in the conflict between local and national approaches to the criminalisation of begging. Arguments in favour of banning begging, which have disproportionate effects for the Swedish Roma-minority, and ignore historic and systemic exclusion and assimilation polices, are increasingly being mounted at a municipal level, notwithstanding recent European Court of Human Rights judgments supporting rights that protect against destitution. Using the concept of 'pragmatic decency', Stendahl critiques the legal response to begging as an indication of a shrinking welfare state and argues for the protection of begging not simply as an expression of free speech, but as a social—and human—right.

Issues of human rights, austerity and administrative justice are taken forward in the final chapter of this collection (Chapter 10), where Jackie Gulland revisits some of the questions that animated her PhD, supervised by Mike 20 years ago. Her topic then was administrative justice and social care, and in her chapter she revisits the topic in light of two major developments that have occurred since she began her doctoral research: the embedding of human rights law within the UK legal systems; and austerity. Social care is a particularly interesting topic for an administrative justice lens because it is a service that combines public sector professionalism (in the form of social work expertise) with private sector service provision. Those in need of social care thus find themselves as both citizens and clients. And whilst they have a legal right to a needs assessment, they do not have any absolute rights to social care itself.

Gulland's review finds that there is only limited evidence of practical change in enabling access to social care services across the UK's four nations in the last 20 years. The economic realities of austerity have significantly stymied efforts to resource equal and full access to social care and continue to negatively affect most decision-making about social care services, notwithstanding promising rhetoric. As for human rights, social work professional values certainly point to the importance of human rights thinking in assessments for social care. Thus, there is, Gulland suggests, potential for radical reconsideration of how social care might work. Yet, again, whilst there has been some positive rhetoric in this regard, there is little sign of sufficient funding being in place to enable meaningful implementation in the near future. And for as long as there is no specific right to services, it is difficult to imagine, she suggests, how a rights-based appeal process would work in practice, although the principle of a right to challenge a decision may enable people to recognise their right to participate in the process.

Conclusions

It is clear from the contributions to this volume of essays that Mike's work has had a profound and continuing legacy. He has engaged with a range of questions and ideas that have been central to socio-legal studies, pushing forward and enriching its intellectual agenda. Yet, Mike's legacy is not just restricted to the development of ideas, we would suggest. One of the facets of Mike's career that emerges clearly from our 'bird's-eye view' of some of his main contributions is that he has long worked in a deeply collaborative way. Indeed, alongside his intellectual curiosity, one of Mike's most appealing and enduring qualities is that of loyalty. Having recognised a person's ideas as interesting, Mike becomes that person's champion, closely reading their work and extolling their virtues at every available opportunity, regardless of their status as a student, early career academic or more seasoned professor. Countless academics have benefited from this intellectual largesse, some of whom have received an unsolicited email from Mike telling them that he has read their insightful and provocative book, article or report, and that he would like to engage them in conversation about it or invite them to participate in an event or publication he is organising. As a constructively critical academic friend, or as a research collaborator, Mike is a powerful ally. He has been without doubt enormously influential for generations of scholars in ways we cannot fully recount here, building capacity and inspiring new work in immeasurable ways.

Outwith the academy, we must add, he is also the most generous and inclusive sort of friend one could hope for. We hope that in bringing together this collection of scholars, we can reflect back to Mike not only how important his work and his pedagogy have been across the last five decades, but also how much we, and the others in this book, would like to offer our respect and admiration, and to thank him for being quintessentially and inimitably, Mike.

References

Adler, M. (2003). A Socio-Legal Approach to Administrative Justice. *Law and Policy, 25*(4), 323–352.

Adler, M. (2018). *Cruel, Inhuman or Degrading Treatment? Benefit Sanctions in the UK*. Basingstoke: Palgrave Pivot.

Adler, M., and Asquith, S. (eds.). (1981). *Discretion and Welfare*. London: Heinemann.

Adler, M., and Bradley, A. (eds.). (1975). *Justice, Discretion and Poverty*. Abingdon: Professional Books.

Adler, M., and Simon, J. (2014). Stepwise Progression: The Past, Present and Possible Future of Empirical Research on Law in the United States and the United Kingdom. *Journal of Law and Society, 41*(2), 173–202.

Barlow, A., Hunter, R., Smithson, J., and Ewing, J. (2017). *Mapping Paths to Family Justice: Resolving Family Disputes in Neoliberal Times*. London: Palgrave Macmillan.

Bradney, A. (1998). Law as a Parasitic Discipline. *Journal of Law and Society, 25*(1), 71–84.

Brodkin, E., and Majmundar, M. (2010). Administrative Exclusion: Organisations and the Hidden Costs of Welfare Claiming. *Journal of Public Administration Research and Theory, 20*, 827–848.

Bumiller, K. (1988). *The Civil Rights Society: The Social Construction of Victims*. Johns Hopkins University Press.

Calder, G. (2012). Performance, Pedagogy and Law: Theatre of the Oppressed in the Law School Classroom. In Z. Bańkowski and M. Del Mar (eds.), *The Moral Imagination and the Legal Life: Beyond Text in Legal Education*. Routledge.

Collier, R. (2014). 'Love Law, Love Life': Neoliberalism, Wellbeing and Gender in the Legal Profession—The Case of Law School. *Legal Ethics, 17*(2), 202–230.

Cotterrell, R. (2002). Subverting Orthodoxy, Making Law Central: A View of Sociolegal Studies. *Journal of Law & Society, 29*(4), 632–644.

Cowan, D., and Halliday, S. (2003). *The Appeal of Internal Review: The (Non-) emergence of Disputes*. Oxford: Hart Publishing.

Cownie, F. (2004). *Legal Academics: Cultures and Identities*. Oxford: Hart Publishing.

Douglas, M. (1982). Introduction to Grid-Group Analysis. In Mary Douglas (ed.), *Essays in the Sociology of Perception*. Abingdon: Routledge and Kegan Paul.

Epp, Charles. 2009. *Making Rights Real: Activists, Bureaucrats, and the Creation of the Legalistic State*. Chicago: Chicago University Press.

Esping-Andersen, G. (1996). After the Golden Age? Welfare State Dilemmas in a Global Economy. In G. Esping-Andersen (ed.), *Welfare States in Transition: National Adaptations in Global Economies*. London: Sage Publications.

Friere, P. (1970). *The Pedagogy of the Oppressed*. Herder and Herder.

Garland, D. (2016). *The Welfare State: A Very Short Introduction.* Oxford: Oxford University Press.
Griffiths, A. (2002). Legal Pluralism? In R. Banakar and M. Travers (eds.), *An Introduction to Law and Social Theory*, pp. 289–310. Oxford and Portland Oregon: Hart Publishing.
Halliday, S., Meers, J., and Tomlinson, J. (2024). Procedural Legitimacy Logics Within the Digital Welfare State. *Journal of Social Security Law 31*(1), 64–81.
Harris, D. (1983). The Development of Socio-Legal Studies in the United Kingdom. *Legal Studies, 3,* 315–333.
Hawkins, K. (ed.). (1992). *The Uses of Discretion.* Oxford: Oxford University Press.
Hood, C. (1991). A Public Management for All Seasons? *Public Administration, 69*(1), 3–19.
Kersing, M. van Zoonen, L. Putters, K., and Oldenhof, L. (2022). The Changing Roles of Frontline Bureaucrats in the Digital Welfare State. *Data & Policy, 4,* 1.
MacCormick, N. (1994). Four Quadrants of Jurisprudence. In W. Krawietz, N. MacCormick and G.H. von Wright (eds.), *Prescriptive Formality and Normative Rationality in Modern Legal Systems*, pp. 53–70. Berlin: Duncker and Humblot.
Marshall, T. H., and Bottomore, T. (1992). *Citizenship and Social Class.* London: Pluto.
Mashaw, J. (1983). *Bureaucratic Justice: Managing Social Security Disability Claims.* New Haven: Yale University Press.
Roman, D. (2016). France. In S. Civitarese Matteucci and S. Halliday (eds.), *Social Rights in Europe in an Age of Austerity.* London: Routledge.
Sparks, J. R., and Bottoms, A. E. (1995). Legitimacy and Order in Prisons. *British Journal of Criminology, 46*(1), 45.
Thomas, P. (1997). Socio-Legal Studies: The Case of Disappearing Fleas and Bustards. In P. Thomas (ed.), *Socio-Legal Studies.* Aldershot: Dartmouth.
Tyler, T. (2006). *Why People Obey the Law*, 2nd ed. Princeton: Princeton University Press.
Twining, W. (1993). Remembering 1972: The Oxford Centre in the Context of Developments in Higher Education and the Discipline of Law. *Journal of Law and Society, 22*(Special Issue), 35–49.
Valenzuela, R., and Cordero, R. (2023). The Making of Neoliberal Legality: The Legal Imagination of Business Elites and the 'Social Constitutionalization' of 'Free Enterprise' in Latin America. *Journal of Law and Society, 50*(4), 517–537. https://doi.org/10.1111/jols.12451.
van Zoonen, L. (2020). Data Governance and Citizen Participation in the Digital Welfare State. *Data & Policy, 2,* 1.
Weber, M. (1978). *Economy and Society.* Berkeley: University of California Press.
Wheeler, S. (2020). Socio-Legal Studies in 2020. *Journal of Law and Society, 47*(S2), S209–S226.

2

The Man, His Politics and Intellectual Origins: A Short Biography of Mike Adler

Linda Mulcahy

Introduction

Mike Adler has been one of the most influential people of his generation in the development of socio-legal studies in Europe. With degrees in Chemistry, Economics and Political Science, and Sociology, he is increasingly unusual in the UK socio-legal movement in coming from the 'socio' disciplines. This chapter explores the stories behind his impressive curriculum vitae; focusing on the factors that have fuelled his life-long interest in street-level bureaucracies, justice and the welfare state. Far too much material has been collected for the space available and as a result the main emphasis is on the period before he became an established academic. Other contributions in this collection will pick up narratives surrounding his publications and academic influence. The focus here is not on his academic work but on the man who produced it and his motivations for doing so.

This chapter draws on interviews with Mike conducted over a two-day period, correspondence with him and archival research which was only possible once he had sketched out his life. Like other contributions in this collection, it has been a labour of love, and Fig. 2.1 shows Mike doing what he does best, talking, elucidating and challenging an audience. However, it has to be acknowledged that Mike is not the easiest of subjects; claiming throughout the interviews that he has had the good fortune of working with

L. Mulcahy (✉)
Statutory Chair of Socio-Legal Studies, University of Oxford, Oxford, UK
e-mail: linda.mulcahy@csls.ox.ac.uk

S. Cowan and S. Halliday (eds.), *Socio-Legal Generation*, Palgrave Socio-Legal Studies,
https://doi.org/10.1007/978-3-031-67244-6_2

some very able people and does not deserve the treatment given to him in this collection. Along with the editors and my co-contributors, I disagree, and the process of researching his life has only increased my admiration for him. His tireless activism, engagement with the world around him and dogged refusal to ignore unfairness and discrimination are markers of his compassion, generosity and commitment to progressive politics which exists both within, and outside of, his work as an academic. Indeed, as I will argue in this chapter, the connection between his activism and his academic work is symbiotic. His research within the academy has invariably been motivated by what he has experienced outside of it, and his experiences as an activist have challenged him to look beyond the particular in search of broader theories about why things are the way they are and how they could be different.

Fig. 2.1 Mike Adler lecturing in China, 2015

The Early Years

Mike's parents were both refugees from Nazi Germany and met in England after escaping the horrors of the Third Reich. His mother Lia worked as an assistant to a GP who, like her, came from the Monchengladbach in the Rhineland. She later became a very successful schoolteacher. His father Max was an engineer who graduated from the Technical University in Munich who then did a doctorate at the Max Planck Institute in Gottingen. Unfortunately, in 1933, the year in which he obtained his doctorate, engineering and other professions were barred to Jewish people in Germany (see further Jarausch 1986). Realising that he had no future in Germany, he moved to Sweden and, nine months later, to London, where he obtained a job as a research engineer with the General Electric Company (GEC). The company was a major British industrial conglomerate involved in the manufacture of consumer products, defence systems, communications and engineering. Later on, when he became redundant, he became a lecturer in engineering at Borough Polytechnic (now South Bank University).

Mike was born in 1942, followed, three years later, by his sister Jane. He lived for the first seven years of his life with his family in Sidcup, a suburb in Southeast London. When he was seven, following the relocation of GEC's research laboratories to Wembley in North West London, his family moved across London to Pinner. Served by the Metropolitan Railway, this was classic 'Metroland' where urban expansion had occurred in tandem with the railway.[1] John Betjeman was later to describe the area as a child of the First World War which had been forgotten by the second.[2] Although Mike was to live in Pinner until he left home for University in 1960, he demonstrated sympathy with this sentiment by claiming no abiding connection to it.

Mike does not consider himself to be religious but acknowledges that his religious heritage forms an important part of his identity. For many years, he edited the *Edinburgh Star*, the magazine of the Edinburgh Jewish Community. He also served as President of the Edinburgh Jewish Literary Society for two periods and on the Management Committee of the local Synagogue. His parents' experience of the horrors of the Third Reich left a much more profound effect on his family. Mike's mother worked tirelessly to arrange for two of her siblings to leave Germany and settle in England. This was a feat she achieved, but her parents were murdered in Sobibor, an extermination

[1] Later known as the Metropolitan Line.

[2] See further *Metro-land* (1973 film), a BBC TV documentary (1973) narrated by Sir John Betjeman about the area and directed by directed by Edward Mirzoeff.

camp in Poland. This tragedy left its mark. In Mike's view his mother never really got over it and his parents refused to go back to Germany for many years. In all other ways Mike enjoyed a happy middle-class upbringing with extremely tolerant liberal parents.[3] At a time when many of Mike's friends were busy rebelling against their parents, he felt that he had the good fortune to have nothing to rebel against. It seems natural to wonder, however, how much his parents' experiences have fuelled Mike's life-long outrage against racism and discrimination.

Mike passed his eleven plus exam and progressed to the local selective grammar school, Harrow County School.[4] Figure 2.2 shows Mike in his second year at the school in 1954, third from the left in the middle row. Other records in the school archive record him taking part in the drama society productions in successive years at the school. His debut was as Hermia in Midsummer Night's Dream in his second year and his final role was as Roderigo, a Venetian gentleman in Othello, in his final year in 1960.[5] Acting pursuits were not the only extra-curricular activities at the school. There was considerable pressure on boys joining either the cadet force or the scouts. Unenthusiastic about the idea of boys playing soldiers and the militaristic ethos associated with the cadets, Mike joined the scouts and remembers several enjoyable camping expeditions with them.

Not all aspects of the school were so palatable. Mike remembers the school as 'terrible, hugely meritocratic'. He also found the Scottish headmaster of the school for the whole period he was there, Dr A R Simpson, to be an 'unpleasant, authoritarian bully'. These negative views have been shared by many others.[6] The official history of the school notes that the years of Dr Simpson's headship were the most nakedly authoritarian period of the school's history. He modelled Harrow County on the leading public schools of the time. This was reflected in his vehement opposition to comprehensive education, his social conservatism, his insistence on a strict hierarchy of

---

[3] An indication of their politics is that they read the *News Chronicle* and then when it ceased circulation *The Guardian*. The *News Chronicle* was a paper owned by the Cadbury family which merged with the Daily Mail in 1960. It has been described as a Liberal party leaning and occasional Labour party supporting paper (Membery 2010).

[4] The eleven plus was an exam for eleven-year-olds in their final year of primary school. It determined whether children should go to grammar schools where they were expected to prepare for university entrance, secondary modern schools or technical colleges. The school ceased being a selective school in 1974 and became a comprehensive school with a different name (Gayton High School) on account of the school being located on Gayton Road in Harrow). Pupils who attended the school are known as Old Gaytonians. The school has since been renamed Harrow High School.

[5] For a collection of Harrow County School for Boys photographs see http://www.jeffreymaynard.com/Harrow_County/index.htm (last accessed September 2023).

[6] See Old Gaytonians recollections of the school at: http://www.jeffreymaynard.com/Harrow_County/History1960s.htm (last accessed September 2023).

Fig. 2.2 Harrow County School for Boys Form 2A 1954

command and the rigorous enforcement of rules relating to school uniform, his expectation that the boys joined either the cadet force or the scouts, the re-introduction of gowns for prefects and his almost obsessional focus on the brightest pupils gaining entry and scholarships to Oxford (May 1975).[7] Dr Simpson's success in achieving the latter is undisputed and on the date of his retirement in 1965 Harrow County School had progressed through national league tables to become the leading state grammar school for getting pupils into Oxford.[8] Judged by Dr Simpson's standards, Mike was a success. He gained an exhibition to study Chemistry at Brasenose College Oxford, following impressive A'level results in Maths, Physics and Chemistry. These early experiences of a strict disciplinary institution go some way to explaining Mike's self-professed and life-long dislike of being told what to do or think.

[7] See further evidence of this in Simpson (1968).

[8] Doubt has been cast on the extent to which this was a successful strategy for those boys at the school who were not destined for Oxford who were frequently marginalised (May 1975).

The Oxford Years

Life at Brasenose College Oxford proved to be much more fun and, while he was there, Mike became involved with a range of societies. The College was all-male at the time, but was one of the first to admit women in 1974.[9] Mike recalls that although it was a very friendly place, it was dominated by athletic boys from public schools. However, he soon found a set of like-minded friends on the left of the political spectrum who were interested in political debate and activism.[10] It is worth noting, given his later prominence as a socio-legal scholar, that Brasenose enjoyed a first-rate reputation for law at the time Mike was there, with fellows including Barry Nicholas, Ron Maudsley and Otto Kahn Freund.[11] While law was not of interest to him at the time, Mike recalls becoming friendly with Barry Nicholas, a much-liked comparative lawyer, who took him under his wing.[12]

Studying Chemistry was a path that Mike drifted into, and it soon became something of a burden. The most able boys at his school had been encouraged to study science but were given no other careers advice. Studying Chemistry required students to spend a lot of time in the laboratory and this increasingly got in the way of his interest in politics. While he was an able scientist and might have gone into medicine, his girlfriend (Ruth), who he subsequently married, persuaded him that this was not where his real interests lay. Despite serious doubts about the subject, Mike completed his four-year Chemistry degree. However, he then transferred to the social sciences by taking a one-year Diploma in Economics and Political Science under the tutelage of A.H. 'Chelly' Halsey, the renowned sociologist of education. Halsey influenced Mike's career path in a number of ways, not least of which was that he encouraged Mike to go to Harvard. Halsey was a friend of Harrison White, a fellow sociologist interested in mathematical modelling who went on to play an influential role in the 'Harvard Revolution' in social networks

---

[9] Brasenose did not admit women until 1971 when it became one of the first colleges to do so (https://www.bnc.ox.ac.uk/about-brasenose/history/212-college-history/397-a-brief-history-of-brasenose), last accessed September 2023. In 1960–1961, the year that Mike started studying in Oxford, there were 7,392 undergraduates at Oxford, 6,321 of whom were men and 1,071 of which were women. The fact that there were only five women's colleges meant that there was fierce competition for places (McLeod 1962).

[10] Contemporaries of Mike have pointed out that relatively few students at Oxford were politically engaged or interested in serious debate and that only about 20 students attended the CND or Socialist Societies (O'Connell 1964).

[11] This appears to be a generally held view. See for instance https://www.bnc.ox.ac.uk/about-brasenose/princblog/1856-principal-s-blog-great-brasenose-lawyers (last accessed September 2023) and Birks (2004). They were later to be joined by Peter Birks and Hugh Collins.

[12] See further the address by Francis Reynolds at Brasenose College, https://www.bnc.ox.ac.uk/downloads/princ_blog/Francis_Reynolds_-_Barry_Nicholas.pdf (last accessed September 2023).

and the New York School of relational sociology. White was looking for a graduate student with a science background to help him with his work and Halsey told Mike that the position 'had his name on it'. The result was that after a further year at Oxford, Mike was awarded a Diploma and moved to the United States with his new wife Ruth, to undertake a PhD at Harvard.

Mike remembers the Social Relations department that he joined at Harvard as a 'crazy dysfunctional place', a department full of 'extinct volcanoes'. The Faculty at the time included Talcott Parsons, George Homans, Seymour Martin Lipset and David Riesman, each of whom ploughed their own furrow and avoided teaching the required courses, which were taught instead by junior Faculty or visiting academics. Parsons made it clear that his graduate seminar was only open to those students who agreed with the basic premises of his approach to sociology.[13] Ever the free thinker, this was an invitation that Mike declined to take up. Instead, he took a course taught by Barrington Moore, a very distinguished neo-Marxist sociologist who worked at the Russian Research Centre. Significantly, Mike was to learn nothing of the sociology of law movement during his time at Harvard and never finished his PhD, leaving to return to England in 1968 after completing his PhD coursework with an MA in Sociology.

Mike returned to Oxford in 1968 to take up an ESRC doctoral studentship at Nuffield College under the supervision of Chelly Halsey. His chosen topic was private medicine and the National Health Service. He recalls that the two years that followed were some of the unhappiest of his life, despite his respect for Halsey and the 'lovely distraction' of his first son being born in 1969. His disquiet was largely due to the competitive and hierarchical nature of the College and tutorials with Fellows he found to be didactic in their approach. Once again, he did not complete his PhD but recalls that not having a doctorate mattered much less then than it does today. He explained that:

> After two heady years in the USA, I returned to the UK, ostensibly to write my thesis, but my funding ran out before I had really got started and it became clear that I needed to apply for a job. In those days, a completed PhD was still an 'optional extra' and I was offered the second job I applied for, a lectureship

[13] Lidz (2021) argues that Parsons was a typical academic liberal of his time. He was an early and active opponent of Nazism in the 1930s and, after the war, argued for government support of the social sciences. In the 1950s, he wrote a famous critical analysis of the McCarthy movement in American politics and, in the 1960s, he contributed supportive essays to the Civil Rights movement. However his structural functional approach to sociology is by its very nature viewed as conservative in that it recognises that a political system's first objective is to ensure its own survival (Lidz 2021; Staubmann 2021; Lipset 1992).

in what was then called 'social administration' at Edinburgh University, with special responsibility for teaching research methods. (Adler 2017)

His years as a doctoral student at Oxford were far from being a waste of time. Halsey's work on the sociology of education inspired Mike's interest in parental rights in education that in turn led to an interest in socio-legal studies.[14] Despite being unsure about what Social Administration was, Mike applied for the job in Edinburgh with the encouragement of Halsey and was appointed. He initially imagined that he would stay for a couple of years but 50 years later he is still there.

The Activist

Mike's activism and interest in politics has been hinted at in the account above but its importance is deserving of much more attention because of the many ways in which his uneasiness about levels of inequality in the world around him has fuelled his academic research. The seeds of his activism were sown early on. Despite the Headmaster banning the discussion of the Campaign for Nuclear Disarmament (CND) during his time at school, Mike was an active member of the movement while at school and went on the early CND Aldermaston marches.[15] Tony Smith, an older boy at school who also went on to Brasenose College, and later became President of Magdalen College, Oxford, recruited him into the Labour Party in Willesden. Mike soon became involved in canvassing for Reg Freeson, Ken Livingstone's predecessor as MP for Brent East. Freeson was a leftwinger with an impressive record of resisting racism, including editing the anti-fascist magazine *Searchlight* from 1964 to 1967. He also opposed the Vietnam War, championed the underprivileged, was a founding member of CND and one of the first five Labour MPs on the initial Aldermaston march (Roth 2006). Mike was very taken with him.[16]

---

[14] Mike was an Associate member of the Edinburgh Centre for Educational Sociology from 1982 to 1996 and published extensively on education during this period.

[15] The Aldermaston marches were anti-nuclear weapons demonstrations in which took place from 1958 to 1965 though there were revivals in 1972 and 2004. Originally organised by the Direct-Action Committee against Nuclear War, they later became closely associated with CND. They took place on Easter weekend from the Atomic Weapons Research Establishment at Aldermaston to London.

[16] *Born in St Pancras*, Reg Freeson was abandoned by his parents when he was 5 years old and brought up until the age of 15 at the Jewish Orphanage in West Norwood, South London. He was elected as the MP for Willesden East in 1964 but was deselected after what was described as 'a bitter struggle' in 1985. He was replaced as Labour candidate in Brent East by Ken Livingstone, who won the seat at the 1987 general election.

According to Mike, he had two passions while at Oxford: the civil rights movement in the US and the anti-apartheid struggle in South Africa. At the end of his first year, together with two friends, Mike went to the USA to take part in a voter registration drive organised by the Student Nonviolent Coordinating Committee (SNCC) in Albany, Georgia.[17] This was far from being a safe activity. Retaliation against those who tried to help people register to vote led to various forms of retribution, including intimidation, violence and even death.[18] Mike had direct experience of this when he was arrested and thrown into a police cell. After demanding to see the British consulate he was eventually released on the understanding that he would get out of town and never come back. Chris Allen, a Brasenose friend of his who later became a colleague at Edinburgh, got shot doing the same work.

Mike was heavily involved with the Joint Action Committee Against Racial Discrimination (JACARI), an organisation founded by Oxford students in 1956 with the aim of raising awareness of racial intolerance in countries such as the US and South Africa amongst students.[19] It did so through a series of student discussion groups, high-profile lectures given by people such as Barbara Castle and James Callaghan, and campaigns and appeals. By the 1960s it claimed to be supported by over 50 University clubs, including all the major political societies, and by the time Mike joined the University it had 1,250 members. A particularly important JACARI initiative was its campaign to raise funds for a South African student to study at Oxford for three years. The first South African to benefit from this campaign was Jeppe Mei who arrived in Oxford in 1959. In due course, Mike was to play an important role in raising funds for Winston Nagan, a graduate of the University of Fort Hare, to study for a BA at Oxford and even persuaded Brasenose College to waive their fees for him. Winston was to go on to enjoy a successful career as an academic lawyer in the US specialising in human rights and international law and to serve as chair of Amnesty International in the US.[20] Mike and Winston became life-long friends.

[17] One of the major goals of the US Civil Rights Movement of the time was to register voters across the 'Deep South' so that African Americans could exercise their rights and gain political power. Voter registration drives involved a variety of activities including driving voters to the polls, teaching literacy classes and encouraging African Americans candidates.

[18] See further https://www.loc.gov/collections/civil-rights-history-project/articles-and-essays/voting-rights/.

[19] Jacari still exists as an educational charity with offices in Oxford and Bristol. Its focus today is on providing free tuition to children who have English as a second language. See further https://www.jacari.org. For a fuller history of the organisation see https://www.jacari.org/history (last accessed September 2023).

[20] See further: http://worldacademy.org/ga-waas60/speakers/winston-nagan (last accessed September 2023).

During his time at Oxford, Mike also joined the staff of *Isis*, the longest-running independent student magazine in the UK,[21] and rose to become its political editor.[22] From the nineteenth century until the end of World War Two *Isis* had primarily been a magazine for trivial student gossip and a painstaking recorder of University minutiae (Billen and Skipworth 1984; Gillman 1964). But there was a significant shift in approach from the late 1950s onwards as the beneficiaries of the 1944 Education Act agitated to bring more serious political debate to the fore. From the 1950s onwards it switched from what Billen and Skipworth (1984) have called an infatuation with the arts to an obsession with politics. By way of example, the 1958 *Isis* special issue on the subject of the bomb caused sufficient controversy that it led to the prosecution of two of the editors.

An analysis of copies of the *Isis* for the four years that Mike was an undergraduate provides extensive evidence of its left-wing leanings in the first half of the 1960s.[23] Alongside its standard diet of poetry, short stories, reviews of lectures, music, films, art, and parochial accounts of student life in Oxford, there was also political commentary on the problems of the press, labour rallies, comprehensive education, racial tensions in Birmingham, CND activity, American civil rights, prison, the future of the Labour party, and inequality of opportunity and profiles of workers at Cowley.[24] Mike recalls that, as political editor, he didn't write very much. Most of his time was taken up commissioning articles from the likes of Tariq Ali, Mary Kaldor and Fred Halliday; attending weekly editorial board meetings; copy editing and ensuring that the articles he commissioned were submitted on time or that there was a reasonable spread of political articles in every issue. He did, however, write the occasional piece, including an article on 'Democracy in America' (Adler 1963) and a letter to the editor, co-authored with his friend Chris Allen, criticising inaccuracies in accounts of the American civil rights movement and extolling the virtues of Martin Luther King (Adler and Allen 1964). On moving to Harvard, Mike maintained his interests in civil liberties

[21] See further: https://isismagazine.org.uk/about-us/ (last accessed September 2023).

[22] Lists of students involved in the production of *Isis* were not regularly included in the publication. On the first date on which Mike is mentioned (16 October 1963), his name is included in a list of 34 staff members and 13 members of the Editorial Board. The editor at this time was Roy Lockett who went on to become the deputy general secretary of the Broadcasting, Entertainment, Cinematograph and Theatre Union (see further: https://historyproject.org.uk/interview/roy-lockett-1 [last accessed September 2023]).

[23] During Mike's time at Oxford, *Isis* was supported and published by the infamous Robert Maxwell who at the time owned Pergamon Press and was a Labour candidate for North Buckinghamshire. He won the seat as part of the Labour victory of 1964 and held it until 1970. He went on to fight for Labour at Buckingham in the February and October 1974 elections (Barker and Sylvester 1991).

[24] Cowley is a working class suburb of Oxford where a significant number of workers are employed at the car production plant.

and spent a considerable amount of time there involved in protests about the Vietnam War.[25]

Mike continued as an activist when he moved to Edinburgh. One of his most significant achievements was the part he played in setting up the Citizen's Rights Office in Edinburgh, the shop front of which is shown in Fig. 2.3. This was a successful voluntary sector agency that gave advice to local people on welfare benefits, published accessible information guides provided representation at social security appeal tribunals and undertook campaigning work on housing law, social security and employment law. Mike played a central role in raising funds for the organisation, finding premises and recruiting volunteers and was later to act as an adviser and advocate. Sadly, The Edinburgh Citizens' Rights Office was forced to shut down when Lothian Regional Council withdrew its funding and opened its own in-house welfare benefits service in 1976. Although the new service was better resourced, in Mike's view it became very bureaucratic and subject to political control.

Fig. 2.3 Edinburgh Citizens' Rights Office 1991 reproduced with the kind permission of Peter Stubbs[26]

[25] While in Boston, Mike and Ruth also got involved in a downtown Boston project for deprived children.

[26] See further http://www.edinphoto.org.uk/0_STREET/0_street_views_-_broughton_street_37_1ag32.htm (last accessed September 2023). This was far from being a popular move with some

For Mike, bringing 'welfare rights' to the fore was an attempt to focus on shortcomings in the welfare state in the UK in the way that the US civil rights movement had been designed to focus on shortcomings in the electoral and wider political system. Debate about the issue was particularly influential in his new-found discipline of social policy and administration. This was a new academic space in which public intellectuals, or what would now be called 'scholactivists' such as Peter Townsend, Brian Abel-Smith and David Donnison played critical roles in the rediscovery of poverty in the UK; a problem which, until then, was too often complacently discussed in the past tense (Clark 2009).[27]

Mike's own contribution to the welfare rights movement manifested itself in a number of ways. From the earliest stage of his career in 1976 he produced a string of policy-orientated research reports and other publications on welfare and decision-making in the welfare state focusing on subjects ranging from the treatment of welfare benefit recipients, those living in public housing, tenants with rent arrears or people in debt. They ranged from people's experience of appeal tribunals, the characteristics of low-level grievances, the treatment of prisoners, begging, the nature of destitution and poverty and, above all, on procedural fairness (see for instance Adler and Bradley 1975; Adler and Feu 1976; Adler and Asquith 1981; Adler et al. 1985).

Outside the academy he became a member of the Executive Committee of the Child Poverty Action Group and of the Management Committee of the Edinburgh Citizen's Advice Bureau. Later, after the closure of the Edinburgh Citizens' Rights Office, he sat as a lay member of the Supplementary Benefit Appeal Tribunal for 20 years. He subsequently served on the Scottish Committee of the Administrative Justice and Tribunals Council for four years and produced two important research reports for them (Adler, 2012a, 2012b). The experience and insights gleaned from these activities became a consistent feature of his intellectual achievements, which in Mike's words were mere reflections of where his activism had taken him. Reflecting on the interface between academic scholarship and the research on debt recovery he undertook for the Scottish Law Commission, Mike said:

seeing it as an example of the Scottish Labour party towing the Westminster line. See Gardiner (2006).

[27] Notable academic publications on the topic in this period include Abel-Smith and Townsend (1965) and Townsend (1979). Peter Townsend's two most important insights were that poverty is best understood as being relative rather than absolute (Abel-Smith and Townsend 1965) and that poverty is less about shortage of income and more about the inability of people on low incomes to participate actively in society (Townsend 1979).

> Those who commissioned the research took the view that research should be value free and that researchers should not concern themselves with questions of policy, but I took the view that researchers were stakeholders and that the knowledge obtained from the research they undertook enabled them to make an informed contribution to discussions about policy. (Adler 2017)

In interview, he expanded on his experience of the policy-academic interface and spoke to an issue which has received some attention in socio-legal circles, the so-called pull of the policy audience (Sarat and Silbey 1988) or danger of capture:

> Looking back, I was never asked to become an adviser to a government department or a parliamentary committee. Over the years, I applied to become a member of a few public bodies such as the General Medical Council's panel that considers complaints against doctors and the Parole Board, but I was never appointed. I eventually concluded that I was seen as an outsider not an insider. I wanted to do some research at some point on judicial discretion and submitted a proposal to the Scottish Government for funding. I had a lot of supporters, but the proposal was turned down. I later heard from a neighbour [with connections][28] that I was considered totally unsuitable because I was no more than a Trotskyist agitator (laughs). I have never been someone who has been welcomed into government circles as a confidential adviser. I don't think civil servants felt they could trust me. I have never been someone who sits quietly in the corner. Fair enough! I wasn't one of them and they kept me at arm's length.[29]

Mike's characteristic directness makes clear the perils of what would now be called the impact and engagement agenda in higher education but also makes clear his strong sense of independence.

---

[28] The neighbour in question was an advocate who informed Mike that she had been told this by her father who was a Sheriff Principal.

[29] Mike could think of only one instance when he had had an influence on policy. In 2001, together with Tony Bradley (see note 35 below), he wrote two papers for a seminar organised by Sir Andrew Leggatt, who was conducting a review of tribunals, later published as *Tribunals for Users: One System, One Service* (Leggatt 2001). In these papers (Adler and Bradley 2001a, 2001b), they suggested a two-tier structure of first instance and appeal tribunals and argued that, at both levels, individual tribunals should be grouped by subject matter into divisions with common rules and procedures. Leggatt was attracted by this proposal, and it was incorporated in his report and subsequently adopted by the new Tribunals Service.

Intellectual Trajectory

Mike was promoted to a Senior Lectureship in Social Policy in 1984, to a Readership in Social Policy in 1991 and to a Personal Chair in Socio-Legal Studies in 1996. This trajectory reflects a gradual shift in his academic interests from that of a sociology student, to social policy lecturer and then to socio-legal researcher. Four key factors influenced this shift in focus. The first of these was that Mike's work with the Citizen's Rights Office made him realise how incredibly complicated and important the law was. The second was that his early years at Edinburgh University provided ample opportunities to become involved with lawyers and the emerging field of socio-legal studies. Shortly after arriving in Edinburgh he became friends with Tony Bradley, who was Professor of Constitutional Law in the Law Faculty. Tony shared Mike's concerns about the workings of Supplementary Benefit Appeal Tribunals[30] and they successfully applied to the Nuffield Foundation for funding to hold a conference on the place of discretion in the supplementary benefits scheme. This was subsequently published as a jointly edited book entitled *Justice, Discretion and Poverty* in 1975. Together with the 'mercurial' Colin Campbell, who was then a lecturer in the sociology of law at Edinburgh University, Mike also became responsible for running a regular series of socio-legal seminars which facilitated exchanges between lawyers and social scientists (Adler 2017). He went on to get ESRC funding with Stewart Asquith to organise a series of workshops on discretionary decision-making in law and social policy which also resulted in a book *Discretion and Welfare*, published in 1980 (Adler and Asquith 1981).[31] Soon afterwards, he came into contact with the legal establishment when he undertook a study of diligence, the technical term for debt recovery in Scotland, for the Scottish Law Commission. In these various ways the legal began to become inextricably implicated in his work on the social.

The third influence on Mike's movement to socio-legal studies came about as a result of spending a sabbatical at the Center for Law and Society at the University of California in Berkeley. The Center, which has now been established for over fifty years, had been set up as an adjunct to the Law School by Philip Selznick. For Mike, it was the institutional embodiment of the 'sociological jurisprudence' associated with Selznick and his close colleagues

[30] Tony Bradley was an important public lawyer, author of a well-known textbook on Constitutional and Administrative Law and, for many years, editor of *Public* Law. He was also a part-time Chairman of a National Insurance Local Tribunal and taught an honours course on welfare law at Edinburgh University.

[31] At this early stage, Mike used the concept of ideology to explain the exercise of discretion.

Philippe Nonet, Jerry Skolnick and Bob Kagan. He has described meeting them and the graduate students in the Jurisprudence and Social Policy (JSP) programme as a formative influence. His engagement with Selznick's work in particular helped him think about broader theoretical frameworks for his own work (Adler 2017).[32]

Finally, as readers of Mike's work will know, Jerry Mashaw's 1983 book on *Bureaucratic Justice: Managing social security disability claims,* prompted a life-long fascination with administrative justice and attempts to make sense of the field. His review of the book with Jack Tweedy (Adler and Tweedie 1984) described Mashaw's study of the US Disability Insurance scheme as ambitious, innovative, original and rich in complexity. But perhaps more importantly, they credit Mashaw with providing a new lens through which to view administrative justice which was to become highly influential in socio-legal circles. More particularly, they drew attention to his focus on front-line decision-making rather than the appellate courts, tribunals and ombudsmen, all of which consider an extremely small proportion of administrative decisions in the welfare state. Reflecting on the influence of this work in the *Journal of Law and Society,* Mike acknowledged Mashaw's work as being something of an intellectual watershed for him (Adler 2006). But in doing so, he also provided a more sophisticated account of his critique of Mashaw's model than in his earlier book review, informed by his own subsequent work in the field. In the intervening years Mike developed Mashaw's work to take more account of external legal influences on decision-making and subsequent shifts in prevalent political ideology in Anglo-American circles, not least of which has been the arrival of managerialism, consumerism and the re-emergence of market-based principles (Adler 2006). While the two authors have never engaged at a personal level, the contribution that Mike has made to the field is acknowledged in an essay Mashaw wrote in 2022 in which there is a whole section dedicated to 'Mike Adler and his Critics' (Mashaw 2022). In this chapter, Mashaw describes Mike as one of the most active contributors to the administrative justice literature and one of his fellow academics who is most interested in specifying 'models' or 'ideal types'.

When understanding the influences which played a part in the story behind these achievements, it is also important to mention the third major influence cited by Mike alongside Selznick and Mashaw. Neil McCormick was Regius Professor of Public Law and the Law of Nature and Nations at the University of Edinburgh from 1972 until 2008. Mike remembers him as an exceptional person who was probably the cleverest person he ever met.

[32] See, also Adler (2013).

He had known Neil from a distance at Oxford describing how he 'came down to Oxford' and took it 'by storm', doing his law degree in two years, gaining a starred first and becoming President of the Oxford Union. He moved to Edinburgh shortly after Mike, where he taught jurisprudence and the philosophy of law. It was with his encouragement that Mike organised the socio-legal seminar series referred to above together with Colin Campbell. Though he was not a socio-legal scholar himself, Neil was supportive of the burgeoning socio-legal movement and more particularly the development of Mike's research. He also played the role of mentor, encouraging Mike to apply for a Readership and then a Chair. While Mike did engage with Neil's scholarship, not least as an active participant in the reading groups he ran, the influence he had on him was distinct from that of Selznick and Mashaw. In Mike's words:

> Neil was incredibly supportive of me. I learnt so much from him about the nature of law and legal argument, about legal rights and about the concept of justice from him. His suggestion that I apply for a chair was a great accolade coming from him. He was a colossal influence intellectually and personally, especially after the death of my first wife, Ruth, who had been a PhD student of his.[33] He inspired me. Did he influence me? Not in a direct way like Philip Selznick, who I did not know well personally or have a sustained relationship with like I did with Neil. Not like Jerry Mashaw, who was the starting point for my fascination with administrative justice and my attempts to make sense of that field. But in a more general way, he was an inspiration and shaped my thinking. In different ways, these are the people to whom I owe the most.

These influences and Mike's own passion for the subjects with which he engaged have led to an impressive academic profile. His books and articles include publications on parental rights in education (Adler 1990, 1993a, 1993b), on the computerisation of social security (Adler and du Feu 1976), on debt and debt enforcement (Adler 1983, 1986), and his recent book on benefit sanctions *Cruel, Inhuman and Degrading Treatment? Benefit Sanctions in the UK* (Adler 2018). In Mike's view, his most ambitious work, and the one he is most proud of, is his book, written together with Brian Longhurst,

[33] Mike's first wife, Ruth, was a founder of Scottish Women's Aid, and a long-term member of the Children's Panel, who drew on her experience as a panel member to undertake a PhD, with Neil MacCormick as her supervisor. Her thesis was subsequently published as a book (Adler 1985). Ruth also helped to establish the Scottish Child Law Centre and went on become Assistant to the Lay Observer for Scotland, subsequently the Legal Services Ombudsman. She sat in the District Court as a Justice of the Peace and was the first Scottish Development Officer for Amnesty International. She died from cancer at the age of 49. Neil was especially supportive to Mike after Ruth's death in 1994.

on decision-making in prisons *Discourse, Power and Justice: Towards a New Sociology of Imprisonment* (Adler and Longhurst 1994).

In the course of his career, Mike was successful in gaining 25 grants from the Economic and Social Research Council (ESRC) as well as grants from the Scottish Office, the Department of Social Security, the Lord Chancellor's Department, the Nuffield Foundation, the European Community and IBM (UK) Ltd to pursue empirical research and bring scholars together in workshops and conferences. He wrote three books and was the editor of six more in addition to 14 research reports, 63 sole-authored and 37 jointly authored articles and book chapters.

When asked what he thought his main contributions to socio-legal research have been, Mike said that he saw himself as an exponent of theoretically informed empirical research. In terms of methodology, he described himself as a methodological pluralist who believes that the problem should determine the choice of method rather than vice versa. In his view, the focus of his research from the early days has been on the concept of fairness, and he has tried to explore what that means in a variety of different contexts. Unlike John Rawls, he does not think that there are any invariant principles of fairness but, rather, that its' meaning is context dependent and can be studied empirically. In his research, he has attempted to demonstrate that a socio-legal approach, rather than a doctrinal or philosophical one, is ideally the best one for exploring these questions. His concerns have always been not only to understand why administrative justice is as it is but also how it could be improved. On reflection, he argued that his focus on the justice of administrative procedures rather than legal doctrine reflected his background as a social scientist. The fact that much of his research has been collaborative is because he feels we all gain a great deal from working closely with others with different backgrounds and skill sets.

Conclusion

It has been an absolute pleasure to write this biographical note and to talk to Mike about his long and illustrious career as academic and activist, and there are still so many stories to tell. So many have benefited from Mike's capacity-building work in the field of socio-legal studies. He has been an active member of the Socio-Legal Studies movement since 1979. He hosted the socio-legal group conference in Edinburgh in 1989 when the idea of setting up a formal association was first mooted, and then served on the Executive Committee for several years. He led the Scottish response to the

Nuffield Foundation inquiry into socio-legal studies (Genn et al. 2006). For many years, he was involved with the ESRC's research training activities and was Chair of the Socio-Legal and Criminology Committee for several recognition exercises and for the award of postgraduate studentships. He also played a role in establishing and sustaining journals as co-editor of the *European Journal of Social Security* with Frans Pennings from the University of Utrecht from its foundation in 1999 until 2020.

There are also tales to tell about Mike Adler as friend, collaborator and adviser. Many, including me, owe much to him for his scholarship, generosity and support. He has mentored numerous early career academics who have themselves become names in the field including Roy Sainsbury, Simon Halliday, Paul Henman, Jackie Gulland and Grainne McKeever. He has also supervised 35 research students, many of whom have gone on to have very successful careers in the academy or in the policymaking arena. Roy Sainsbury, who was his sixth PhD student and remains a friend, summed up his influence in the following way:

> Mike supervised with a deceptive light touch, always encouraging and supportive whilst simultaneously pushing and challenging. And all done with the utmost warmth and charm. I learned an immense amount under his supervision – about the business of doing applied social research, about aiming to achieve clarity and precision in communicating to different audiences, and about the importance of studying areas of social policy like social security too often neglected by the academy. I have carried those lessons with me ever since. (Personal correspondence, 2023)

Alongside his important body of academic publications he will also be remembered by many of us for his informal mentorship over the odd glass of whisky. Together with his second wife Sue, he continues to be a generous host, to be active in local community groups, and continues to write. The surface of the stories to honour him has only been scratched and there will be time to tell more.

References

Abel-Smith, B., and Townsend, P. (1965). *The Poor and the Poorest*. London: G. Bell and Sons.

Adler, M. (1963). Democracy in America. *Isis*, 27 November.

Adler, M. (1983). Debt Enforcement and Social Security. *Journal of Social Welfare Law*, September, 265–283.

Adler, M. (1986). The Economic and Social Situation of Consumer Debtors in Great Britain. In Günter Hörmann (ed.), *Consumer Credit and Consumer Insolvency*, pp. 37–65. Bremen: University of Bremen Press.

Adler, M. (1990). Rights as Trumps: The Case of Parental Choice of School in Scotland. *Education and the Law*, 2(2), 67–72.

Adler, M. (1993a). A New Approach to Parental Choice. *NCE Briefing No.13*, London: National Commission on Education, March; reprinted in National Commission on Education (1993), *Briefings*, pp. 183–198. London: Heinemann.

Adler, M. (1993b). Parental Choice and the Enhancement of Children's Interests. In Pamela Munn (ed.), *Parents and Schools: Customers, Managers or Partners?*, pp. 47–64. London: Routledge.

Adler, M. (2006). Fairness in Context. *Journal of Law and Society, 33*(4), 615–638.

Adler, M. (2012a). *Right to Appeal: A Review Of decisions Made by Scottish Public Bodies Where There Is No Right of Appeal or Where the Appeal Procedure is Inaccessible or Inappropriate.* A Report for the Scottish Committee of the Administrative Justice and Tribunals Council, Edinburgh.

Adler, M. (2012b). *Understanding the Differences Between Appeals, Complaints and Reviews: Some Empirical Evidence.* A Report for the Scottish Committee of the Administrative Justice and Tribunals Council, Edinburgh.

Adler, M. (2013). Review of Martin Krygier: Philip Selznick—Ideals in the World. *Social and Legal Studies, 22*(1), 133–136.

Adler, M. (2017). 'An Outline of My Career', Address Given at the SLSA Conference 2017 on Being Awarded the Lifetime Achievement Award. Available from Mike Adler.

Adler, M. (2018). *Cruel, Inhuman and Degrading Treatment? Benefit Sanctions in the UK*, London: Palgrave Macmillan.

Adler, M., and Allen, C. (1964). Letter to the Editor, *Isis*, 7 November.

Adler, M., and Asquith, S. (eds.). (1981). *Discretion and Welfare.* London: Heinemann.

Adler, M., and Bradley, A. W. (eds.). (1975). *Justice, Discretion and Poverty: Supplementary Benefit Appeal Tribunals in Britain.* Abingdon: Professional Books.

Adler, M., and Bradley, A. (2001a). 'The Case for Systematic Reform and the Establishment of a Unified Administrative Tribunal' in Martin Partington (ed.), *The Leggatt Review of Tribunals: Academic Seminar Papers*, (pp. 1–30). Bristol: The Bristol Centre of Administrative Justice, Faculty of Law, University of Bristol.

Adler, M., and Bradley, A. (2001b). 'The Organisation of the Proposed Tribunal Service' in Martin Partington (ed.), *The Leggatt Review of Tribunals: Academic Seminar Papers*, (pp. 169–177). Bristol: The Bristol Centre of Administrative Justice, Faculty of Law, University of Bristol.

Adler, M., and du Feu, D. (1976). *A Computer Based Welfare Benefits Information System: The Inverclyde Project*. Scientific Centre Report No.78, Peterlee Co, Durham.

Adler, M., Himsworth, C., and Kerr, S. (1985). *Public Housing, Rent Arrears and the Sheriff Court: A Study of the Early Implementation and Impact of the Tenants'*

Rights Etc. (Scotland) Act 1980. Edinburgh: Scottish Office Central Research Unit Papers.
Adler, M., and Longhurst B. (1994). *Discourse, Power and Justice: Towards a New Sociology of Imprisonment*. London: Routledge.
Adler, M., and Tweedie, J. (1984). Jerry L. Mashaw, Bureaucratic Justice: Managing Social Security Disability Claims, Yale University Press, New Haven and London. *Journal of Social Policy, 13*(4), 491–493.
Adler, R. (1985). *Taking Children's Rights Seriously*. Edinburgh: Scottish Academic Press.
Barker, D., and Sylvester, C. (1991). Obituary: Robert Maxwell. *The Guardian*, 6 November.
Billen, A., and Skipworth, M. (eds.). (1984). *Oxford Type: An Anthology of Isis, the Oxford University Magazine*. Robson Books Limited.
Birks, P. (2004). Nicholas, J.K.B.M., 1919–2002. *Proceedings of the British Academy, 124*.
Clark, P. (2009). Obituary: Peter Townsend. *The Guardian,* 9 June.
Gardiner, M. (2006). *From Trocchi to Trainspotting in Scottish Critical Theory Since 1960*, Edinburgh: Edinburgh University Press.
Genn, H., Wheeler, S., and Partington, M. (2006). *Law in the Real World: Improving our Understanding of How Law Works: Final Report and Recommendations*. London: Nuffield Foundation.
Gillman, P. (1964). Parish Pump Runs Dry. *Isis*, 25 January, 5.
Jarausch, K. H. (1986). The Perils of Professionalism: Lawyers, Teachers, and Engineers in Nazi Germany. *German Studies Review, 9*(1), 107–137.
Leggatt, Sir Andrew. (2001). *Tribunals for Users: One System, One Service*. London: The Stationary Office.
Lidz, V. (2021). Politics and the Academic Social Scientist; The Record of Talcott Parsons. *The American Sociologist, 52*, 63–87.
Lipset, S. M. (1992). The State of American Sociology. *Sociological Forum, 9*(2), 199–220.
Mashaw, J. (2022). Models of Administrative Justice. In M. Hertogh, R. Kirkham, R. Thomas and J. Tomlinson (eds.), *The Oxford Handbook of Administrative Justice*. Oxford: Oxford University Press.
May, T., (1975). *The History of the Harrow County School for Boys*. London: Harrow County School for Boys.
Mcleod, K. (1962). Women in Oxford. *Isis*. 30 May.
Membery, Y. (2010). Who Killed the News Chronicle? *British Journalism Review, 21*(1), 3–88.
O'Connell. (1964). Only Connect. *Isis*, 23 January, 3.
Roth, A. (2006). Reg Freeson, Long Serving Labour Housing Minister Ousted by Ken Livingstone. *The Guardian*, 11 October.
Sarat, A., and Silbey, S. (1988). The Pull of the Policy Audience. *Law and Policy, 10*(2–3), 97–166.
Simpson, A. R. (1968). The Custodians of Western Democracy. Self-published.

Staubmann, H. (2021). 'C Wright Mills' The Sociological Imagination and the Construction of Talcott Parsons as a Conservative Grand Theorist. *The American Sociologist, 52*(1), 178–193.

Townsend, P. (1979). *Poverty in the United Kingdom: A Survey of Household Resources and Standards of Living*. Harmondsworth: Penguin Books.

3

Just AI: Using Socio-Legal Studies of Fairness to Inform Ethical AI in Government

Paul W. Fay Henman

Introduction

Writing this chapter in the middle of 2023, I am surrounded by a cacophony of voices about the latest developments in Generative Artificial Intelligence (AI). These new technologies and the discourses they generate are the latest movement in an ongoing crescendo over the last five or so years variously hyping and critiquing "AI", a catch-all phrase that coincides with an uptick in machine learning (ML[1]) capacities.

Chief among the critiques has been the investigation of the ethics of AI. The phrase "ethical AI" captures a constellation of considerations, concepts and principles, including human rights, bias, transparency, explainability and so on. As the new shiny object for academics, ethical AI is the latest hot topic on which to postulate, gesticulate and promulgate; to make one's reputation and build one's career. As with many intellectual hot topics, the race to be visible, to be cited, to be *the* expert, has meant that too few works in the field of ethical AI have built on past work conceptualising and researching

[1] Machine learning is a form of computer programming to produce another program. Using large volumes of input data, a (structured) machine learning program adjusts internal data and calculations to process the input data to generated desire output data (e.g. Naqa and Murphy 2015). The result is an machine learning AI model.

P. W. F. Henman (✉)
School of Social Science, The University of Queensland, Brisbane, QLD, Australia
e-mail: p.henman@uq.edu.au

S. Cowan and S. Halliday (eds.), *Socio-Legal Generation*, Palgrave Socio-Legal Studies,
https://doi.org/10.1007/978-3-031-67244-6_3

ethics, fairness and justice. Yet, to avoid reinventing the wheel, research on ethical AI fundamentally *needs* to become informed by (and build on) ideas about fairness and justice from socio-legal and policy studies so that it can translate abstract ethical concepts into practical, grounded realities of how people experience our rapidly evolving AI-enabled and mediated world. To that end this chapter, dedicated to and inspired by the work of Emeritus Professor Michael (Mike) Adler, from the University of Edinburgh, seeks to highlight the ways in which socio-legal and policy ideas about justice and fairness may advance thinking about, developing and deploying ethical AI in government.

For clarity, ethical AI encompasses a wide range of concepts and normative values. For example, in their review of ethical AI literature, Fjeld et al. (2020) identify nine themes including accountability; safety and security; transparency and explainability; and fairness and non-discrimination. This chapter focuses heavily on procedural fairness that I denote as "just AI" using the contraction of justice. Other aspects of ethical AI are not considered here.

In preparing this chapter, I revisited Adler's works on computerisation, social policy and administrative justice. The aim of this chapter is to use Adler's insights to stimulate critical engagement with contemporary ethical AI research. I begin with a few provocations arising from Adler's first body of work on computerisation in social policy from a Scottish Office Social Work Services Group-funded study (1977, 1975, 1974). Written almost 50 years ago by Adler (then Lecturer, Department of Social Administration, University of Edinburgh) and his research fellow David du Feu, they wrote:

> Technical experts frequently prescribe simple technical 'solutions' to complex social problems. In this article, the authors describe an experimental project which was designed to increase the take-up of means-tested benefits. The project incorporated a computer-based information system which provided individuals who supplied details of their financial and other household circumstances with personalized information about their entitlement to a wide range of benefits. Although the project was a technical success, it made little impact on take-up rates. In attempting to explain why this should have been so, the authors point to the complexity of the problems involved and advocate the need to examine and simplify existing administrative procedures at the same time as investigating the potential of computerization, rather than assuming that a technical device can of itself side-step the problems. They also point out that administrative simplification is itself no easy task and is fraught with political and organizational problems. (Adler and Du Feu 1977, p. 431)

In light of contemporary discussions on AI, I drew several insights from this paper.

First, much AI innovation and resulting tools seem driven by a will to automate, to replicate and replace human activity, with the goal of generating efficiencies and cost savings. Think of Amazon's automated warehouses, calculations of government benefit or service eligibility or automated border controls. Another motivation for AI innovation is more abstract; to enact or surpass complex human abilities; for example, to become grandmasters in Chess or Go, drive cars, or evaluate X-rays for cancer. AI is also often developed, marketed and deployed to control humans based on ideas of detecting crime and enhancing security, such as facial and voice recognition systems and fraud risk-profiling. What I found compelling by Adler and du Feu's (1977) study was its focus on developing digital tools to address a social problem, that of people in the UK not receiving the benefits or services to which they are entitled to receive. This is the first key lesson that ethical AI research needs to do more of: *rather than building digital tools then finding a purpose, start with important social purposes and then building the tools to achieve that purpose*. Called "Human Centred Computing" (HCC), this is an approach that has been in operation for over 30 years!

Second, Adler and du Feu found that it was not enough to simply build the technology and the social problem will be solved. Rather, "complex social problems" may often require the support of digital technological solutions, but the technologies do not inherently solve the problem, in and of themselves. This is a second lesson for ethical AI research: *eschew techno-solutionism, that is, the idea that technology in of itself will solve social, political or economic challenges* (Morozov 2013). *AI needs to be designed, built for and enacted within socio-technical systems.* Tools designed to be used by abstract imagined users are a recipe for failure, because human diversity and circumstances do not fit these neat conceptual models. Concurrently, Adler and du Feu's study highlighted the revision work required by government in improving social policy and administrative processes, as well as changing negative social valorisations of welfare to solve the social problem of underutilisation of social welfare benefits.

The study implicitly acknowledges that there are ethical dimensions in the design and use of digital tools; engaging marginalised people to support and empower their lives through technology-generated information. This approach points to a third lesson for ethical AI researchers: *analysing AI tools using abstract principles in isolation from its use case is unlikely to achieve ethical AI or ethical outcomes.* Ethical AI requires more grounded analysis based on specific use cases and co-designed with the people that are likely to be users or affected by its use. In this regard, ethical AI researchers can draw on a large body and long history of Participatory Design literature (Schuler and Namioka 1993).

Having highlighted Adler's very early and innovative work, in the next section I reflect on Adler's larger body of work relating to computerisation and administrative justice. This will then be followed by a section on how contemporary studies of algorithmic/AI fairness and justice have conceptualised fairness and justice and their obverse, bias. The concluding discussion draws out the threads and lessons from Adler's contributions to highlight future directions for researching and creating just AI.

Bringing Socio-Legal Ideas of Administrative Justice into Digital Technology Research

It would be approximately another 15 years until Adler turned his attention to computerisation again, first undertaking work in the late 1980s/ early 1990s and then again in the early 2000s. Focusing once again on social security, Adler was concerned about how computerisation may be transforming the operation of administrative justice (or procedural fairness) defined as follows:

> Whereas substantive fairness generally equates justice with desert, procedural fairness defines justice as the outcome of a fair process. Procedural fairness therefore does not allow dissatisfaction with the substance of an outcome to impeach the fairness of the process. (Rich 2017: 662)

Adler's innovation was to first modify then expand on Jerry Mashaw's work in *Bureaucratic Justice* (1983), then Professor of Law at the Yale Institute of Social and Policy Studies and a 1969 University of Edinburgh PhD graduate. See the chapter by Arvind et al. in this volume for a full discussion of Adler's contribution to thinking about administrative justice.

The UK DSS Operation Strategy

In the early 1980s, the UK Department of Social Security (DSS) initiated a computerisation project, called the *Operational Strategy,* to improve administrative efficiency and reduce costs, to enhance service quality to the public and to modernise and improve the work of staff. By the late 1980s, the *Strategy* had experienced long delays and costs overruns, and the achievement of its service goals was in doubt. In this context, the DSS commissioned Adler and his former PhD student Roy Sainsbury to investigate how to enhance service delivery through enacting a "whole person" approach and was funded by the UK Department of Social Security (DSS).[2]

Adler and Sainsbury (1991b, 1991a) argued that the activities of the *Operational Strategy* would lead to a strengthening of the *bureaucratic* mode of administrative justice at the expense of *professional* and *legal* modes, through its top-down approach to computerisation focused on the interests of government rather than staff or social security beneficiaries and claimants; "the overall effect of the program was certainly to alter but not necessarily to enhance the procedural fairness of administrative decision-making in social security" (Adler 2003: 337).

Comparative Studies of Computerisation in Social Security

I discovered this work in the early-1990s while undertaking my PhD at the University of Queensland, on computerisation of social security in Australia, and this was the basis for Adler being selected a thesis examiner in 1996. While undertaking a postdoctoral fellowship, I worked with Mike in 2000 at the University of Edinburgh. Building on our own previously separate studies, we undertook an international comparative study of computerisation in social security systems, partly inspired by comparative welfare state research.

Supported with a small grant from IBM-UK we asked two expert informants per country from 13 OECD countries[3] to complete a survey to assess the impact of computerisation on each of Mike's six modes of administrative justice. Most of these contacts were colleagues of Mike's, highlighting his capacity to build diverse and wide professional networks. The survey was repeated in late 2004 covering 8 of the original 13 countries.[4] The first survey covered the period 1985 to 2000, while the second survey covered 2000 to 2004. The earlier period was dominated by the introduction of "online" computers systems (compared with batch processing), whereas the latter was dominated by the growing use of the Internet.[5]

[2] Publications from this work include Adler and Sainsbury (1990, 1991a, 1991b, 1996).

[3] Australia, Belgium, Canada, Denmark, Finland, France, German, Ireland, Netherlands, Norway, Sweden, UK and USA.

[4] Australia, Canada, Denmark, France, Netherlands, Sweden, UK, USA.

[5] The publications from this work include Adler and Henman (2001, 2005a, 2005b, 2009), Henman and Alder (2001, 2003) and also appeared in Adler's PhD thesis (2002).

Our study found that the *bureaucratic* mode of procedural justice was the strongest across national social security administrations, and that computerisation had consolidated and strengthened it over the period 1985 to 2004. The *legal* model was also strong, but remained largely unaffected by computerisation. In contrast, the relatively low levels of *professional* modes of procedural justice were further weakened by computerisation, whereas computerisation (alongside other public sector reforms) seemed to have furthered *managerial* modes of procedural justice, coming second behind the bureaucratic mode by 2004. We also concluded that "computerisation appears to have had little effect on the availability and structure of appeal procedures, but has had a greater effect on the procedures for determining entitlement to benefit" (Adler and Henman 2009: 79).

This work with Mike has been formative for my subsequent intellectual and normative considerations of computerisation in government, with concerns for both administrative and substantive justice. Responding to the growing use of risk-profiling for government policy, service delivery and administration, I explored its ethical and legal challenges (Henman 2005). Most recently I have had cause to reflect on the administrative justice implications of the growing use of automated decision-making (ADM) in government (Henman 2021).

Implications of Adler's Computerisation and Administrative Justice Research

Going back over 50 years, Adler's previous research on computerisation and administrative justice highlights and foreshadows issues that are increasing in their frequency and intensity, given the now ubiquitous digital mediation of social, market and governmental interactions. Unfortunately, collectively we still have not given sufficient consideration to the justice and ethical considerations of traditional modes of computerisation. While that earlier work examined traditional forms of computerisation, that is coding computers to undertake well-defined tasks, ML-based AI accelerates these challenges and provides new ones. In the light of this earlier work, what might be the lessons and insights for understanding and investigating the ethicalness and fairness of AI?

First, Alder's work evidences a long history of interest in the ethical and fairness implications of digital technology that readers and authors of the recent rush of writing in ethical AI often overlook and depreciate. Although AI *qua* ML is quite new, this does not mean that it represents a rupture in the development of digital technology nor its social impacts. Nor does it mean that earlier research on the ethics of digital technology is irrelevant in understanding the ethicality of present technology. Indeed, I have often found older work inspirational by seeking parallels with and similarities in past technologies and their usages to think through and about current circumstances. Indeed, Weizenbaum's (1976) classic *Computer Power and Human Reason* contends with many issues that have repeatedly reoccurred since then. In short, *researchers of ethical AI need to draw more on the insights of past research*, as I detail below.

Second, Adler's work specifically highlights diverse ways of thinking about fairness; both procedural and substantive. In addition to Adler's important contribution of delineating six different modes of administrative (i.e. procedural) justice, there is a long history in the discipline of social policy articulating different modes of *substantive* justice, that the earlier quoted definition relates to "desert" or deservingness. Fairness can be assessed by a concept of equality, contrasting procedural equality (treating everyone equally) with substantive (or outcome) equality that might involve treating everyone according to their different circumstances, sometimes called equity. In providing public services, fairness may be based on "need", or "desert", that may include meritocracy, blame (or lack thereof), capability, or rights (Wolfson 2015). Importantly, due to these multiple and situated ways of thinking about fairness, unsurprisingly people have different normative expectations on fairness that also vary by context (Rasinski 1987). Accordingly, *research into ethical AI thus need to be more cognisant of the different ways in which fairness can be operationalised and situated,* otherwise studies will wrongly assume a universal understanding of fairness. Mehrabi et al.'s (2021) review paper, which delineates 19 different notions of AI bias, is an important development.

Third, because meanings of fairness are situated in a particular context, whether a process or outcome is regarded by those effected as fair is likely to depend on how, when and where a digital tool is used, and not on an independent attribute of the digital tool. Much ethics of AI research solely focus on the tool, not on its use case. Consider facial recognition systems, which have been widely critiqued for being inaccurate, creating too many false positives and false negatives, with greater inaccuracy rates for people of colour than White people (Leslie 2020; Buolamwini and Gebru 2018). When used in criminal justice settings, their use can reproduce and exacerbate racial inequalities and racist policing systems and hence are unfair (Gentzel 2021). However, when used in disaster or war to identify bodies, it is likely to be regarded as appropriate and ethical (Harwell 2022). However, this apparent fluidity of the ethics of facial recognition systems should not be taken to support the "ethical neutrality of the tool" argument. Rather than assume an agreed universal definition of fairness, *research investigating the ethics of AI needs to determine the most appropriate definition of fairness based on how, where and with whom it is used*.

Fourthly, in reading and writing with Adler, I was repeatedly reminded of the numerous ways in which digital technologies are designed and deployed, that naturally have quite diverse outcomes. Technology interacts with diverse people and within complex social relationships. Accordingly, ethical AI designers need to look beyond the sole focus of tech, and even "imagined users", to understand and investigate how AI is grounded in human and organisational practice. For example, Australia's notorious Robodebt algorithm calculated potential social security debt by averaging annual income to fortnightly amounts. This in itself was not new nor unlawful as this approach was previously used to flag individual cases for further evidence and in-depth investigation. What was unlawful was using this average as evidence to *assert* a debt that was owed (Carney 2019). Similarly, we know that there are diverse ways in which human operators make use of risk assessment tools (e.g. in child protection, criminal justice, education), whether the tools are forms of input or decisive for human action is materially important. We also know that people have different levels of trust to automation (Glikson and Woolley 2020). *Building and deploying ethical and just AI thus requires an understanding of the social and organisational dynamics with technology that gives rise to ethical dilemmas. Ethnographic research and street level perspectives provide fertile means for such research.*

Given these lessons for contemporary ethical AI research arising from Adler's work on procedural justice, the next section engages with contemporary considerations and conversations concerning ethical AI.

Procedural Justice and AI Fairness

Bias (as a concept) is a key touchstone for ethical AI. Fairness in ethical AI research is defined by its opposite:

> In the context of decision-making, fairness is the *absence of any prejudice or favoritism toward an individual or group based on their inherent or acquired characteristics*. Thus, an unfair algorithm is one whose decisions are skewed toward a particular group of people. (Mehrabi et al. 2021: emphasis in original)

Therefore, AI (or algorithmic) bias has multiple meanings and arises from various locations. As Mehrabi et al.'s (2021) review of the field demonstrates, bias (or fairness) can be conceptualised as operating at individual, group or subgroup levels. Bias can also arise from biased datasets used for training an AI model using ML or designing a biased algorithm. While rejecting bias and creating fairness is seemingly universally embraced in AI, what counts as bias/fairness is not always straightforward—as Adler's earlier work on administrative justice foreshadowed. The following discussion critically examines some examples of AI design and use with the hope of advancing the conceptual and practical formation of just AI, while engaging with contemporary ethical AI literature.

Understanding the Origins of AI Bias

An iconic example of biased datasets is policing datasets of crime and recidivism, as highlighted in *ProPublica*'s seminal piece "Machine bias" (Angwin et al. 2016). It has long been understood that policing data on crime, conviction rates and so on have considerable bias along racial/ethnic, class, gender and disability/impairment categories. This is because of police bias in attitudes towards different groups, of where police focus surveillance, of decisions about arrests, of reporting patterns and of ongoing dis/advantages in the criminal justice system. Training AI with such historically biased data simply embeds such bias into the AI/ML model and replicates and even exaggerates such bias in their use in decision-making.

Even with unbiased training data, AI bias can be built into the algorithm or ML model. This might be due to intentional or unintentional human bias by coders—embedding their ways of thinking and their models of the world into the algorithmic model. An example is bias in facial recognition systems. While this can result from the lopsided nature of training datasets, understandably with fewer examples from minority groups, Leslie (2020) observes that facial recognition technologies are built on photogenic biases from digital and earlier cameras, whereby maximising for contrast was based on people of paler skin tones, meaning that photography performed poorer on darker skin tones. Digital image construction was therefore "racist" from the beginning and is not easy to fix (Raji et al. 2020).

Bias in the data and in the subsequent AI model is relatively easy to acknowledge, though fixing such bias is not conceptually easy. A typical approach in ethical AI is to pre-process training datasets to remove potential data bias. A starting point is to remove (protected) personal identifiers, such as race/ethnicity and sex/gender. The challenge with this approach is that indirect bias can occur as other data categories can be proxies for these protected categories, such as postcode, name or education, or a combination of these.

To provide checks on these challenges, a second way in which to assess data and subsequent AI bias is to compare the algorithmic outcomes from input cases with a given protected characteristic (e.g. Black, female) with outcomes from input case except the protected characteristic is changed (e.g. to White, male). This is group fairness, based on *demographic parity*, that Mehrabi et al. (2021: 12) defines as: "The likelihood of a positive outcome…should be the same regardless of whether the person is in the protected (e.g., female) group".

The challenge with this approach can be illustrated by considering how to create fair assessments of recidivism. In a study of domestic violence/abuse recidivism in Australia, McNamara et al. (2019) found that seeking demographic parity led to a loss of the predictive accuracy of the resulting model, with:

> non-Indigenous non-reoffenders [being] judged to be more risky [than in reality]. And all reoffenders – particularly Indigenous reoffenders – [being] judged to be less risky, which is not in the interests of potential victims. (2019: 112)

In short, there is a trade-off between model (or algorithmic) fairness and model accuracy. Seeking to reduce systematic disadvantage by removing racial profiling can end up increasing the inaccuracy of the predictions for others. Moreover, identifying when outputs are not biased is conceptually challenging.

Conceptual Complexities in Determining AI Bias

McNamara et al.'s study raises three challenges. First, demographic parity occurs when predictions of Indigenous Australians and non-Indigenous Australians of repeat (non)offending are similar. This assumes that the correct reference, or comparator, group for Indigenous Australians is the entire non-Indigenous group. Noting that Indigenous Australians are more likely to live in regional areas, have lower income and educational levels, would a better comparator group be non-Indigenous Australians with these same geographic, income and educational levels? In short, it is not clear how to assess demographic parity. Secondly, assessing the accuracy of the model involves comparing the predicted risks with actual rates of recidivism, considering both false positives and false negatives. Given that the purpose of unbiasing the model was to correct the bias in the dataset, how can that same dataset then be used to assess the model's accuracy? It is not clear what the "ground truth" is, or how it would even be determined. The McNamara et al. study did not address this, instead pointing to the need to consider the possible outcomes of getting it wrong; those wrongly predicted as reoffending and to the victims of those wrongly predicted to not reoffending. Accordingly, assessments of fairness thus need to consider the impact of algorithmic outcomes—individually (the offender) and more broadly (past/potential victims).[6] Thirdly, a corollary of these two observations is that socio-political or policy judgement is needed to supplement technical considerations; where to set the balance between fairness and accuracy is "a social, political and regulatory" decision (McNamara et al. 2019: 107). Technical AI bias calculations cannot address these considerations.

A further confounding challenge is that *algorithmic bias does not necessarily equate to unfairness*. Consider the use of algorithmic risk-prediction of long-term unemployment which is widely adopted in OCED countries (Desiere et al. 2019). Kern et al. (2021) found that their model for Germany tended to "exacerbate differences between male and female and German and non-German job seekers" (2021: 24). When used to determine individual employment services, this would mean that women would on average receive greater employment support than men, and more than they actually need. This overallocation of and over expenditure on services, may not *prima facie* amount to (negative) discrimination, because the additional employment services do not in themselves amount to negative consequences. However, if higher assessed risk of long-term unemployment is associated with greater surveillance, administrative reporting and potential noncompliance costs, than a greater (and inaccurate) assessed risk for women compared to men would arguably be discriminatory and unfair. Moreover, what counts as negative consequences may also vary by subpopulation group or individual. For example, some women may find the additional (unnecessary) employment support services beneficial, while others find them annoying or demeaning. This example illustrates that the fairness depends on how the risk assessments are used. The context of AI use thus matters. *Bias and fairness are not solely a characteristic of AI to be fixed by technical means, but by considering AI's use context*.

Determining the bias or fairness of AI use is therefore not straightforward but involves complex socio-political considerations. To illustrate further, consider recommender systems; AI systems that determine what product or service to suggest to a user, used widely in the commercial world, but

[6] A similar ethical argument was considered in the Allegheny County's Family Screening tool to assess risk of possible child maltreatment notifications (Dare and Gambrill 2017).

increasingly in government. Imagine a child searching for a toy on an online toyshop. The website is aware that the child's gender and thus recommends toys like Barbie dolls for girls and Hot Wheels cars for boys. Is this recommender system biased or fair? According to Pitoura et al. (2022), who state "a recommendation is fair, if the values of the protected attributes of the users, or, the items, do not affect the outcome of the recommendation", such a recommendation is unfair because the outcome varies by a protected attribute (i.e. sex/gender). Yet, many people would say that this "biased" algorithm is fair; it curates recommendations to the most likely consumer choices. Now consider the situation for the same algorithm recommending Black Barbies to Black girls, and White Barbies to White girls. It is fair? On the one hand it may reflect consumer patterns, but on the other hand, it reinforces racial stereotypes and biases that children should only have dolls of the same colour/race as themselves. How would the online toy store determine fairness in this case? More than likely the answer would be to defer to the algorithm that maximises profit, which is Adler's market form of procedural justice. Moreover, this example highlights the problematic nature of using the term bias (with its normative connotations) when it is *differentiation*, suggesting instead a *need to consider when differentiation denotes bias/discrimination and when it does not*.

Given what counts as fairness or bias is often subjective, determined by human judgement, a recent body of research has emerged seeking to understand which measure of AI bias/fairness people prefer. For example, Srivastava et al. (2019) undertook experiments and found that demographic parity (that is ensuring one's gender or ethnicity does not affect the outcome) was the concept of fairness most akin to people's thoughts about algorithmic fairness. Whereas, Wang et al. (2020) found that people were more likely to regard automated decisions as fair if the decisions are in their favour. In their systematic review of 58 papers on perceived fairness of automation, Starke et al. (2022) conclude that:

> the perceived fairness of ADM systems is highly context-dependent. Fairness perceptions are determined not only by the technical design of the algorithm but also by the area of application (e.g. pretrial risk assessment, hiring) and the specific task at hand (e.g. high-stakes vs. low-stakes). (2022: 10)

Importantly, individuals' background experiences can also elicit different fairness (and trust and safety) concerns. For example, Benjamin (2023) observes that in a context of their constant policing and surveillance, it is hard for African-Americans to not approach new AI as yet another technology of state control. The outcome of this socially embeddedness of perceived AI fairness leads to Dolata et al. (2022) to suggest a socio-technical view of algorithmic fairness is necessary. Additionally, in riffing off the common terminology of human-in-the-loop as a way in which to ensure decisions using automation is accountable, Rahwan (2018) calls for a "society-in-the-loop" approach to developing, deploying and evaluating just AI.

This final observation brings us back full circle to this chapter's opening discussion of the Adler study of identifying how computers might contribute to increasing citizens' take up of welfare benefits to which they are entitled. Adler and de Feu started with a socio-economic and policy problem and designed and evaluated a digital tool that may help address that problem. That study, like the observations from the previous paragraph, point to the need to start with the human, social, or economic problem, to understand the situatedness of people in their diversity. Just AI arises from building and deploying AI in a manner that is alert to not only the technical challenges—such as biased datasets—but to the diversity of social realities, to ensure that the dynamics of its use remain just. Moreover, such human-centred design cannot be achieved without being informed by the people using and affected by such technologies.

Inspired from these insights, I have recently embarked on two projects that hope to build justice-enhancing AI. In one project I am working with Economic Justice Australia, an organisation that represents and advocates for community legal centres providing specialist advice to people about their social security issues and rights. To advocate for their clients, welfare rights lawyers must navigate and make sense of hundreds of pages of client case notes and computer screenshots provided to them by Australia's social security agency. This is tedious, slow work that takes away from the legal issues of a client's case and their representation. With my postdoctoral fellow Dr Awais Hameed Khan and other colleagues from the ARC Centre of Excellence for Automated Decision-Making and Society, we are co-designing with welfare rights lawyers, an automated data extraction tool to provide more user-friendly data summary and navigable documents. It is hoped that such a tool will enhance social security recipients' administrative justice rights.

In a second project with Lyndal Sleep, Suzanna Fay and Suvradip Maitra, we have co-designed with human service professionals a practical framework to assess how well an AI-enabled service accords to trauma-informed principles (Maitra et al., 2024). The project drew together conceptual and applied audit frameworks in trauma-informed principles and ethical algorithms/AI. It is hoped that the tool can be used by human service organisations (and beyond) to better design and deploy AI to provide services that neither generate trauma nor retrigger trauma in those who have previously experienced it. It is the opposite of AI harms.[7]

Concluding Reflections

The dialogical reflections between Michael (Mike) Adler's research on computerisation and fairness and contemporary approaches to ethical AI have highlighted key lessons for people interested in studying, developing and deploying ethical AI. These lessons are curated in Table 3.1.

Bringing together the early work of Adler and his colleagues across the decades with the recent work of AI bias and fairness, several concluding observations are useful in advancing a "Just AI" agenda.

First, it is noteworthy that various rationales for deploying and evaluating algorithms/AI map onto the six different legitimating goals of the six modes of procedural justice. AI can be argued to operate according to accuracy, expertise, legality, efficiency gains, consumer satisfaction and profit making. Adler's work would thus suggest that different modes of accountability and remedies may need to be considered according to the different ways in which AI is used.

Table 3.1 A synopsis of lessons for studying, building and using just AI

1. Rather than building digital tools then finding a purpose, start with important social purposes and then build the tools to achieve that purpose. Adopt Human-Centred Computing
2. Eschew techno-solutionism. AI needs to be designed, built for and enacted within socio-technical systems
3. Analysing AI tools using abstract principles in isolation from its use case is unlikely to achieve ethical AI or ethical outcomes. Adopt Participatory Design
4. Researchers of ethical AI need to draw more on the insights of past research
5. Research into ethical AI needs to be cognisant of the different ways in which fairness can be operationalised and situated
6. Building and deploying ethical and just AI requires an understanding of the social and organisational dynamics with technology that gives rise to ethical dilemmas
7. Ethnographic research and street level perspectives provide fertile means for such research
8. Bias and fairness are not solely a characteristic of AI to be fixed by technical means, but by considering AI's use context
9. Consider when differentiation denotes bias/discrimination and when it does not

[7] The AI Incident Database (https://incidentdatabase.ai/) provides an excellent resource highlighting the harms that AI systems can cause.

Second, there is a need to work on the terminologies and conceptualisation relating to Just AI. Starke et al. (2022: 10) conclude their review that "more theoretical groundwork on human perceptions of algorithmic fairness" is needed. There is also a need to better distinguish between distributive/substantive fairness and procedural/process fairness. Given that this work has normative connotations, it is also necessary to distinguish between differentiation and discrimination. Whenever I hear AI researchers referring to bias, I recall *The Princess Bride's* Inigo Montoya: "You keep using that word. I do not think it means what you think it means".

Third, AI fairness is not an attribute of its algorithmic design. Mathematical measures of fairness provide important insights into an AI's structural design and operation, but they do not determine whether it will be regarded as un/fair. For that, researchers, developers and deployers of AI need to give greater attention to the social and organisational context of their use. For that a socio-technical view of fairness is required.

Fourth, key to determining fairness is the impact of AI(-enabled) decision-making. This includes the immediate effects on those subject to the decisions, recommendations, etc., its negative versus positive consequences and the strength of these consequences (e.g. providing unnecessary employment services versus denying parole), its effects on a person's choice versus their control. It also includes the flow-on consequences to others (e.g. a potential victim of a person wrongly assessed as low recidivism) and society at large (e.g. reproducing social segmentation). This means that practical approaches to auditing AI need to consider the wider AI context.

Finally, just AI starts with society, not the technology. Ethics is about the society we want to build. Given that AI is increasingly a crucial part of our social infrastructure, where we embed, codify and solidify social relations and values into digital devices, we need to design just AI with visions of the social relationships and society we want. Adler's work on administrative justice highlights that justice is achieved not just through a process towards a decision, but also a process after a decision. Similarly, ethical AI requires not just algorithmic design, or the design around its use, but processes of governance and accountability. Accordingly, given human diversity, vulnerability and power, *just AI is co-designed, human-centred AI*. If this chapter and the applied projects I have initiated are able to create enhanced social outcomes through just AI, then this is a just legacy bequeathed from Mike and his personal and professional inspiration.

Acknowledgements I acknowledge the helpful and insightful feedback by Awais Hameed Khan and Sharon Cowan on earlier versions of this chapter, and to colleagues in the Australian Research Council Centre of Excellence for Automated

Decision-Making and Society for the discussions that helped to crystallise my thinking.

References

Adler, M. (2002). *Treating People Fairly: A Socio-Legal Approach to Administrative Justice*. Annexe Thesis Digitisation Project 2017 Block 15.

Adler, M. (2003). A Socio-Legal Approach to Administrative Justice. *Law & Policy, 25*(4), 323–352.

Adler, M., and Du Feu, D. (1974). Using the Computer to Estimate Entitlement: A Feasibility Study. *Policy & Politics, 3*(1), 61–68.

Adler, M., and Du Feu, D. (1975). *A Computer Based Welfare Benefits Information System: The Inverclyde Project: Joint Project Between University of Edinburgh, Inverclyde District Council, IBM United Kingdom*. UK Scientific Centre, IBM United Kingdom.

Adler, M., and Du Feu, D. (1977). Technical Solutions to Social Problems?: Some Implications of a Computer-Based Welfare Benefits Information System. *Journal of Social Policy, 6*(4), 431–447.

Adler, M., and Henman, P. (2001). e-Justice: A Comparative Study of Computerization and Procedural Justice in Social Security. *International Review of Law, Computers & Technology, 15*(2), 195–212.

Adler, M., and Henman, P. (2005a). A comparative international study of computerization and e-government in social security. *Washington, DC: IBM Center for the Business of Government*.

Adler, M., and Henman, P. (2005b). Computerizing the Welfare State: An International Comparison of Computerization in Social Security. *Information, Community & Society, 8*(3), 315–342.

Adler, M., and Henman, P. (2009). Justice Beyond the Courts: The Implications of Computerisation for Procedural Justice in Social Security. *E-Justice: Using Information Communication Technologies in the Court System*, pp. 65–86. IGI Global.

Adler, M., and Sainsbury, R. (1990). *Putting the Whole Person Concept into Practice: Final Report*. Edinburgh: Department of Social Policy and Social Work, University of Edinburgh.

Adler, M., and Sainsbury, R. (1991a). *Administrative Justice, Quality of Service and the Operational Strategy*. The Social Implications of the Operational Strategy, New Waverley Papers, Social Policy Series 4.

Adler, M., and Sainsbury, R. (1991b). *The Social Shaping of Information Technology: Computerisation and the Administration of Social Security*. The Sociology of Social Security, Edinburgh Education & Society Series. Edinburgh: Edinburgh University Press.

Adler, M., and Sainsbury, R. (1996). Alternative Approaches to the Computerisation of Social Security: Reflections on the Delphi Exercise. In *Gazing into the Oracle: The Delphi Method and Its Application to Social Policy and Public Health*, pp. 176–192. Jessica Kingsley Publications.

Angwin, J., Larson, J., Mattu, S., et al. (2016). Machine Bias. *ProPublica*, 23 May.

Bach, R. L., Kern, C., Amaya, A., et al. (2021). Predicting Voting Behavior Using Digital Trace Data. *Social Science Computer Review, 39*(5), 862–883.

Benjamin, R. (2023). *Race After Technology.* Routledge.

Binns, R. (2018). *Fairness in Machine Learning: Lessons from Political Philosophy.* Conference on Fairness, Accountability and Transparency. PMLR, pp. 149–159.

Buolamwini, J., and Gebru, T. (2018). *Gender Shades: Intersectional Accuracy Disparities in Commercial Gender Classification.* Conference on Fairness, Accountability and Transparency. PMLR, pp. 77–91.

Carney, T. (2019). Robo-Debt Illegality: The Seven Veils of Failed Guarantees of the Rule of Law? *Alternative Law Journal, 44*(1), 4–10.

Dare, T., and Gambrill, E. (2017). *Ethical Analysis: Predictive Risk Models at Call Screening for Allegheny County*. Alleghany County Analytics.

Desiere, S., Langenbucher, K., and Struyven, L. (2019). *Statistical Profiling in Public Employment Services.* OECD.

Dolata, M., Feuerriegel, S., and Schwabe, G. (2022). A Sociotechnical View of Algorithmic Fairness. *Information Systems Journal, 32*(4), 754–818.

El Naqa, I., and Murphy, M. J. (2015). *What Is Machine Learning?* Springer.

Fjeld, J., Achten, N., Hilligoss, H., et al. (2020). *Principled Artificial Intelligence: Mapping Consensus in Ethical and Rights-Based Approaches to Principles for AI*. Berkman Klein Center Research Publication.

Gentzel, M. (2021). Biased Face Recognition Technology Used by Government. *Philosophy & Technology, 34*(4), 1639–1663.

Glikson, E., and Woolley, A. W. (2020). Human Trust in Artificial Intelligence: Review of Empirical Research. *Academy of Management Annals, 14*(2), 627–660.

Harwell, D. (2022). Ukraine Is Scanning Faces of Dead Russians, Then Contacting the Mothers. *The Washington Post*.

Henman, P. (2005). E-Government, Targeting and Data Profiling: Policy and Ethical Issues of Differential Treatment. *Journal of E-Government, 2*(1), 79–98.

Henman, P., and Adler, M. (2001). Information Technology and Transformations in Social Security Policy and Administration: A Review. *International Social Security Review, 54*(4), 23–47.

Henman, P., and Adler, M. (2003). Information Technology and the Governance of Social Security. *Critical Social Policy, 23*(2), 139–164.

Henman, P. W. F. (2021). Administrative Justice in a Digital World: Challenges and Solutions. In *Oxford Handbook of Administrative Justice*, pp. 459–480. Oxford University Press.

Kern, C., Bach, R. L., Mautner, H., et al. (2021). *Fairness in Algorithmic Profiling: A German Case Study*. arXiv preprint. arXiv:2108.04134.

Leslie, D. (2020). *Understanding Bias in Facial Recognition Technologies.* arXiv preprint. arXiv:2010.07023.
Maitra, S., Sleep, L., Fay, S. & Henman, P. (2024). *Building a Trauma-Informed Algorithmic Assessment Toolkit*. ADM+S Report. https://doi.org/10.60836/f01c-4a18, https://apo.org.au/node/326724
Mashaw, J. L. (1983) *Bureaucratic Justice: Managing Social Security Disability Claims.* Yale University Press.
McNamara, D., Graham T., Broad E., et al. (2019). Trade-offs in Algorithmic Risk Assessment. *Good Data*, 96–116.
Mehrabi, N., Morstatter F., Saxena N., et al. (2021). A Survey on Bias and Fairness in Machine Learning. *ACM Computing Surveys (CSUR), 54*(6), 1–35.
Morozov, E. (2013). *To Save Everything, Click Here: The Folly of Technological Solutionism.* PublicAffairs.
Pitoura, E., Stefanidis, K., and Koutrika, G. (2022). Fairness in Rankings and Recommendations: An Overview. *The VLDB Journal*, 1–28.
Rahwan, I. (2018). Society-in-the-Loop: Programming the Algorithmic Social Contract. *Ethics and Information Technology, 20*(1), 5–14.
Raji, I. D., Gebru, T., Mitchell, M., et al. (2020). *Saving Face: Investigating the Ethical Concerns of Facial Recognition Auditing*. Proceedings of the AAAI/ACM Conference on AI, Ethics, and Society, pp. 145–151.
Rasinski, K. A. (1987). What's Fair Is Fair—Or Is It? Value Differences Underlying Public Views About Social Justice. *Journal of Personality and Social Psychology, 53*(1), 201.
Rich, S. M. (2017). Procedural Versus Substantive Fairness. In F. M. Moghaddam (ed.), *The SAGE Encyclopedia of Political Behavior*, pp. 661–662. Thousand Oaks: Sage.
Schuler, D., and Namioka, A. (1993). *Participatory Design: Principles and Practices.* CRC Press.
Srivastava, M., Heidari, H., and Krause, A. (2019). *Mathematical Notions vs. Human Perception of Fairness: A Descriptive Approach to Fairness for Machine Learning.* Proceedings of the 25th ACM SIGKDD international conference on knowledge discovery & data mining, pp. 2459–2468.
Starke, C., Baleis, J., Keller, B., et al. (2022). Fairness Perceptions of Algorithmic Decision-Making: A Systematic Review of the Empirical Literature. *Big Data & Society, 9*(2), 20539517221115189.
Wang, R., Harper, F. M., and Zhu, H. (2020). *Factors Influencing Perceived Fairness in Algorithmic Decision-Making: Algorithm Outcomes, Development Procedures, and Individual Differences.* Proceedings of the 2020 CHI Conference on Human Factors in Computing Systems, pp. 1–14.
Weizenbaum, J. (1976). *Computer Power and Human Reason: From Judgment to Calculation.* Freeman & Co.
Wolfson, D. J. (2015). Implementing Fairness in Social Policy. *Journal of Human Development and Capabilities, 16*(2), 272–286.

4

Discretion and Power

Dave Cowan and Sally Wheeler

Introduction

Discretion and Welfare (Adler and Asquith 1981) is an edited collection, published in 1981, but based on a series of seminars funded by the then Social Science Research Council and which took place in 1978–1979. As such, it straddled the back end of the Callaghan government and the front end of the Thatcher government. References, as the editors caustically commented, may have become out of date, but the general themes remained prominent (p. 1). Thatcher's 1979 election victory and first government are often taken to be a paradigm shift, but, quite apart from the historical inaccuracy of such a view, discretion and welfare remained prominent and consistent problems.

The editors of this collection were Michael Adler and Stewart Asquith. At the time, both were early career scholars, and it must have been quite an enterprise organizing the workshops. Michael Adler's life history is beautifully presented by Linda Mulcahy in this collection (Chapter 2). Stewart Asquith, who passed away in 2009, was a child rights' researcher and activist,

D. Cowan (✉)
Cardiff University, Cardiff, UK
e-mail: CowanD1@cardiff.ac.uk

S. Wheeler
VC, Birkbeck University of London and Hon Professor of Law, Australian National University, London, UK
e-mail: s.wheeler@bbk.ac.uk

S. Cowan and S. Halliday (eds.), *Socio-Legal Generation*, Palgrave Socio-Legal Studies,
https://doi.org/10.1007/978-3-031-67244-6_4

as well as a sometime photographer. His career bridged various different disciplines, but, at the time of publication, shortly after he had completed his doctorate at Edinburgh (under the supervision of Neil MacCormick and Alex Robertson), his principal concerns were around justice and welfare in the context of juvenile criminal justice. Mike told us that

> I can't remember anything about how we came to collaborate on the proposal that eventually led to the book except that we sought the advice of Raymond Illsley, who was the Director of the Medical Sociology Research Centre in Aberdeen and the Chair of the ESRC's sociology and social policy committee, and that we went up to Aberdeen to see him. Applying for a grant to organise a seminar series was his idea. We applied and the rest is history.

The assembled cast of scholars now reads as an assembly of the founding parents of socio-legal studies. Most were early career lecturers or researchers at the time. A few, such as Jonathan Bradshaw and Gilbert Smith, were well-known scholars even then. Participants in the workshops included outstanding social administration scholars, then early career, such as Michael Hill.

For those of us graduating into socio-legal studies in the 1980s and 1990s, it was a pioneering collection, the themes of which have been a constant guide throughout our careers. Firstly, the collection sought to be multidisciplinary. The participants in the workshops and the essays produced in the book crossed the social sciences; the very purpose of the workshops appears to have been to counter the predominant positivist versions of the value of law as a control on discretionary power. Secondly, at their heart, the essays raise questions of power, specifically bureaucratic power, and do so—albeit sometimes awkwardly, and certainly not consistently—in a theoretically informed way. Thirdly, the essays themselves speak to each other and offer productive disagreements (perhaps, the current phrase, 'disagree agreeably', is appropriate) about even the conceptual and theoretical salience of the notion of discretion as a unit of analysis. As Zenon Bankowski and David Nelken (1981: 247) begin their essay,

> Practical and theoretical concern over discretion is best seen, not as an invitation to study a particular area of decision-making, but as an index to anxiety over the possibilities of unregulated decision-making.

We are now familiar with interdisciplinary studies of discretion, and there have been a considerable number of such studies, considering discretion generally, as well as in specific case studies. As a result, the pathbreaking nature of *Discretion and Welfare* may be lost on us. Recognized to be a problem requiring solutions, generally legal solutions, discretion had not been the subject of particularly sustained academic analysis in the disciplines. As Hill (1983: 129) wrote in his review of the collection, "That discretion should have come to be given extensive attention in a debate about what the balance between it and rules should be is not something about which those who are interested in social policy should be ashamed". That such a statement could be written may seem shocking to those of us for whom the relationship between discretion and rules is a taken-for-granted analytical variable across numerous case studies.

In this essay, we want to resuscitate the issues and anxieties of this collection, exemplified in both the introduction to the collection and Adler and Asquith's opening chapter, "Discretion and power". In the first section, we draw attention to the themes which the authors sought to develop, and which have subsequently been developed by others. In the second section, we discuss illustrations from our own original research which impinges on these themes, and which we develop in that context.

The first illustration concerns the use of the housing health and safety rating system to regulate housing standards in the private rented sector. We know that poor housing conditions have particular impacts on public and private health, but, statistically at least, local authority environmental health departments (the regulatory bureaucracy) have different levels of performance in terms of regulatory action against landlords and letting agents. The second illustration concerns the disqualification of directors of failed companies under the Company Directors Disqualification Act 1986 (CDDA 1986). The power to disqualify directors rests with the Court on an application from the Insolvency Service made in the public interest and alleging that a director is unfit to be concerned in the management of a company. The statute lists non-exhaustively practices which render a director unfit (Finch 1993). This deceptively simple, apparently rule-based construct is in practice run through with layers of agency, sites of micro-power and instances of the exercise of discretion.

Discretion and Power

In their essay, "Discretion and power", Adler and Asquith pursue a number of interconnected themes about the use and role of discretion in decision-making. In what follows, we draw attention to their approach and its continuing purchase in studies of discretionary decision-making. We focus on their approach to power, which, at that time, was innovative.

Discretion, Law and Power

Their target, however, was a critique of Kenneth Culp Davis' now well-known call for legal controls of discretionary decision-making. As Davis put it, "… we have to penetrate the unpleasant areas of discretionary determinations by police and prosecutors and other administrators, where huge concentrations of injustice invite drastic reforms" (1971: 216). In so doing, Davis counterposed rules with discretion, arguing that formal rules would contain and provide boundaries for administrative discretion. It was a nuanced argument, which recognized that discretion remained whenever one had formal rules—as Harlow and Rawlings (2022: 232) note, "Modern managers, with their faith in box-ticking, have tended to lose sight of this important point". The point of departure, for Davis, was the kind of individual bureaucrat decision-making routines and simplifications which were described by Lipsky and which virtually become the policies which are delivered (Lipsky 1980: 84).

The essential insight of Adler and Asquith's analysis, though, was that the relationship between the individual welfare-seeker and the bureaucrat-administrator was structured by relations of power. Lipsky (1980: 180) had already noted that street-level bureaucracy was "embedded in a larger system that creates and fortifies working conditions". Adler and Asquith's focus on power, however, enabled them to acknowledge the classic structure-agency problem. As they put it, it followed that "… attempts to modify the nature of these [bureaucratic] relationships must acknowledge the social and political forces sustaining forms of decision-making which have to be overcome for the achievement of meaningful social reform" (Adler and Asquith 1981: 12).

Further, their analysis of power was multi-faceted. They were early adopters of Foucauldian understandings of the micro-physics of power, and, although they did not put it this way, their analysis of power was linked to the disciplines/discipline and knowledge (here citing Giddens 1976). In so approaching power, they were pioneers in social policy (Hillyard and Watson 1996) and their analysis predated by some years the reception of Foucault's ideas around government and the administration of life. These approaches to power now seem *de rigueur* within socio-legal studies, such that they are taken-for-granted understandings and rarely explicitly discussed.

However, Adler and Asquith adopted a more peripatetic approach to power. Rather, the way they framed their analysis was by reference to ideology, and, more particularly, professional and lay ideologies (23–26). This complex analysis gave them the purchase to critique other studies of discretion:

> By ignoring the social derivations of differing ideologies, insufficient consideration is given to the fact that the powerful and authoritative position of the professions in the wider social and political arena renders the relationship between the decision-maker and the person who is subject to the decision a hierarchical one and one which is imbued with power. (26)

Accordingly, returning to the critique of the Davis's line of reasoning about legal controls of administrative discretion, they were able to argue that such controls do not touch on the inequalities in society upon which they depend and to which they actually contribute. Welfare state capitalism remained immune from, and diverted from, critique by the superimposition of legal control. This relationship between structure and agency was, they argued, the key to the study of discretionary decision-making (29). Drawing on Tay and Kamenka (1975), they argued that the superimposition of legality would lend further weight to the shift to Gesellschaft law, focusing on the atomization of society and avoiding the societal structure/s. As a result of this analysis, they advocated interpretative and phenomenological sociological methods.

Perhaps the best illustration of most of these methodological points about discretion lies in Jeffers and Hoggett's (1995) classic analysis of the approach taken by Haringey and Lambeth in the 1980s to counter subjective and institutional racism in council housing allocation. Since 1935, councils had powers to allocate their housing as they wished but had to give "reasonable preference" to certain statutorily identified groups. In the 1970s and 1980s, numerous studies found subjective and institutional racism in council housing allocation, which was regarded as the product of discretionary decision-making (Henderson and Karn 1987; CRE 1984). Discretion "… was the smokescreen behind which housing departments infused an agreed hierarchy of needs with a range of other, more dubious, allocative principles" (Smith and Mallinson 1996: 341).

Haringey and Lambeth, with anti-racist commitments, sought to avoid this problem by moving towards a more rule-based approach, but found that, despite that commitment, black households were being allocated poorer quality housing in worse areas in the boroughs, which was causing residential segregation. Part of the reason for this was that black households approaching the authority disproportionately as homeless re-interpreted the question "where would you like to live" as "how soon do you want to be re-housed"—thus, selecting worse areas; "street knowledge" of allocation schemes amongst applicants affected housing chances and was differentially distributed. Officer discretion still impacted on the choice of area, steering households closer to their family connections (for example), and what to do if a household refused an offer of accommodation. However, the key finding was that it was structural racism, for example as a result of the disproportionate number of black people approaching as homeless, which accounted for differential and disadvantaged outcomes (341–342). Reading this study in the light of Adler and Asquith's analysis, one can see how the retreat to rules opened up new areas for discretion; how the micro-physics of power worked in tandem with professional power, statistics and population (viz. structural inequalities) to produce not dissimilar outcomes to the previous system, in spite of the best intentions of the programme designers.

Towards Co-production

One strand of their analysis, which may seem odd to today's readers, lies in their partial focus on the significance of lay decision-makers and a more open-textured decision-making process, influenced by Luhmann's ideas. One can see this partial focus as a product of its time—the rise of the idea of the consumer as a counter-hegemonic device to challenge professional power (for discussion, see Loveland 1991). A similar set of understandings about regulation and accountability permeates the tripartite technique of responsive regulation (Ayres and Braithwaite 1992: ch 3).

Adler and Asquith raise concerns about the capture of such lay participation, and note that community participation "may help to impart a spurious legitimacy to the institutions concerned" (31). Their instincts in this regard remain pertinent as the dominant research and regulatory motif has become "co-production", a new way to describe this old problematic of government (see generally, McDermont et al. 2020).

Current Research Agendas

The analytical purchase of the ideas and diverse strands in their chapter can be demonstrated by the kind of research agenda and taken-for-granted knowledge which we have today. Hawkins' influential multidisciplinary collection of essays, published 11 years later, covered the same ground and a number of the essays made not dissimilar points albeit in a lengthier format (see Hawkins 1992; Daly 2020). The literature has branched out into diverse subdisciplines around administrative and bureaucratic justice (see Mashaw 1983; Adler 2004). The nuanced co-relationship between rules and discretion has been a focal point for analysis (for example, Sainsbury 1992). The failures of the legal model have been consistently remarked upon (see, for example, Handler 1992; Loveland 1995), and concerns have been raised about the impact of the legal model on decision-making (for example, Cane 2004; Halliday 2000). The concerns about the salience of due process are frequently considered in the context of ideas around legitimacy and why people obey the law (Tyler 1990), provoking the kinds of critique which are redolent of Adler and Asquith's analysis (Galligan 1996: 90–95).

These kinds of issues, however, remain of considerable ongoing importance, raising questions for scholars considering bureaucratic decision-making in the new public management inflected machine age. The shift to screen-level, system-level and even algorithmic-driven bureaucratic decision-making raises similar issues and can pose much sharper questions about structure and inequalities (Bovens and Zouridis 2002; Eubanks 2018). And structures are deeply implicated—indeed, imbricated—within digital decision-making (Daly et al. 2021; Raso 2022). As Bovens and Zouridis noted (2002: 181), there are new implications of these bureaucracies in constitutional state, with system designers the locus of discretionary power (see also Yeung and Harkens 2023); and further, the capacity of machines to learn within certain boundaries raises added issues for administrative justice (Harlow and Rawlings 2022: 251–255).

Perhaps most importantly, studies of discretionary decision-making routinely build in nuanced understandings of structure-agency, drawing on a rich sociological heritage. Consider, for example, Hawkins' and Manning's approach to the influences on regulatory decision-making, which relies on a kind of triptych between surround-field-frame (see, in particular, Hawkins 2002; Manning 1992). Changes to one level may prompt changes to another. Using this methodology, Hawkins establishes how and why criminal sanctions for health and safety breaches are regarded as the last resort. Reminiscent of Adler and Asquith's approach, he argues that "legal decisions, like other kinds of decision, are made not in a vacuum, but in a broader context of demands and expectations arising from the environment in which the decision-maker lives and works" (2002: 31).

Illustrating Discretion and Power

In the previous section, we discussed the core themes of Adler and Asquith's essay, and demonstrated their continuing salience to the project of understanding discretionary decision-making. In this section, we draw on two illustrations from our own original work to draw out these themes.

Regulating Landlords

In their essay in *Discretion and Welfare*, Bankowski and Nelken refer to Nelken's own data on the way in which discretion was used in relation to the powers of local authorities to prosecute private landlords for harassment. Their argument was that discretion could be used sometimes "... to insulate the relatively powerless from the full force of legal or administrative action at their expense" (1981: 253). Instead of prosecuting poor landlords, local authorities engaged in social work techniques to avoid prosecution.

Subsequent research found that these practices were facilitated and enhanced by a discursive narrative about the affected landlords as "amateurs"; only the most egregious breaches might be prosecuted (Cowan and Marsh 2001). These social work techniques or simply sending a warning letter to a landlord also reflected a significant shift in housing provision. The large-scale decline in social housing from the mid-1970s meant that there was greater reliance on private landlords. Local authorities had to work with them, under "the halo effect" of partnership (Valverde et al. 2020: 48).

As the housing crisis, underpinned by a local authority austerity-induced funding crisis, in England has proceeded apace, one might have expected these trends to continue. In two projects conducted with colleagues at the University of Bristol between 2018 and 2022 on the related area of housing conditions, we found that authorities were more willing to engage in enforcement action (see Harris et al. 2020). The reasons for this shift have been unpacked elsewhere. Here, we reflect on three issues—the relationship between rules and discretion; co-production; the role of discursive narratives in discretionary decision-making.

(i) Rules and discretion

The particular issue with which we are concerned in this chapter is local authority regulation of housing standards in the private rented sector. The 2004 Housing Act requires authorities to take action when health and safety hazards in a property fall below a certain threshold. These are termed Category 1 hazards and are assessed on the basis of the risk of harm associated with the occurrence of 29 matters, such as damp and mould growth, excess cold/heat, asbestos, crowding, light and noise (see Housing Health and Safety Rating System (England) Regulations 2005, SI 2005/3208). The assessments of these risk were evidence-based (Burridge and Ormandy 2007; although the evidence-base itself has not kept pace with the evidence, the guidance last being updated in 2006).

What we have, then, is a clear rule—enforcement action must be taken—underpinned by a scientific assessment process. However, as was pinpointed by the Upper Tribunal, that scientific assessment process was, in fact, undercut by discretion:

> The complicated set of provisions is designed to produce a numerical score for each hazard that is under consideration so that it can be seen to fall within a particular band and in either category 1 or category 2. The great danger of a numerical score produced in this way is that it creates the impression of methodological accuracy, whereas the truth may be that it is the product of no more than a series of value judgments based on little understood statistics of questionable validity. (*Bolton MBC v Patel* [2010] UKUT 334 (LC), at [38])

Further, although there was a clear rule about enforcement, aspects of discretionary judgement seeped in to frontline action, even in authorities which had moved towards a more hard line enforcement process. The statutory enforcement guidance itself appeared to mandate this move by being less than clear about enforcement. It recognized the importance of "informal working" and suggested the need for "judgment as to the necessity for intervention, given the authority's priorities and wider renewal policies and, where appropriate, their knowledge of a landlord and his or her compliance history" (ODPM 2006). That firm statutory rule on enforcement had been rolled back, giving a green light to more informal working practices, including the types of practice found by Nelken.

A particular example demonstrates how, even in enforcement-oriented authorities, discretion might play out. There was discretion at the margins as to how long an officer might give a landlord before sending out the enforcement notice. If the landlord was able to conduct the repairs or have the repairs in train before the notice was served, then there would be no need for the notice itself. Some authorities institutionalized this practice by using the threat that, if they did have to serve the notice, the landlord would have to pay a fee. During COVID-19, such periods were extended because of the difficulty in finding building contractors.

Some authorities, recognizing differences in practice between officers and landlords' common complaint of differential treatment, had sought to develop IT systems and co-ordinated practices to avoid such issues. Some, also, had institutionalized the "breathing space" between inspection and enforcement on the basis that it was appropriate to give landlords the opportunity before more heavy-handed action. However, the heart of the difference lay in the subjective opinions that officers might have about the willingness of the landlord to comply with their requirements. This might be constructed in part as a risk judgement based on past history of engagement with the particular landlord. The officer's self-orientation about the purposes of enforcement was also significant. For example, an officer may disagree with the authority's enforcement standpoint and work at its margins in a particular case.

Different versions of the rationale for enforcement were also employed. It may have been about housing standards, but there were differences about whether this concerned the particular occupiers. The assessment process assumed in rational scientific style a particular occupier, but the role of the actual occupier affected by the housing conditions was less clear. A more vulnerable occupier might give rise to stronger enforcement. Equally, the occupier's reasons for making a complaint in the first place might affect enforcement—they might be regarded simply as seeking to obtain more priority for social housing, for example, as a result of their living conditions.

Adler and Asquith noted that one of the problematic aspects of law and discretion was that individuals may be unaware of their rights. Socio-legal scholars around the same time as Adler and Asquith's collection were seeking to understand how disputes emerged, developing their ideas under the rubric of naming, blaming and claiming (Felsteiner et al. 1981–2). They also argued for the significance of "agents of transformation". In our study, an agent of transformation was a set of processes which had been developed to filter complaints which were uniformly labelled "triage". That is a label which has been used in welfare bureaucracies, but, in contradistinction to its medical etymology, it means that systems are put in place to identify the worst cases on which there will be primary focus. In some areas, triaging systems were electronic and required tenants to upload veracious information on to a web site before a complaint would be registered. Photographs of areas of concern and details of interactions with landlords (including landlord refusals to comply with their repairing obligations) may be required before being able to pursue the complaint. The concern about such systems is perhaps obvious—they do not necessarily identify the most serious issues, but allow the most technically able to pursue complaints, leaving potentially vulnerable households at the mercy of poor housing conditions. These kinds of systems bake in various assumptions about workload management, and, perhaps, a management view that, if your complaint is serious enough, you will persevere with it.

(ii) Co-regulation

In two study areas, it emerged that the local authorities had sought to engage with the local landlord associations in what was described to us as "co-production". The broad understanding of co-production involved was that the landlord association would take primary responsibilities for policing the housing management standards of their members. Reductions in licensing costs were given to members of those organizations. We can see here the operation of the proto-co-production model which Adler and Asquith discussed. Whether or not this relationship between the authority-qua-regulator and the landlord association created the spurious legitimacy to the latter or not, these relationships were failed experiments. Co-production is hard to do, but even harder when the expectations of both organizations are different. The authority expected effectively to contract out their roles to the associations but the associations had only limited ability to remove members from their roll. Accordingly, the outcome was that, for the duration of the relationship, it provided a spurious legitimacy to the authority exercising its enforcement role through the landlord association.

(iii) Narratives at work

Ewick (2008: 87) argues that narratives are powerful techniques of legitimation and sustain power relations. Adler and Asquith's focus on power in the context of welfare bureaucracies emphasizes the need for us to see how narratives predetermine particular types of action through the production of a particular type of power/knowledge. In earlier studies, landlords had been constructed by local authorities and their officers as partners in meeting housing need (Cowan and Marsh 2001). This partnership meant that authorities had to balance their enforcement roles with a recognition that they relied on landlords to fulfil the role of meeting households' housing needs, the authorities themselves having insufficient stock so to do.

However, it was notable across both of the studies being discussed here that the narratives had changed. Landlords were commonly regarded as running a profit-making business. Accordingly, the idea of the partner meeting housing need, or of accidental landlords requiring training, was shifting towards a commercial crime keying in which the authority's role was to "break the business model". This tied in with changing government narratives which have emphasized the rise of the "rogue landlord"—whilst the participants in both studies deprecated this label, it gave rise to the recognition that some landlords were "crooks", and some authorities had either received short-term grants from central government to deal with them, and/or set up units to deal with the worst offenders. This re-keying also brought the authorities closer to other organizations, like the police, which had different, more pro-prosecution orientations, and which "rubbed off" on the authorities' approach.

Disqualifying Directors

(i) The process

The current regime around the disqualification of directors emerged from the deliberations of the Cork Committee on the reform of insolvency law (Cork 1982). Disqualification had been possible before (since 1929) but was available only in very limited circumstances. The 1986 legislative intervention introduced a much broader regime requiring the Court to disqualify a director for a period of 2–15 years upon a finding of unfitness on foot of an application by the Secretary of State made in the public interest. Carruthers and Halliday characterized it as offering an underpinning of prevention, retribution, punitiveness and restitution, in deep contrast to the US. The US-inspired approach was normatively much more neutral using insolvency as a mechanism for removing "less fit" organizations from the ranks of business institutions, or placing poorly managed assets under the stewardship of more able managers (Carruthers and Halliday 1998: 266, 274–277). The UK legislation imposed a brake on the otherwise prevailing rhetoric of "free enterprise", "entrepreneurship", and the small business as a route to prosperity (specifically a grocery store in Grantham) so valourized by Thatcherism (CPC 1984; Wheeler 1993).

This brake has its roots in two other components of Thatcherism. One was the Premier's own moral stance, founded in the tenets of Methodism, that personal responsibility and hard work as opposed to acquisitiveness and incompetence were the key to a good life (Heelas and Morris 1992; Cooper et al. 2022). The second was the need to support and protect key policies such as the organization and marketization of utilities and other large industries with demonstrable governance of market morality and policing of market failure (Halliday and Carruthers 1996). The absence of an automatic disqualification for directors of failed companies hints at a distinction being drawn between legitimate attempts at self-advancement that end unfortunately in failure, on the one hand; and, on the other, activities or decisions which are considered to be irresponsible and commercially immoral. In this framing, we can see how the insight of Adler and Asquith, about the significance of structures, remains true in the way in which deviance is framed.

In the first empirical survey of the disqualification legislation, it was clear that those disqualified from being directors were primarily owner-managers of small companies (Hicks 1998; cf Bankowski and Nelken 1981). A perusal of the Insolvency Service database of disqualified directors indicates that this remains the case (Insolvency Service 2023a). The immorality and irresponsibility that are being punished are the use of the shelter of limited liability by shareholders (owners) for the companies' debts generated by their own activities in the guise of managers (directors). As Bankowski and Nelken (1981: 254) put it, "… it is to be expected that, on the whole, officials will use their discretion to ease their tasks by directing their unpleasing attentions at those who cannot fight back". However, the point here is that the legislation itself was devised to produce such low-hanging fruit.

Corporate insolvency and within that directors' disqualification is less conceptually centred than landlord and tenant law, and housing conditions. Within insolvency law there are different types of proceedings and overlapping interest groups—for example, directors are often employees, shareholders and creditors of the failed company simultaneously in addition to their role as directors. Most disqualification orders occur as a result of Creditors' Voluntary Liquidation (CVL) proceedings. That process is by far and away the most numerically significant insolvency proceeding used in England and Wales each year. In 2022, there were 18,825 CVLs but only 1959 compulsory liquidations with even fewer company voluntary arrangements and administrations. In 2019, there were 12,058 CVLs and 2945 compulsory liquidations, respectively (Statista 2023). The organization of CVLs is such that they are essentially a private process between the company and its creditors. Once the state administered system of disqualification is grafted on to this process, we are then confronted with a quite unique mix of state regulation, public interest, private actors and private funding. In one sense, then, this is the kind of democratized understanding of how discretion might be used to operate in society through co-opting society into its operation; but, this ideological model was far from that conceived by the authors in *Discretion and Welfare*, as this model represented the atomization of individual private actors with the state only as backup of last resort.

A CVL begins with a resolution by a company's shareholders to wind it up. At the same time an Insolvency Practitioner (IP), an individual in private practice (often accountancy) licensed to act, is invited by the directors of the company to prepare a statement of the company's assets and debts for its creditors; a summary of the company's trading and financial history; and an account of its transactions since its last audited accounts. To prepare these documents the IP works closely with the directors of the company. These documents are sent to the creditors of the company who vote formally at a meeting on whether to approve the appointment of the IP as liquidator of the company. As voting rights are determined by the value of the creditor's debt and most directors of failed companies are, on paper at least, large creditors of their company the appointment is invariably approved.

Directors of failed companies are rarely "repeat players" in the sense of being involved in successive corporate failures, despite sensationalist media stories which might suggest otherwise (Williams 2007). This means that often they fail to understand the pivotal significance for them of the appointment of the IP as liquidator by the creditors. The Adler and Asquith insight about the nuance of disciplinary power is evident here: from this moment onwards there is a power shift in the IP-director relationship. The IP's key constituencies now do not include the directors from whom they originally sourced this work and appointed them. The IP becomes the central actor in the disqualification process for company directors as the disqualification system (CDDA 1986, section 7A, and the Insolvency Rules 2001) requires that the liquidator in a CVL completes a form for the Insolvency Service commenting on the conduct of the directors. These forms are known as Director Conduct Reports and are submitted at the level of the company.

(ii) Rules and discretion

Prior to April 2016, the IP was expressly asked to make a yes/no determination on whether a director was "unfit" to be concerned in the management of a company, and to give details of what they thought the unfit conduct was. After April 2016, the IP has not been required to exercise discretion as to whether the conduct amounts to unfitness or not. That determination is performed by an algorithm within the Insolvency Service which sorts out which matters require further investigation. Accordingly, the critical moment of discretion has slipped back to the IP Report and its framing. The discretion of the IP now sits at the level of the thoroughness of the investigation that they carry out around the director's conduct and the quality of evidence that they include in the Director Conduct Report.

The Creditors' Meeting is also a critical juncture for IP and the creditors themselves. The interplay between private interests and the requirements of the regulatory state make this meeting a micro-power site where expectations are voiced and promises are made (Wheeler 1994). It is here that the IP provides and gets agreement on their fees for winding up the company. These fees might be based on a time cost basis (the hours that will be spent on the liquidation) or expressed as a percentage of the assets recovered. As the company is in liquidation because it can't pay its debts, whatever the IP charges is money taken from the limited funds recovered and so is money not available to creditors to satisfy their debt.

If the creditors want the directors' conduct to be investigated with a view to civil recovery personally against them—a recommendation for disqualification or a compensation order—they have to recognize the financial cost of the IP doing this and trust that they will do it. For the IP, fees can't be excessive partly because of the rather remote risk of losing reputational capital with local trade associations and the like, and partly because of the much bigger risk of individual creditor complaints to their licensing body. Conversely, if fees are set too low, then the investigation of the directors' conduct that creditors might request and that the Insolvency Service requires for the disqualification regime will need to be subsidized by the IP. At the point of setting fees at the Creditors' Meeting, the IP will have had time for only the briefest of consideration of director conduct, so gauging the amount of work required is difficult. Whilst conduct reports are required to be made about directors "in the public interest", the cost of protecting the public interest here is borne not by the state but by the creditors or the IP.

The IP controls the asset recovery process and the compilation of the disqualification reports for the Insolvency Service. A Schedule to the CDDA 1986 provides an indicative list in very broad terms of the type of activities that might render a director unfit if an application to disqualify them is made by the Insolvency Service to the Court—misfeasance, breach of fiduciary duty, and breach of legislation or other obligations to be set alongside the frequency of conduct and responsibility for the failure of the company. There is no legislative guidance on how these factors are to be weighed or assessed. The Director Conduct Report form translates these criteria into a requirement for details of how the company has been conducted over the previous three years of its existence. The IP decides how they present the company and what evidence they provide to support their narrative.

There is clearly a discretion filter residing in IPs in the compilation of the report. The vast majority of companies that are placed in CVL have both poor quality records and accounting compliance history. They are likely to have been in a state of disarray for some time. The IP will have to decide how much time they spend on reconstructing the company's history and the decisions of the directors, and who will be interviewed (Wheeler 1995). Evidence will need to be gathered and analysed to be presented in the Director Conduct Report.

The "Rules Engine", as the Insolvency Service describes its algorithm, makes the first sift of Director Conduct Reports, and depends on language recognition to allocate the case for human review. If a case is not sifted for review at this stage, then there is no possibility of proceedings being launched by the Insolvency Service. In 2020, changes were made to the algorithm to lower the number of cases being captured for human review. In the financial year 2021–2022, the Insolvency Service received 9826 Director Conduct Reports of which 4165 were sifted by the rules engine for human review. From that sub-sample, 802 directors were subsequently disqualified. What we do not know is how many individual directors were caught in the 9826 submitted conduct reports or in the 4165 sifted reports as they are at the level of the company (Insolvency Service 2022).

(iii) Decision-maker professionalism

Insolvency Practitioners are one of the UK's youngest professions, yet the professional knowledge analysis of Adler and Asquith can be applied to them. IPs' professional status and licensing regime came into being in 1986 coterminously with the legislative framework for disqualifying directors. Whilst their reports on directors go to the Insolvency Service and their primary client relationship is with the directors of insolvent companies, individuals facing bankruptcy and their respective creditors, licensing occurs through one of four Recognized Professional Bodies (RPBs). The two largest such bodies are the Insolvency Practitioners Association (IPA) and the Institute of Chartered Accountants in England and Wales (ICAEW), with around 600 and 800 members, respectively.

Creating a new profession to administer the frontline of a new disciplinary regime was key to avoiding direct regulation by the state of this process, which would not have suited the prevailing ideology at the time of smaller government and less regulation. It might be said that the ethic of the legislation through which they owe their powerful social and political existence is replicated in their approach and understandings.

Professional status was something for which elite professionals involved in insolvency work had been asking since the 1960s (Cork 1982)—for recognition within their own professional groups as much as for professional status in and of itself. This creates a micro-power site between the individual IP and the RPB that provides their licence. RPBs are required to undertake compliance checks on their members and respond to complaints about their service with any complaints to the Insolvency Service about IPs being referred to them.

The complaint handling and compliance visit system by the RPBs is, like nearly all self-regulation systems, financed by membership fees. The number of complaints concluded across the full spectrum of IP work for IPA regulated IPs was 162 in 2022. Five of these were referred to the Regulation & Conduct or Disciplinary & Appeals Committees (IPA 2022). The Insolvency Service holds the key to RPBs maintaining their status as regulators. The number of RPBs has reduced from eight to four since the IP profession was created. All of this is perhaps indicative of the insight of Adler and Asquith (1981: 22) that such organizations are "carriers of a welfare ideology and are a very important means by which certain conceptions of social reality are sustained and by which particular forms of social order are maintained".

In September 2023 a Government Consultation Response to the Future of Insolvency Regulation challenged the RPBs to deliver measurable improved outcomes to their regulatory activities around the timeliness of complaint handling and disciplinary decision-making, and to deal with the potential for internal actual or perceived conflicts that arise from self-regulation (Insolvency Service 2023b). Perhaps the sun is slowly setting on a regulatory style of a particular time; a discretion based system of private action, privately funded, supporting a rarely applied but inflexible state sanction.

Conclusions

In this chapter, we have demonstrated how the analytical insights of the pioneering work of Mike Adler and Stewart Asquith in their collection remain both perspicacious and so significant to our understandings of the role of discretion that they are automatically implicated in our studies. *Discretion and Welfare* has become a key reference point without being referenced. We have sought to resuscitate it here by giving credit where it is due. We corresponded with Mike about this chapter and, like us, he "... was surprised at how many of the ideas that have informed my research over the years were flagged up in this early piece". The same is true for us. Our illustration reflects the ongoing significance of the key themes of that chapter—the micro-physics of power; how discretion apparently written into legislation comes to be used against the interests of the poor; and how professional and lay knowledges combine with unequal outcomes. Although our illustrations are different, and the actors differently constituted, both demonstrate how that relationship between structure and agency becomes implicated in the practice of discretion.

References

Adler, M. (2004). A Socio-Legal Approach to Administrative Justice. *Law and Policy, 25*(4), 323–352.

Adler, M., and Asquith, S. (eds.). (1981). *Discretion and Welfare*. London: Heinemann.

Ayres, I., and Braithwaite, J. (1992). *Responsive Regulation: Transcending the Deregulation Debate*. Oxford: OUP.

Bankowski, Z., and Nelken, D. (1981). Discretion as a Social Problem. In M. Adler and S. Asquith (eds.), *Discretion and Welfare*. London: Heinemann.

Bovens, M., and Zouridis, S. (2002). From Street-Level to System-Level Bureaucracies: How Information and Communication Technology Is Transforming Administrative Discretion and Constitutional Control. *Public Administration Review, 62*(2), 174–184.

Burridge, R., and Ormandy, D. (2007). Health and Safety at Home: Private and Public Responsibility for Unsatisfactory Housing Conditions. *Journal of Law and Society, 34*(4), 544–566.

Cane, P. (2004). Understanding Judicial Review and Its Impact. In M. Hertogh and S. Halliday (eds.), *Judicial Review and Bureaucratic Impact: International and Interdisciplinary Perspectives*. Cambridge: CUP.

Carruthers, B., and Halliday, T. (1998). *Rescuing Business*. Oxford: OUP.

Commission for Racial Equality (CRE). (1984). *Race and Council Housing in Hackney*. London: CRE.

Conservative Political Centre (CPC). (1984). *Small Today, Bigger Tomorrow*. London: Conservative Party.

Cooper, C., Tweedie, J., Andrew, J., and Baker, M. (2022). From 'Business-Like' to Businesses: Agencification, Corporatization, and Civil Service Reform Under the Thatcher Administration. *Public Administration, 100*(2), 193–215.

Cork. (1982). *Insolvency Law and Practice: Report of the Review Committee*, Cmnd 8558. London: HMSO.

Cowan, D., and Marsh, A. (2001). There's Regulatory Crime and Then There's Landlord Crime: From 'Rachmanites' to 'Partners'. *Modern Law Review, 64*(6), 831–853

Daly, P. (2020). The Inevitability of Discretion and Judgment in Front-Line Decision-Making in the Administrative State. *Journal of Commonwealth Law, 2*, 99–134.

Daly, P., Raso, J., and Tomlinson, J. (2021). Administrative Law in the Digital World. In C. Harlow (ed.), *Research Handbook on Administrative Law*. Aldershot: Edward Elgar.

Davis, K. C. (1971). *Discretionary Justice: A Preliminary Inquiry*. Urbana: University of Illinois.

Eubanks, V. (2018). *Automating Inequality: How High-Tech Tools Profile, Police, and Punish the Poor*. New York: St Martin's Press.

Ewick, P. (2008). Consciousness and Ideology. In A. Sarat (ed), *The Blackwell Companion to Law and Society*. Oxford: Blackwell.

Felsteiner, W., Abel, R., and Sarat, A. (1981–2). 'The Emergence and Transformation of Disputes: Naming, Blaming, Claiming ...', *Law and Society Review, 15*(3), 631–654.

Finch, V. (1993). Disqualifying Directors: Issues of Rights, Privileges and Employment. *Industrial Law Journal, 22*(1): 35–43.

Galligan, D. (1996). *Due Process and Fair Procedures: A Study of Administrative Procedures*. Oxford OUP.

Halliday, T., and Carruthers, B. (1996). The Moral Regulation of Markets: Professions, Privatization and the English Insolvency Act 1986. *Accounting, Organizations and Society, 21*(4), 371–413.

Handler, J. (1992). Discretion: Power, Quiescence, and Trust. In K. Hawkins (ed), *The Uses of Discretion*. Oxford: OUP.

Harris, J., Cowan, D., and Marsh, A. (2020). *Improving Compliance with Private Rented Sector Legislation: Local Authority Regulation and Enforcement*. Glasgow: CaCHE. https://housingevidence.ac.uk/wp-content/uploads/2020/08/200803_ComplianceReport_Final.pdf.

Halliday, S. (2000). The Influence of Judicial Review on Bureaucratic Decision-Making. *Public Law*, 110–124.

Harlow, C., and Rawlings, R. (2022). *Law and Administration*. Cambridge: CUP.

Hawkins, K. (1992). The Use of Legal Discretion: Perspectives from Law and Social Science. In K. Hawkins (ed.), *The Uses of Discretion*. Oxford: OUP.

Hawkins, K. (2002). *Law as Last Resort: Prosecution Decision-Making in a Regulatory Agency*. Oxford: OUP.

Heelas, P., and Morris, P. (1992). Enterprise Culture: Its Values and Value. In P. Heelas and P. Morris (eds.), *The Values of the Enterprise Culture*. London: Routledge.

Henderson, J., and Karn, V. (1987). *Race, Class and State Housing: Inequality and the Allocation of Public Housing in Britain*. Aldershot: Gower.

Hicks, A. (1998). *Disqualification of Directors: No Hiding Place for the Unfit?* London: ACCA Educational Trust.

Hill, M. (1983). Review of Michael Adler and Stewart Asquith, *Discretion and Welfare*, Heinemann, London, 1981. *Journal of Social Policy, 12*(1), 128–129.

Hillyard, P., and Watson, S. (1996). Postmodern Social Policy: A Contradiction in Terms? *Journal of Social Policy, 25*(3), 321–346.

Insolvency Rules. (2001). *The Insolvent Companies (Reports on Conduct of Directors) (Amendment) Rules 2001*, SI 2001/764.

Insolvency Service. (2022). *The Insolvency Service* 'Annual Reports and Accounts 2021–2022'. https://assets.publishing.service.gov.uk/government/uploads/system/uploads/attachment_data/file/1113783/221012_Annual_Report_and_Accounts_2021-22_FINAL.pdf (accessed September 13, 2023).

Insolvency Service. (2023a). https://find-and-update.company-information.service.gov.uk/ (accessed September 9, 2023).

Insolvency Service. (2023b). *The Future of Insolvency Regulation*. https://www.gov.uk/government/consultations/the-future-of-insolvency-regulation (accessed September 16, 2023).

IPA. (2022). https://insolvency-practitioners.org.uk/about/annual-reports-and-accounts/ (accessed September 16, 2023).

Jeffers, S. and Hoggett, P. (1995). Like Counting Deckchairs on the Titanic: A Study of Institutional Racism and Housing Allocations in Haringey and Lambeth. *Housing Studies, 10*(3), 325–344.

Lipsky, M. (1980). *Street-Level Bureaucracy: Dilemmas of the Individual in Public Services*. New York: Russell Sage Foundation.

Loveland, I. (1991). Square Pegs, Round Holes: The 'Right' to Council Housing in the Post-War Era. *Journal of Law and Society, 19*(3), 339–364.

Loveland, I. (1995). *Housing Homeless Persons*. Oxford: OUP.

Manning, P. (1992). 'Big Bang' Decisions: Notes on a Naturalistic Approach. In K. Hawkins (ed.), *The Uses of Discretion*. Oxford: OUP.

Mashaw, J. (1983). *Bureaucratic Justice: Managing Social Security Disability Claims*. New Haven: Yale UP.

McDermont, M., Cole, T., Newman, J., and Piccini, A. (2020). *Imagining Regulation Differently: Co-creating Regulation for Engagement*. Bristol: Policy Press.

ODPM. (2006). *Housing Health and Safety Rating System: Enforcement Guidance*. London: DLUHC.

Raso, J. (2022). Implementing Digitalization in an Administrative Justice Context. In M. Hertogh, R. Kirkham, R. Thomas and J. Tomlinson (eds.), *The Oxford Handbook of Administrative Justice*. Oxford: OUP.

Statista. (2023). https://www.statista.com/statistics/310422/uk-insolvencies-total-number-of-company-liquidations/ (accessed August 21, 2023).

Sainsbury, R. (1992). Administrative Justice: Discretion and Procedure in Social Security Decision-Making. In K. Hawkins (ed), *The Uses of Discretion*. Oxford: OUP.

Smith, S., and Mallinson, S. (1996). The Problem with Social Housing: Discretion, Accountability and The Welfare Ideal. *Policy and Politics, 24*(3), 339–357.

Tay, A., and Kamenka, E. (1975). Beyond Bourgeois Individualism: The contemporary Crisis in Law and Legal Ideology. In E. Kamenka and R. Neale (eds), *Feudalism, Capitalism and Beyond*. London: Edward Arnold.

Tyler, T. (1990). *Why People Obey the Law*. New York: Princeton.

Valverde, M., Briggs, J., Tran, G., and Montevirgen, M. (2020). Public Universities as Real Estate Developers in the Age of 'the Art of the Deal'. *Studies in Political Economy*, *101*(1), 35–58.
Wheeler, S. (1993). Disqualification of Directors: A Broader View. In H. Rajak (ed.), *Insolvency Law and Practice*. London: Sweet & Maxwell.
Wheeler, S. (1994). Empty Rhetoric and Empty Promises: The Creditors Meeting. *Journal of Law and Society*, *21*(3), 350–373.
Wheeler, S. (1995). Directors' Disqualification: Insolvency Practitioners and the Decision-Making Process. *Legal Studies*, *15*(2), 283–305.
Williams, R. (2007). Disqualifying Directors: A Remedy Worse Than the Disease? *Journal of Corporate Law Studies*, *7*(2), 213–242.
Yeung, K., and Harkens, A. (2023). How Do "Technical" Design Choices Made When Building Algorithmic Decision-Making Tools for Criminal Justice Authorities Create Constitutional Dangers? *Public Law*, 265–286 and 448–472.

5

Examining Prison Discourse: Extending 'Discourse, Power and Justice' to Front-Line Prison Officers

Shelley Eder

Introduction

Adler and Longhurst's (1994) classic study of prison management in Scotland significantly advanced our understanding of the internal dynamics of the penal institution and provides one of the few comprehensive examinations of high-level actors within the prison complex (Duke 2002; Bennett et al. 2013). Turning, as they did, the academic lens towards the 'powerful in preference to the poor', they extended into an at the time innovative sociological terrain, providing the groundwork for a succinct conceptualisation of the conflicts and complexities of pressures at the heart of the carceral matrix. Part of the book's appeal is that it turns the lens of administrative justice to the field of penology, and by doing so lays the groundwork for a reframing of penal power in terms of the institutional forces on which it rests.

Here it is argued that Adler and Longhurst's model may provide a good basis from which to analyse the discourses of power employed by prison officers on the ground. It is accepted that systemic discourse analysis is a useful tool for analysing power relations in prison, although it is asserted here that the most important expression of power in prison is to be found in the day-to-day interactions between officers and inmates. On this level the narratives involved in the assertion of power and authority may stem from the formal structures identified in the models or may be generated by more

S. Eder (✉)
Charles Darwin University, Darwin, NT, Australia
e-mail: Shelley.Eder@cdu.edu.au

S. Cowan and S. Halliday (eds.), *Socio-Legal Generation*, Palgrave Socio-Legal Studies,
https://doi.org/10.1007/978-3-031-67244-6_5

informal cultural understandings. An interesting and fruitful way of picking up this research where it left off may be to investigate whether and/or how far the identified formal discourses are adopted and mobilised by the front-line prison officer.

The substantial barriers to conducting qualitative research inside prisons may be particularly acute where the focus is more on the prison officers than inmates, and in the current climate these questions are, admittedly, not easy to investigate. One suggestion proposed here to overcome the notorious inaccessibility of prison in this sense might be to investigate the interactions of prison officers over social media. The following discussion unpacks the case for extending our examination of narratives to incorporate those that form part of the world views of officers acting at the coal face and proposes a means of investigating this question via analysis of certain kinds of online data. This kind of examination, it is argued, allows us to access a more comprehensive picture of the reality of prison institutional authority.

Background: Discourse, Power and Justice Explained

The initial study innovatively merged the fields of socio-legal studies and the sociology of knowledge. Drawing on the work of Manheim (1952, 1953, 1986) and Foucault (1979, 1981) in these respective arenas, the book is designed as a platform for the formulation and development of a 'new sociology of imprisonment'. Here discourse analysis provides the underlying theoretical framework for an investigation of organisational rationalities that allow for the contestation and negotiation of power dynamics. Adler and Longhurst argue that the prison is a natural site for studying these kind of processes, as it provides a stark example of the means of social domination:

> We are ... much concerned with the discursive nature of social domination, which is particularly evident in the case of prisons. An institution, which in many respects seems to be built upon violence and brutal repression is, we would argue, also structured and maintained by discursive relations and interactions. (1994: 28)

The focus here is very much on the pressures that create change. They locate these pressures largely within the policy and report documents, formal mechanisms for oversight and accountability, and the way in which various grievances are handled. By analysing these documents and supplementing this data with observations of high-level meetings and selective interviews, they are able to provide a comprehensive overview of governance styles and the infiltration of certain modes of thought into prison policy and practice.

Adler and Longhurst present their analysis as a way of building on Foucault's theoretical perspective by focusing attention on 'the detailed mechanics of power relations which are neglected in his more general account' (1994: xxi). Noting that discursive relations are reflective of broader attitudes and beliefs, they map these narrative patterns and then home in on the 'competitive struggle' that occurs between the different actors mobilising various discourses within the penal institution, with a particular focus on formal decision-making and policy. The whole basis of their thesis is that these struggles are central to the way organisational power manifests:

> It is possible for the analyst to identify the patterns and structures of such discourses, which in turn act as resources to be used by social groups engaged in struggle. Further, such discourses affect the nature of domination- the result of struggles- and give it a particular cast. (1994: 31)

Overlaid on this theoretical foundation is a form of identification and classification drawn from the field of administrative justice. Administrative justice is concerned with the way governmental institutions operate towards citizens; in particular, how administrative decisions are made and challenged. Adler and Longhurst use the frameworks developed in this context as a basis for a classificatory system that identifies and analyses the kinds of discursive struggles in decision-making that are occurring at the site.

The map they develop of the discourses infiltrating decision-making at prison management level is classified broadly under the banner of 'ends discourses' and 'means discourses'; where ends discourses are concerned with the overall justification of prison in society and means discourses are concerned with how prisons should be run. Adler and Longhurst asserted that each of these discourses represented the interests of certain groups and that 'such discourses affect the nature of domination... and give it a particular cast' (1994: 31). Thus, the identified external and internal discursive models create pressures that are essentially in constant conflict, entailing that 'the penal system is the site of struggles between different social actors mobilising, constructing and re-interpreting particular discourses' (1994: 45). They explore further these apparent tensions and their model (see table below) highlights how the various influences, the assumptions underpinning them, and their flow on effects, are prevalent in various aspects of prison administration. The resulting analysis provides us with a systematic conceptual framework for understanding the discursive foundations underpinning the exercise of power in this institution.

End Discourses

Ends discourses are concerned with the underlying purpose of the prison. Adler and Longhurst categorise prevalent ends narratives in terms of rehabilitation, normalisation or control. Rehabilitation concerns itself with the 'deviant individual' (1994: 37) who is socially maladapted in some way, where the prison aims to re-socialise and re-integrate the prisoner back into society in a way that reduces future offending. Normalisation refers to the framing of offenders as ordinary people 'who have committed a crime', and that aside from custody and security, life should remain as normal as possible for the inmate, 'merely aiming to ensure the individual will not become 'worse' during the period of incarceration' (1994: 39). Normalisation frames the criminal justice system in terms of retribution and reduces the role of the prison in this sense, instead focusing primarily on sentencing as the retributive act. Here, then, the prison itself has no role in exacting additional punishment (the famous saying being that a person is sentenced *as* punishment not *for* punishment) and the aim becomes 'humane containment' of the inmate. Adler and Longhurst highlight the deep conflict between the normalisation and rehabilitation discourses that is not always apparent to those involved in the development of prison policy (1994: 39).

The control discourse is clearly central to contemporary understanding of the role of the prison, and within this frame the inmate is a source of potential trouble or difficulty (1994: 40). Control is about 'managing' difficult behaviours; 'it maintains that the individual should conform to whatever measures are deemed to be necessary for the maintenance of order and discipline in the prison' and focuses on conformity of behaviours (1994: 40). Adler and Longhurst have highlighted that within the institution itself the control discourse is ubiquitous and primarily concerned with the protection of prison officers (1994: 40).

Ends discourses table:

Discourse	Rehabilitation	Normalisation	Control
Source of legitimacy	*Improving the individual	*Prevent negative effects *Treating prisoners like individuals in the community	*Control of disruption *Smooth functioning of the prison
Focus	Deviant individual	Normal individual	Disruptive individual

(continued)

(continued)

Discourse	Rehabilitation	Normalisation	Control
Dominant concerns	*Socialising the individual back into society E.g. training/ treatment	*Minimum security Contact with family *Improved living conditions	*Good order and discipline *Protection of prison staff

Source Adler and Longhurst (1994: 41)

Means Discourses

In addition to the ends discourses concerned with the external justification of imprisonment, Adler and Longhurst also identified 'means' discourses in the prison setting; ways of framing *how* a prison should be run. Utilising Mashaw's (1983) well-known framework of analysis of public organisational accountability in the field of administrative justice scholarship, Adler and Longhurst identify how the day-to-day routine operation of the prison can be framed in legal, bureaucratic and professional terms. As with the ends discourses, the means discourses are often not congruent and may be competing forces within the organisation (1994: 43). As ideal types, they each have their own conceptual framework, and according to this theory, a higher reliance on one will lead to a lessening of the others (1994: 47, 44).

The bureaucratic discourse is concerned with enforcement of rules and regulations where the employee is viewed more in terms of their role as a civil servant. From this perspective, the prison officer is a member of an administrative organisation and is accountable in hierarchical terms. The focus here is on the application of managerially dictated rules, and the bureaucratic concern should be with conformity and consistency under this administrative structure. The professional discourse views the roles within the prison in terms of their acquired knowledge and expertise and is more focused on the individual and their professional networks. Accountability here stems from the peer group and professional associations. The legal framework is instead concerned with the courts and the application of legal concepts and the rule of law in the institution. Accountability from this framework is more centred around individual rights and justice for the inmates. In the study all three frames were encountered, although the bureaucratic and professional discourses were found to be more widely adopted and the legal discourse to be 'relatively muted' (1991: 45).

Means discourses table:

Model	Bureaucracy	Profession	Legal
Mode of Decision-making	Applying rules	Applying professional knowledge	Weighing up arguments
Legitimating Goal	Accuracy	Service to client	Fairness
Nature of Accountability	Hierarchical	Interpersonal	Independent
Characteristic Remedy	Administrative review	Complaint to professional body	Appeal to court or tribunal

Source Adler and Longhurst (1994: 43)

Adler and Longhurst use the model above as a basis for analysing and critiquing the prison system in Scotland in a tightly specified period (1985–1990) and to make recommendations aimed at improving the system to promote a more just decision-making framework. At the same time, they argue that this model might form the basis for further research:

> … it is clear that our analytic framework could equally be applied to the situation of other groups of prisoners, to other areas of decision-making, to other periods of time and to other prison systems. Although we have not done this ourselves, we are keen to encourage further work of this nature.

At the time, it was suggested that this investigation was perhaps 'the first study of imprisonment in which the concept of discourse has been brought into the analysis in such a systematical way' (Vegheim 1996), which is not an insignificant contention considering the attention that Foucault (1979) famously brought to this very subject. We might then find it surprising that this invitation was not taken up more widely in subsequent research, and it is argued here that there is room for revival of work of this nature. Still now, the focus of the vast majority of prison research is on the incarcerated and, for various reasons, there has been a consistent neglect of the equally important side of the prison story; that of management and the front-line officers. It is argued here that far more of the academic gaze could be directed towards the state actors within carceral institutions, and that this could produce fruitful results as far as the potential for understanding and reform. Further, the field of penal research could be enriched by applying a discourse analysis framework in a more methodical and systematic way, and Adler and Longhurst provide a solid conceptual framework from which to base future investigations of this type.

Later Developments

Whilst the model developed in *Discourse, Power and Justice* was not employed as widely as it could have been at the time, it was picked up and modified theoretically by Carrabine (2000), who explored how it could be adapted to explain the changes in management style of the Strangeways prison in Manchester from 1965 to 1990. Carrabine reinforces this idea of the centrality of discourse to the very existence of the prison, and fundamental to this perspective is an understanding that institutional action is not possible without it:

> The penal system can be regarded as a composite of divisive forces, techniques, rationalities and devices which seek to regulate the actions and decisions of individuals and groups in relation to certain authoritative criteria. These criteria and the ability to *act* are performed through discourse. (2000: 316)

For Carrabine, the discursive model provides us with a means for conceptually bridging the macro-micro divide by turning our attention to the way in which power is 'translated' in prison in a Foucauldian sense (Callon and Latour 1981; Law 1993). Translation concerns the technologies of governing; the means by which power filters outwards from the central government echelons and constrains or enables action in the periphery. A focus on the mechanics of translation enables us to understand the very means by which macro-institutional forces create the capacity for micro-institutional action.

The focus from this perspective is on the political rationalities that infiltrate the 'capillaries' of power (Foucault et al. 1991). Carrabine draws theoretically on Garland (1997) who provides a succinct explanation of this dynamic:

> Power is not a matter of imposing a sovereign will, but instead a process of enlisting the cooperation of chains of actors who 'translate' power from one locale to another. This process always entails activity on the part of the 'subjects of power' and it therefore has built into it the probability that outcomes will be shaped by resistance or private objectives of those acting 'down the line'. (Garland 1997: 182)

Conceptualising the prison in these terms, Carrabine argues, enables us to view it in terms of its place amongst a system of networks 'with each member actively involved in the translation of thought and action' (2000: 319). Carrabine argues that state power filters across networks via 'relatively durable associations through discursive alignments to achieve particular ends' (2000: 318), and that an examination of discourse matrices enables us to make sense of the struggles involved in this space, and how new ways of thinking take hold (2000: 326).

In terms of mechanics, Carrabine's model omits the 'legal' means discourse from the original and replaces it with 'authoritarianism' which he argues is particularly prevalent within the institutional landscape of the prison. The authoritarianism frame is derived from the militaristic style of management that is embodied in carceral institutions, where the emphasis is on 'firm but fair' routines and disciplinary procedures that are grounded in historical developments and related traditions (2000: 318). This style, he argues (2000: 323), was largely subsumed with the introduction of new managerialism and its focus on a more bureaucratic means of governance, leading to the widely observed and discussed conflict between the 'old school' and 'new school' type approaches to doing prison officer work (Feeley and Simon 1992; Tait 2011; Warr 2008: 25). In any case, the suggested modification indicates that the models presented by Adler and Longhurst are not apparently fixed or complete representations of the discursive landscape of the prison, and at the same time re-enforces their initial assertion about the weakness of the legal discourse.[1] It could also be the case that both the authoritarian and the legal modes of framing are influential at the level of decision-making and governance—indeed, there is no reason to limit the map to three categories—and in any event it might be best to include both in any mapping exercise, even if it is to address the absence or weakness of a certain frame.

The mapping of formal narrative frameworks in this manner takes us to the very heart of an institution and allows us to scrutinise the very mechanisms on which it rests. By identifying and unpacking these dynamics we can plainly see the ways in which various concerns may arise, compete and create pressures in various directions. Conducting this kind of analysis allows us to identify the way penal policies and practices may be developed, justified and carried out, and to deconstruct the ways in which this complex web of understandings encourages the promotion of certain concerns and the subsuming of others. Further, as Adler and Longhurst did, it allows for the identification of weaknesses in prison governance and the making of very concrete recommendations for reform. It should be highlighted, however, that the discourses outlined above are very much related to the formal framework of the prison and are to do with conceptions underpinning the institutions on a more structural, and largely managerial and political level. The means

[1] Nor were they intended to be, of course, and Adler (2003) himself later expanded the administrative justice model to include 'market' and 'consumerist' forces; frames which might expected to be very muted or absent in the prison sphere, although further investigation is possible on this point.

and ends discourses are closely intertwined with the formal mechanisms of power in the prison; the written rules and policies, the physical technologies in use, the formal bodies of oversight and the overall organisational structure. The question explored here is whether the narrative model might be usefully developed and adapted to incorporate the understandings of prison officers on the ground.

Possible Future Developments—Informal Discourses and the Prison Officer

There is no question that our institutions are constructed and maintained through discourse; even when viewed from a concrete physical perspective, the discourses prevalent about a certain institution will have flow on effects on all aspects of the institution including the kinds of technologies employed, the type and amount of resources allocated and the built environment (Jewkes and Johnston 2012). Whilst the models discussed above provide a solid foundation for understanding the formal aspects of power within prison, a more comprehensive understanding would need to encompass the discourses involved in the exercise of power and authority from the perspective of prison officers on the front line. This would need to include more informal narratives, which would allow us to acknowledge and explore the gap between the formally generated, ideal types of justificatory frameworks already outlined, and the culturally generated ways of understanding, as well as personal perspectives, that will invariably have a great deal of influence over the way the officer behaves and asserts authority. A comprehensive understanding of institutional control will always need to account for this.

Revisiting Foucault as a starting point, one of his main contributions to our understanding of power in society is that he focused our attention on the 'micro-physics of power' (Leib 2022), where power is the 'capacity to act on others' and is 'something that is operational between agents' (Dore 2010: 739–740). For Foucault the study of 'the state' should focus on the micro-interactions between individuals which may then be utilised to infer broader social patterns (1980: 102). He advocated exploring institutional power dynamics initially from the perspectives understood and shared at a ground level, that is from the perspective of individual agency, rather than as a centrally generated phenomenon. As summarised by Jessop (2007):

> The study of power should begin from below, in the heterogeneous and dispersed micro-physics of power, explore specific forms of its exercise in

> different institutional sites, and consider how, if at all, these were linked to produce broader and more persistent societal configurations. One should study power where it is exercised over individuals rather than legitimated at the centre; explore the actual practices of subjugation rather than the intentions that guide attempts at domination; and recognize that power circulates through networks rather than being applied at particular points. (Foucault 1979). (2007: 36)

Understanding, as we do, that power has both formal and informal dimensions (Helme and Levitsky 2004; Jacobs 2011), and that, as has been famously and strikingly observed, the informal dimensions of power dynamics have the capacity to compel human action in extreme and sometimes confronting ways (Zimbardo et al. 1971; Milgram 1974), we can safely assume that the shared cultural understandings concerning the exercise of power in any institution can be as, if not more, important than the formally generated narratives, particularly at the individual level. A vast array of prison research suggests that informal mechanisms of control can be an essential and all-important tool for prison officers (Sykes 1958/2007; Ibsen 2013; Marquart 1986; Crewe 2009; Symkovych 2018), and that interaction between prison management and lower-ranked officers may in ordinary circumstances be rare (Ibsen 2013; Symkovych 2018). Gilbert (1997), for example, has highlighted that the militaristic reputation of the correctional space often belies the degree of actual management control over the front-line officers, who are expected to work in an environment where the rules designated from above are often unworkable or otherwise repugnant to their interests and views or the practical realities of front-line work. This kind of working environment encourages 'staff resistance', which means 'formal bureaucratic controls are unlikely to be effective as a guide for individual discretionary behaviour' (1997: 58). Prison officer work is largely about managing relationships (Liebling et al. 2010) and involves substantial emotional labour (Crawley 2004), and prison officer culture is a strong and persistent influence on officer behaviour (Garrihy 2020). Thus, whilst the managerial level analysis will be appropriate for the task of identifying the social pressures that drive changes in penal policy, there is a good case to be made for extending the analytic lens to account for the more informal aspects of power as understood by front-line officers, who really are the coal face of the state towards the inmate.

Previous research has highlighted that aspects of soft-power such as interpersonal skills, morality, the quality of officer-inmate relationships and language and 'mythology' colour the very fabric of the prison, and significantly contribute to, or conversely detract from, authority and legitimacy and thus the experience of prison for officers and inmates alike (see for example Tyler 2021; Jackson et al. 2010; Crewe 2011; Liebling 2004; Mayr 2003). As Sparks et al. (1996) have highlighted, prisons are not cold, rational places:

> .. in reality prisons quite commonly seethe and boil with human agency, passion, and conflict- in ways that are not infrequently magnified and rendered more intense precisely by the constraints and frustrations encountered there. (Sparks et al. 1996: 68)

The personal world of any individual is in fundamental ways narratively constructed. Cultural understandings and morality, as it is understood locally, provide one of the main foundations for individual expectations of behaviours in interactions; breaches of these expectations are quite often what ultimately provoke strong emotional responses. Thus, an understanding of these informal narratives will be central to an understanding of power in any institution overall.

Administrative Justice, Discretion and Accountability

As stated above, one of the innovations of Adler and Longhurst's analysis was in the merging of some of the tenets of administrative justice scholarship into the field of penology. Administrative justice is concerned with the way public institutions interact with citizens and it is concerned overall with the quality of public institutional decision-making (Mullen 2010). Administrative justice is not often considered part of the corrections landscape academically. However, much can be usefully brought from this body of knowledge. It is widely acknowledged that the moral imperative for good governance is particularly strong in the corrections context, where inmates are extremely reliant on the state and therefore acutely vulnerable to inappropriate exercises of power (Liebling 2004, 2011; Scraton et al. 1991; Calavita and Jenness 2015). Indeed, the effects of arbitrary, oppressive or apparently unfair uses of power have been widely documented (Woolf and Tumim 1991; Sparks et al. 1996; Bierie 2013; Liebling et al. 2013). The concern of administrative justice scholarship with 'good governance' in a qualitative sense and its focus on institutional actors at the coal face means we can draw on many useful analytical tools that have been developed in this arena.

The manner and degree to which the various kinds of formal narrative have infiltrated the institutions themselves at a ground level can only be understood from the perspective of the front-line prison workers that implement these narratives on a daily basis. Administrative justice scholarship provides some useful observations in this sense, as it concerns exercises of decision-making power in public organisations as well as the broader institutional contexts in which these decisions occur. At its most fundamental, it provides an analytical context for exploring the relationship/s between the citizen and state bureaucratic agents and agencies.

One of the cornerstones of administrative justice research is understanding how discretion is exercised. As Lipsky (1980) notably explored, discretion is central to the role of the street-level bureaucrat, and 'the rules' and policy will only be one part of the overall picture they consider when exercising authority in a certain kind of way. The discretionary aspect of decision-making is generally justified in rational and reasoned terms. However, as Lipsky and others have highlighted, emotions and personal biases can and do play a part in this process. Often there will be a substantial gap between what is formally designated and what might be occurring on the ground and explaining this gap has been an ongoing concern in this arena (see for example- Halliday 2004; Halliday 2021; Mcneill et al. 2009; Hertogh 2010; Maynard-Moody and Musheno 2022). The mobilisation of formal discourses towards the promotion of officially sanctioned policy aims is not an either/or question, and studies have suggested that (a) this dynamic is best viewed as fluid and on a continuum, and (b) the degree of infiltration of the ideal/formal into the daily practices of street-level bureaucrats can vary dramatically from person to person, or in different circumstances (Halliday 2004). Broader influences such as institutional culture, personal attitudes, emotions and practical considerations have consistently been shown to have an impact on the way discretion is exercised at the street-level bureaucratic level (Hunter et al. 2016; Sabbe et al. 2021; England 2022).

Prison officer discretion has also been widely discussed in penal research, although it is not usually explored in depth as a phenomenon (Liebling 2000; Calavita and Jenness 2015; Garrihy 2020; Haggerty and Bucerius 2021). Prison officers are street-level bureaucrats intensified; they exercise an immense degree of discretion in interpreting formal legislation and applying rules compared with other institutional actors, but also do so in the environment of a total institution, so that they necessarily have ongoing and close (at least in terms of physical proximity) relationships with their detainees. Prisons are *hyperlegal* in nature (Calavita and Jenness 2013: 76), although paradoxically, this overload of rules and regulations has the effect of *increasing* officer discretion; where it is impossible to enforce all of the rules, selective non-enforcement is essential to maintaining order and getting through the day

(Haggerty and Bucerius 2021: 144, 147). Not only is there excessive regulation, prison rules are intentionally ambiguously drafted in order to afford a large degree of discretion to prison authorities (Maguire et al. 1985: 5; Scraton et al. 1991: 80–86). The often vague nature of prison regulations can make them difficult to understand and interpret, which may also permit or encourage arbitrary application.

Gilbert argues that the tension between the formal system of rules and the practical daily requirements of the role 'puts officers in an untenable position' (1997: 61), and the discretionary aspect of officer power is 'guided less by the formal rules and hierarchy than by an explicit understanding of the shared [62] operational values and ethical principles that govern correctional practice' (1997: 61–62). Further, prison powers and administrative regulations can be co-opted by officers and/or prison authorities and applied in ways that are apparently in conflict with formal policies, sometimes in disturbing ways (Gostin and Staunton 1985: 87–88). Where the officer has the power to frame events in formal written reports, and significant structural and cultural barriers exist for the inmate in pursuing formal means of accountability (Calavita and Jenness 2015; De Kretser 2007), the informal prison culture and informal social sanctions may take on a more primary role in shaping behaviour.

Adler and Longhurst, in devising their model, were particularly concerned with the different frames of accountability and the flow on effects in terms of governance. One important means for ensuring that decision-making and discretionary power is exercised in accordance with regulatory requirements is through the provision of an accessible and effective system for the independent review of first-instance decisions, and in prison, the primary driver of internal accountability will necessarily be the inmate (Harding 1997: 53, Feeley and Rubin 2000). The carceral organisation by its very nature lacks transparency and involves a stark power imbalance between the inmate and the custodial officer. Hence, what may appear on the surface to be a legitimate formal structure for the fair resolution of complaints and review of decisions can in reality operate as nothing more than a symbolic mechanism for absorbing confrontational friction. This effect has been observed in prison ethnographic studies. Crewe, for example, observed that in terms of grievance processing, from the perspective of inmates, '[i]n practice.. 'paperwork' was the institutional black hole into which problems could be cast without further explanation' (2009: 112), and Calavita and Jenness (2015) in their comprehensibly in-depth study noted that internal grievance processing disadvantaged inmates to such an extent that 'the very term *dispute* seems quaintly euphemistic' (Calavita and Jenness 2015: 186). This brings into question the degree to which the concerns arising from existing formal accountability structures become real concerns of the institutional actors on the ground.

Accountability has a cultural dimension; however, prison officers may feel themselves informally accountable to each other, to inmates and to their own internal sense of morality. Cultural understandings about the exercise of authority in prison will underpin the way officers conceptualise the scope of legitimate action and thus the way they act. The informal attitudes, values and beliefs of prison officers have been shown to have a significant effect on the way they carry out their work (Gilbert 1997; Liebling et al. 2010; Tait 2011), and internalised discourses are the very building block of these. Additionally, many scholars have noted that the formal prison governance structure often belies the actual power of the inmate; and officers are often discussed as somewhat disempowered in real-life terms. Sykes unpacks this in detail, highlighting how the 'defects of total power' in practice may undermine the institutional authority afforded the officer (1956: 52–58), and the informal constraints on the use of the officer's institutional authority have also been discussed in much subsequent prison literature (Liebling 2008; Crawley 2013; Arnold et al. 2012). Where formal controls over social order are insufficient or lacking, an informal social order may emerge that relies on prisoner self-rule and extra-legal governance (Symkovych 2018). Informal normative frameworks have their own, perhaps less obvious, means of motivating behaviour, which will invariably include informal consequences (violent and non-violent) for breaching shared expectations.

Inmates' use of informal social sanctions was observed by Mathiesen as a specific type of *censoriousness* (2012: 12–14). Censoriousness is the 'pointed finger' whereby inmates may draw attention to shortcomings in the way officers exercise their power and can include appeals to generally held values, such as fairness and equality. Censoriousness by its very nature requires shared understandings, and even when there is intense ideological struggle between groups, various discourses will be mobilised to that aim. Mathiesen highlights how these individual acts of censure can reinforce the normative framework of the prison and can operate as an important check on excesses and improper use of power (2012: 187).

Legitimate authority becomes undermined when an officer deviates from accepted boundaries of conduct, allowing an inmate a means to criticise the officer's use of power by referring to shared norms. For Mathiesen, censoriousness is a means by which an otherwise 'weak' inmate can influence an officer. Although Mathiesen was mostly concerned with the effect of this on the inmate, he does describe how the 'pointed finger' can be felt on a personal level by officers; along with a loss of face and legitimacy in the eyes of the prison community, an act of censure has the potential to impact an officer's self-esteem. The exercise of authority in prison requires a considerable degree of confidence, and constant legitimate censure can undermine authority, both in the way an officer feels internally, and in the way others respond to them. The potential effects of this should not be underestimated; if a criticism is felt personally by an officer, repercussions have the potential to extend well beyond the event/s at hand. This is how personal narratives can become central to institutional action.

Social Media and the Research of Professional Cultures

The beliefs and perceptions of front-line officers and the way they frame the exercise of power in prison are not an easy topic to study. Up-close observation, shadowing, interviewing officers and gaining their trust over an extended period have traditionally been the best way to access the kind of data needed to pierce the institutional veil in this manner. Scholars have noted that, even whilst prison populations have exploded in recent times, unfortunately, prison ethnography and other in-depth qualitative sociological enquiry into this site has declined (Wacquant 2002; Simon 2000). Institutional challenges to access abound, and even where access is granted, constraints on researchers are the order of the day (Sloan and Wright 2015; Rhodes 2015). Only the most determined researchers will be able to overcome these barriers, and even with substantial perseverance it may often be the case, as with my own research, that the prison remains closed off. This has led researchers to become increasingly creative in terms of how they access this space (Jardine 2022; Ellis 2021), and we have been more or less forced to reconsider how we might be able to access pertinent data.

Whilst the physical world of the prison officer in many ways may remain an enigma, the way they think and feel about their work may be accessible in other ways. In our contemporary society, many of our social interactions have moved online and people's informal online interactions are more accessible than ever. Social media provides us with a direct and highly personalised window into the lives of all kinds of groups, and a proliferation of professionally oriented chat rooms allows us to examine the way people discuss their working environments. It is asserted here that it is possible to use these kinds of discussions to examine the prevalent narratives involved in doing prison officer work. Although online data is one step removed (at least) from any given physical space, it is also one step closer to the internal world of the social media user, and thus this data has the capacity to inform us in a more personal and authentic manner of the narratives and belief frameworks including more informal culturally generated understandings.

In my own project I have proposed using the Reddit sub-group 'r/ontheblock' as a way of accessing the informal aspects of the prison officer world. Social media chat groups such as Reddit allow for users to post topically and communicate with their peers, and this includes professional peer groups such as prison officers. The anonymous nature of Reddit, the fact that it is in some ways less restrained than other sites (e.g. Twitter with its restricted character limit), and the manner in which the site is organised into topical *sub-reddits*, means that the site is more conducive to frank discussion of relatively sensitive topics than other social media sites (Henninger 2020). The amount of research conducted into Reddit has been increasing significantly in recent years (Proferes et al. 2021: 5), and the capacity of Reddit to elicit sensitive information means it has increasingly gained the attention of many researchers into these areas (see for example Bohrer et al. 2020; Maxwell et al. 2020; Du et al. 2020; Lavis and Winter 2020).

Relevantly, Reddit has also been identified as a useful space for accessing data in relation to professional and or trade-related interactions such as the collective curation of knowledge (Gray and Kou 2019) or the formation of professional identities (Staudt Willet and Carpenter 2020). Henninger (2020), for example, looked at the interactions of medical professionals on the site and found that it provided a window into the expression and resolution of professional problems, the validation of decisions, comfortable exchange of opinions and an invaluable informal arena for professional support. In terms of reliability of research data, comparisons between participant recruitment via Reddit and other recruitment methods suggest overall that the data can be reliable and relatively representative (at least when compared to on-campus recruitment, for example; Jamnik and Lane 2017).

In granting us access into a more personal kind of interactive space, the anonymous professional online group on Reddit may allow us to examine the ways in which prison officers make sense of their working lives. In focusing on discussions around the topic of power and authority in this site, we can examine some of the informal dimensions of power and the associated narratives. Although these will, of course, very much be determined and influenced at a local cultural level and will likely vary significantly from place to place, it is also likely that common patterns will emerge and that these patterns will include both formal and informal narratives concerning power and authority.

This might enable us to fill in or explain some of the potential gaps in the more formal kinds of maps outlined above.

Conclusion

Adler and Longhurst brought our attention to the discursive technicalities involved in the development and maintenance of the prisons in their study, and in conducting their in-depth analysis they laid the groundwork for further work in this area. The ideal-type models they developed were intended to be applied beyond their initial study and here it has been argued that they can used as a basis for examining whether and to what extent formal policy discourses are adopted by front-line officers, and even extended to account for the informal discourses that may subsume them.

Prison officers on the ground are at the very core of this institution and occupy the interface between the state and the individual in this intensely regulated site. The question of how power is understood and justified by them is central to our understanding of carceral authority. It is argued here that for various reasons, formal rationalities will invariably form only part of the world-view of the prison officer, and that more informal discourses and rationalisations will also be influential to varying degrees. A more complete model may be developed that allows for the incorporation of more informally generated narratives. To this aim we might extend more of the academic gaze into the world of prison officers and also seek out more innovative research methods. It is argued here that one fruitful way of learning about the way prison officers make sense of their work is to study online social media interactions in specialised professional online sites. Although this is not a perfect way of studying officers, online interactions do make narrative contents available in ways that other kinds of interactions do not, and this kind of research may compliment some of the more immersive research that has and is being conducted in this arena.

References

Adler, M., and Longhurst, B. (1994). *Discourse, Power and Justice: Towards a New Sociology of Imprisonment*. Routledge.

Adler, M. (2003). A Socio-Legal Approach to Administrative Justice. *Law & Policy*, *25*(4), 323–352.

Arnold, H., Liebling, A., & Tait, S. (2012). Prison Officers and Prison Culture. In *Handbook on prisons*, pp. 501–525. Routledge.

Bennett, J., Crewe, B., and Wahidin, A. (2013). *Understanding Prison Staff*. Willan.
Bierie, D. M. (2013). Procedural Justice and Prison Violence: Examining Complaints Among Federal Inmates (2000–2007). *Psychology, Public Policy, and Law, 19*(1), 15.
Bohrer, B. K., Foye, U., and Jewell, T. (2020). Recovery as a Process: Exploring Definitions of Recovery in the Context of Eating-Disorder-Related Social Media Forums. *International Journal of Eating Disorders, 53*(8), 1219–1223.
Calavita, K., and Jenness, V. (2013). Inside the Pyramid of Disputes: Naming Problems and Filing Grievances in California Prisons. *Social Problems, 60*(1), 50-80.
Calavita, K., and Jenness, V. (2015). *Appealing to Justice: Prisoner Grievances, Rights, and Carceral Logic*. University of California Press.
Callon, M., and Latour, B. (1981). Unscrewing the Big Leviathan: How Actors Macro-Structure Reality and How Sociologists Help Them to Do So. *Advances in Social Theory and Methodology: Toward an Integration of Micro-and Macro-Sociologies, 1.*
Carrabine, E. (2000). Discourse, Governmentality and Translation. *Theoretical criminology, 4*(3), 309–331.
Crawley, E. M. (2004). Emotion and Performance: Prison Officers and the Presentation of Self in Prisons. *Punishment & Society, 6*(4), 411–427.
Crawley, E. (2013). *Doing prison work*. Routledge.
Crewe, B. (2009). *The Prisoner Society: Power, Adaptation and Social Life in an English Prison*. OUP Oxford.
Crewe, B. (2011). Soft Power in Prison: Implications for Staff–Prisoner Relationships, Liberty and Legitimacy. *European Journal of Criminology, 8*(6), 455–468.
De Kretser, H. (2007). Prison Litigation: Barriers to Justice. *Precedent (Sydney, NSW), 81*, 29–33.
Dore, I. (2010). Foucault on Power. *UMKC Law Review, 78*(3), 737.
Du, C., Lee, W., Moskowitz, D., Lucioni, A., Kobashi, K. C., and Lee, U. J. (2020). I Leaked, Then I Reddit: Experiences and Insight Shared on Urinary Incontinence by Reddit Users. *International Urogynecology Journal, 31*(2), 243–248.
Duke, K. (2002). Getting Beyond the 'Official Line': Reflections on Dilemmas of Access, Knowledge and Power in Researching Policy Networks. *Journal of social policy, 31*(1), 39–59.
Ellis, R. (2021). Prisons as Porous Institutions. *Theory and Society, 50*(2), 175–199.
England, E. (2022). 'You're Having us on… That's What It Felt Like.': Frontline Workers Navigating the Introduction of Moral Commitments to Domestic Abuse Support within a Statutory Homelessness System. *Social Policy and Society*, 1–15.
Feeley, M. M., and Rubin, E. L. (2000). *Judicial Policy Making and the Modern State: How the Courts Reformed America's Prisons*. Cambridge University Press.
Feeley, M. M., and Simon, J. (1992). The New Penology: Notes on the Emerging Strategy of Corrections and Its implications. *Criminology (Beverly Hills), 30*(4), 449–474.
Foucault, M. (1979). *Discipline and Punish: The Birth of the Prison*. Vintage Books.

Foucault, M. (1980). *Power/Knowledge: Selected Interviews and Other Writings, 1972–1977*. Vintage.
Foucault, M. (1981). *The History of Sexuality*. Vol. 1, An Introduction. Penguin.
Foucault, M., Burchell, G., Gordon, C., and Miller, P. (1991). *The Foucault Effect: Studies in Governmentality: with Two Lectures by and an Interview with Michel Foucault*. University of Chicago Press.
Garland, D. (1997). Governmentality and the Problem of Crime: Foucault, Criminology, Sociology. *Theoretical criminology*, *1*(2), 173–214.
Garrihy, J. (2020). 'There Are Fourteen Grey Areas': 'Jailing', Professionalism and Legitimacy in Prison Officers' Occupational Cultures. *Irish Probation Journal, 17*, 128–150.
Gilbert, M. J. (1997). The Illusion of Structure: A Critique of the Classical Model of Organization and the Discretionary Power of Correctional Officers. *Criminal Justice Review*, *22*(1), 49–64.
Gostin, L., and Staunton, M. (1985). The Case for Prison Standards: Conditions of Confinement, Segregation, and Medical Treatment' Chapter 5. In M. Maguire, J. Vagg, and R. Morgan (eds.), *Accountability and Prisons*. Tavistock Publications Ltd.
Gray, C. M., and Kou, Y. (2019). Co-producing, Curating, and Defining Design Knowledge in an Online Practitioner Community. *CoDesign*, *15*(1), 41–58.
Haggerty, K. D., and Bucerius, S. M. (2021). Picking Battles: Correctional Officers, Rules, and Discretion in Prison. *Criminology*, *59*(1), 137–157.
Halliday, S. (2004). *Judicial Review and Compliance with Administrative Law*. Hart Publishing.
Halliday, S. (2021). Administrative Justice and Street-Level Emotions: Cultures of Denial in Entitlement Decision-Making. *Public Law*, 727–746.
Harding, R. (1997). *Private Prisons and Public Accountability*. Buckingham, England: Open University Press.
Helme, G., and Levitsky, S. (2004). Informal Institutions and Comparative Politics. *Perspectives on Politics*, *2*(4), 725–740.
Henninger, N. M. (2020). 'I Gave Someone a Good Death': Anonymity in a Community of Reddit's Medical Professionals. *Convergence (London, England)*, *26*(5–6), 1391–1410.
Hertogh, M. (2010). Through the Eyes of Bureaucrats: How Front-Line Officials Understand Administrative Justice. In M. Adler (ed.), *Administrative Justice in Context*. Bloomsbury Publishing.
Hunter, C., Bretherton, J., Halliday, S., and Johnsen, S. (2016). Legal Compliance in Street-Level Bureaucracy: A Study of UK Housing Officers. *Law & Policy*, *38*(1), 81–95.
Ibsen, A. Z. (2013). Ruling by Favors: Prison Guards' Informal Exercise of Institutional Control. *Law & Social Inquiry*, *38*(2), 342–363.
Jackson, J., Tyler, T. R., Bradford, B., Taylor, D., and Shiner, M. (2010). Legitimacy and Procedural Justice in Prisons. *Prison service journal*, *191*, 4–10.

Jacobs, A. M. (2011). *Governing for the Long Term: Democracy and the Politics of Investment*. Cambridge University Press.

Jamnik, M. R., and Lane, D. J. (2017). The Use of Reddit as an Inexpensive Source for High-Quality Data. *Practical Assessment, Research, and Evaluation, 22*(1), 5.

Jardine, C. (2022). Prison Ethnography by Correspondence? *Criminology & Criminal Justice*, 17488958221111502.

Jessop, B. (2007). From Micro-Powers to Governmentality: Foucault's Work on Statehood, State Formation, Statecraft and State Power. *Political geography, 26*(1), 34–40.

Jewkes, Y., and Johnston, H. (2012). The Evolution of Prison Architecture. In *Handbook on prisons* (pp. 204–226). Routledge.

Lavis, A., and Winter, R. (2020). Online Harms or Benefits? An Ethnographic Analysis of the Positives and Negatives of Peer-Support Around Self-Harm on Social Media. *Journal of Child Psychology and Psychiatry, 61*(8), 842–854.

Law, J. (1993). *Organising Modernity: Social Ordering and Social Theory*. Wiley.

Leib, R. S. (2022). Goffman and Foucault: Framing the Micro-Physics of Power. In *The Routledge International Handbook of Goffman Studies* (pp. 349–360). Routledge.

Liebling, A. (2000). Prison Officers, Policing and the Use of Discretion. *Theoretical Criminology, 4*(3), 333–357.

Liebling, A. (2004). *Prisons and Their Moral Performance: A Study of Values, Quality and Prison Life*. Oxford University Press.

Liebling, A. (2008). Incentives and Earned Privileges Revisited: Fairness, Discretion, and the Quality of Prison Life. *Journal of Scandinavian Studies in Criminology and Crime Prevention, 9*(S1), 25–41.

Liebling, A., Price, D., and Shefer, G. (2010). *The Prison Officer*. Routledge.

Liebling, A. (2011). Moral Performance, Inhuman and Degrading Treatment and Prison Pain. *Punishment & Society, 13*(5), 530–550.

Liebling, A., Durie, L., Stiles, A., and Tait, S. (2013). Revisiting Prison Suicide: The Role of Fairness and Distress. In *The effects of imprisonment*, pp. 229–251. Willan.

Lipsky, M. (1980; 2010). *Street-Level Bureaucracy: The Dilemmas of the Individual in Public Services*. Russell Sage Foundation.

Maguire, M., Vagg, J., and Morgan, R. (eds.). (1985). *Accountability and Prisons*. Tavistock Publications Ltd.

Mannheim, K. (1952). Competition as a Cultural Phenomenon. In *Essays on the Sociology of Knowledge*, pp. 191–229. London: Routledge.

Mannheim, K. (1953). Conservative Thought. In *Essays on Sociology and Social Psychology*. London: Routledge and Kegan Paul.

Mannheim, K. (1986). *Conservatism: A Contribution to the Sociology of Knowledge*. London: Routledge and Kegan Paul.

Marquart, J. W. (1986). Prison Guards and the Use of Physical Coercion as a Mechanism of Prisoner Control *Criminology, 24*(2), 347–366.

Mashaw, J. L. (1983). *Bureaucratic Justice Managing Social Security Disability Claims.* Yale University Press.
Mathiesen, T. (2012). *The defences of the weak : a sociological study of a Norwegian correctional institution.* Routledge.
Maxwell, D., Robinson, S. R., Williams, J. R., and Keaton, C. (2020). A Short Story of a Lonely Guy: A Qualitative Thematic Analysis of Involuntary Celibacy Using Reddit. *Sexuality & Culture, 24*(6), 1852–1874.
Maynard-Moody, S. W., and Musheno, M. C. (2022). *Cops, Teachers, Counselors: Stories from the Front Lines of Public Service.* University of Michigan Press.
Mayr, A. D. (2003). *Prison Discourse: Language as a Means of Control and Resistance.* Palgrave Macmillan Limited.
McNeill, F., Burns, N., Halliday, S., Hutton, N., and Tata, C. (2009). Risk, Responsibility and Reconfiguration: Penal Adaptation and Misadaptation. *Punishment & Society, 11*(4), 419–442.
Milgram, S. (1974). *Obedience to Authority: An Experimental View.* Harper & Row.
Mullen, T. (2010). A Holistic Approach to Administrative Justice? In M. Adler (ed.), *Administrative Justice in Context*, pp. 384–420. Bloomsbury Publishing.
Proferes, N., Jones, N., Gilbert, S., Fiesler, C., and Zimmer, M. (2021). Studying Reddit: A Systematic Overview of Disciplines, Approaches, Methods, and Ethics. *Social Media+ Society, 7*(2), 20563051211019004.
Rhodes, L. (2015). Ethnographic Imagination in the Field of the Prison. In *The Palgrave Handbook of Prison Ethnography*, (pp. 271–283). Palgrave Macmillan.
Sabbe, M., Schiffino, N., and Moyson, S. (2021). Walking on Thin Ice: How and Why Frontline Officers Cope with Managerialism, Accountability, and Risk in Probation Services. *Administration & Society, 53*(5), 760–786.
Scraton, P., Sim, J., and Skidmore, P. (1991). *Prisons Under Protest.* Open University Press.
Simon, J. (2000). The Society of Captives' in the Era of Hyper-Incarceration. *Theoretical Criminology, 4*(3), 285–308.
Sloan, J., and Wright, S. (2015). Going in Green: Reflections on the Challenges of 'Getting in, Getting on, and Getting out' for Doctoral Prisons Researchers. In *The Palgrave Handbook of Prison Ethnography*, pp. 143–163. London: Palgrave Macmillan UK.
Sparks, R., Bottoms, A. E., and Hay, W. (1996). *Prisons and the Problem of Order.* Oxford, England and New York: Clarendon Press.
Staudt Willet, K. B., and Carpenter, J. P. (2020). Teachers on Reddit? Exploring Contributions and Interactions in Four Teaching-Related subreddits. *Journal of Research on Technology in Education, 52*(2), 216–233.
Sykes, G. (1958/2007). *The Society of Captives: A Study of a Maximum Security Prison.* Princeton University Press.
Symkovych, A. (2018). Compromised Power and Negotiated Order in a Ukrainian Prison. *The British Journal of Criminology, 58*(1), 200–217.
Tait, S. (2011). A Typology of Prison Officer Approaches to Care. *European Journal of Criminology, 8*(6), 440–454.

Tyler, T. R. (2021). Why People Obey the law. In *Why People Obey the Law*. Princeton University Press.

Vegheim, B. (1996). Book Reviews—Discourse, Power and Justice: Toward a New Sociology of Imprisonment by Michael Adler and Brian Longhurst [Review of *Book Reviews—Discourse, Power and Justice: Toward a New Sociology of Imprisonment by Michael Adler and Brian Longhurst*]. *Acta Sociologica*, *39*(1), 109. Sage Publications Ltd.

Wacquant, L. (2002). The Curious Eclipse of Prison Ethnography in the Age of Mass Incarceration. *Ethnography*, *3*(4), 371–397.

Warr, J. (2008). Personal Reflections on Prison Staff. *Understanding Prison Staff*, 17–29.

Woolf, L. J., and Tumim, S. (1991). *Prison Disturbances April 1990*. London: HM Stationery Office.

Zimbardo, P. G., Haney, C., Banks, W. C., and Jaffe, D. (1971). *The Stanford Prison Experiment*. Zimbardo, Incorporated.

6

Thought Styles on Administrative Justice Systems

T. T. Arvind, Simon Halliday, and Lindsay Stirton

Introduction

Mike Adler is rightly celebrated for having made significant theoretical and empirical contributions to the study of administrative justice. Relatively early in his career, Adler was much influenced by the publication of Jerry Mashaw's *Bureaucratic Justice: Managing Social Security Disability Claims* (Mashaw 1983), an extended study of social security administration in the USA.[1] Mashaw famously proposed three competitive models of administrative justice: bureaucratic rationality; professional treatment; and moral judgement. During the course of a number of empirical projects, Adler applied, developed and refined Mashaw's analytical schema, culminating in

[1] For an account of the significance of Mashaw's book on Adler's thinking, see Adler (2006).

T. T. Arvind
University of York, York, UK
e-mail: t.t.arvind@york.ac.uk

S. Halliday (✉)
University of Strathclyde, Glasgow, UK
e-mail: simon.halliday@strath.ac.uk

L. Stirton
University of Sussex, Falmer, UK
e-mail: L.Stirton@sussex.ac.uk

S. Cowan and S. Halliday (eds.), *Socio-Legal Generation*, Palgrave Socio-Legal Studies,
https://doi.org/10.1007/978-3-031-67244-6_6

an important article in 2003, which definitively sets out his own framework for understanding administrative justice (Adler 2003). This article has been very influential and is now a standard point of reference for the field. Yet, it has also been the subject of some critique (Halliday 2004; Sainsbury 2008; Cane 2009; Craven 2023), the core of which is that not all of Adler's suggested additions to Mashaw's schema speak squarely to Mashaw's working definition of administrative justice: 'those qualities of a decision process that provide arguments for the acceptability of its decisions' (Mashaw 1983: 24).

In this chapter, we re-visit Adler's seminal essay on administrative justice, offering an interpretation of its contribution which is sometimes overlooked by his critics: that Adler sought to move the agenda on from a narrower focus on frontline administrative decision-making to a broader consideration of administrative justice systems, including modes of redress. Adler's essay, in consequence, represents an important advance in our overall thinking about administrative justice. Indeed, we might suggest that Adler, in effect, developed Mashaw's definition of administrative justice. In contrast to Mashaw's definition, quoted above, implicitly Adler's definition of administrative justice is something like: those qualities of a system that provide arguments for the acceptability of its outcomes.

In reviewing Adler's contribution to administrative justice theory, we also seek to build on it. Adler's work is radical in its potential, and when taken seriously points to an important and far-reaching agenda for administrative justice scholarship. We live in an era where new political narratives centred around populism and radically participatory theories of democracy challenge the narratives of legitimacy that have traditionally been advanced to support administrative government (see the chapter by Kagan in this collection; also Harlow and Rawlings 2023). Adler's work points to the range of legitimating arguments that may be seen as unconvincing to such populist thought styles, and which (to emphasise the flip-side of the coin) pose a challenge to defenders of administrative government, which they must address if they are to offer a response to such provocations. A central feature of this challenge—implicit in Adler's work but which we bring to the surface—is the real possibility of a gap between how system designers, system operators, and system users in the field both imagine and experience administrative justice.

Drawing on Mary Douglas' grid-group cultural theory, we offer a high-level 'map' of thought styles around administrative justice systems—four distinctive ways in which participants in systems of administrative justice—whether users, operators or designers—frame the legitimacy of the system rationality that underpins it. Each of these frames, we argue, presents a distinctive set of challenges to the system's own 'arguments for the acceptability of its outcomes' which, if left unaddressed, could have non-trivial implications for the success of systems of administrative justice.

In re-analysing Adler's work through the lens of grid-group cultural theory, we can observe that, while his work can be read as drawing attention to two families of thought styles, two others remain unexamined. As we argue below, the styles of administrative justice identified by Adler align along what Mary Douglas calls the 'positive diagonal'. The contribution of this chapter, on the other hand, is to draw attention to the neglected 'negative diagonal' of thought styles which are—in different ways—critical of the more familiar legitimacy claims of administrative justice systems. By emphasising this negative diagonal, we argue, this chapter connects mainstream administrative justice theory with a strand of public law scholarship that has in recent decades been overlooked in administrative justice scholarship, no doubt due to its neglect in administrative justice policy, but which administrative justice scholarship would do well to reconnect with.

Mashaw, Adler and Administrative Justice

The details of Mashaw's models of administrative justice are well known. We need not spend too much time rehearsing them here. In essence, Mashaw argued that disability benefits decision-making could be organised variously, according to different legitimating values and goals.

'Bureaucratic rationality' as way of organising decision-making is principally concerned with distinguishing between true and false claims for benefits, within the limits of operational costs. Thus, it cares about accuracy, balanced by a concern for economic efficiency, and operates by way of information processing. To put it at its absolute simplest, the basic operational question underlying this model of administrative justice is: what is the truth of claimant's circumstances? And the core legitimating narrative underpinning the model is: we apply the rules to an accurate understanding of claimants' circumstances.

'Professional treatment' is concerned with how best to support and improve the health and well-being of the claimant. Thus, it cares about service to the client and achieves it through seeking to understand the client's needs and applying professional knowledge to address them. The basic operational question is: what are the needs of the claimant? And the core legitimating narrative is: we apply professional expertise to meet claimants' needs.

'Moral judgement' treats the claimant as someone who is making a contested entitlement claim and who must therefore be afforded procedural protections in the application process. Thus, it cares about procedural fairness and organises itself in a way that secures them a full and fair opportunity to make their case. The basic operational question is: what does the claimant deserve? And the core legitimating narrative is: we give claimants a fair opportunity to present their case and take everything into account before determining what they deserve.

Adler saw great merit in these insights but felt that they could be expanded—both to cater for other facets of the public sector and to reflect trends in public management since the publication of Mashaw's book. Hence Adler added three new models: 'managerial', 'consumerist' and 'market'. If we were to restrict ourselves to a narrow focus on the administrative justice of frontline decision-making processes, we could have sympathies with Adler's critics about the extent to which his three models add something new. As one of us has argued previously (Halliday 2004), there is really only one new frontline decision-making model that emerges: where the decision process approximates that of a market transaction. Here the underlying operational question would be 'what does the claimant want?' And the corresponding legitimacy narrative would be: we are responsive to claimants' input and reach a settlement about what they want. Taken as a fourth model of decision-making legitimacy, Adler's contribution to Mashaw's schema would look as follows:

Model	Bureaucratic rationality	Professional treatment	Moral judgement	Consumerism/ market
Operational question	What is the truth of claimants' circumstances?	What are claimants' needs?	What do claimants deserve?	What do claimants want?
Decision legitimacy narrative	We apply the rules to an accurate understanding of claimant circumstances	We apply professional expertise to meet claimant needs	We give claimants a fair opportunity to present their case	We are responsive to claimants' input

However, as we noted above, Adler's ambition was broader than the ambit of the critique, seeking to include characteristic modes of redress in an understanding of broader administrative justice systems. His first move here was to attach characteristic modes of redress to Mashaw's existing three models: internal administrative review for 'bureaucratic rationality'; second opinion or complaint to a professional body for 'professional treatment'; and appeal to a court or tribunal for 'moral judgement'. His second move was the addition of his three new models, each of which had its own characteristic remedy: publicity for 'managerial'; voice or compensation for 'consumerist'; and exit or private law court action for 'market'.[2]

Model	Bureaucratic rationality	Professional treatment	Moral judgement	Managerial	Consumerist	Market
Characteristic remedy	Administrative review	Second opinion/ complaint to a professional body	Appeal to a court or tribunal	Publicity	Voice and/or compensation	'Exit' or private law court action

Adler's inclusion of modes of redress or accountability within his treatment of administrative justice is significant. While representing distinct stages or dimensions of administrative justice practice, there are important analytical benefits in considering them together. As Adler noted in his 2003 essay, 'internal and external procedures should not be seen as alternatives, and it is important to recognize that, for good reasons, they are frequently combined' (2003: 329). Thus, an individual may experience both frontline and redress decision-making as part of their single claim for a public benefit.

Just as important, however, Adler draws our attention to the fact that modes of redress do not simply revolve around the rectification of individual grievances. To some extent, at least, we may also think of them as being about the shaping of administrative systems: voice, publicity or exit each have clear regulatory potential; but so too could the internal review, complaints or appeals about individualised decisions. In this way, Adler urges us to focus on administrative justice systems, comprising both frontline decision-making and modes of redress or accountability.

But perhaps more fundamentally, Adler's inclusion of external mechanisms within administrative justice points to an important, but often neglected, aspect of administrative justice systems, namely that a system designer's view of what constitutes 'an argument for the acceptability' of the system's decisions may not be shared by system users. A claimant with a competing sense of procedural legitimacy may be left disappointed by their encounters with the decision-making process. Thus, effective external forms of redress and accountability—a more systemic perspective—can contribute to the acceptability of a system's ultimate outcomes from the perspective of users.

[2] For an alternative characterisation of how these new models fit into the administrative justice landscape of the regulatory state, see Stirton and Lodge (2001).

Our ambition in this chapter is to build on Adler's distinctive contribution to administrative justice. To do so, we re-read his schema through the lens of grid-group cultural theory (GGCT)—an analytical resource that has considerable potential for drawing out high-level contrasts between ways of seeing and approaching various social phenomena. It is to this that we turn next.

Thought Styles of Administrative Justice

Models of administrative justice, like all human artefacts, are contingent rather than absolute—a point that Adler has done much to underscore. The model of administrative justice that a particular scholar might propose, or that a given jurisdiction might introduce, is influenced by both the specific temporal and cultural context in which it operates as well as the preferences of the persons who are responsible for the existence of the systems or control the systems. A central challenge for scholars of administrative justice is, accordingly, to understand and critically appraise the impact these contexts and preferences have on models of administrative justice.

There is now an established literature that uses GGCT to answer this challenge (e.g. Halliday and Scott 2010; Lodge and Stirton 2010; Arvind et al. 2022; Kirkham 2022). GGCT was developed by the British anthropologist, Mary Douglas, to study the aetiology of the 'thought styles' that underpin different cultural phenomena, and the cultural biases that are built into them (Douglas 1982). In the context of administrative justice scholarship, GGCT's value lies in the insight it provides into how these thought and cultural biases influence models of administrative justice, that is to say:

- the different worldviews (or 'cosmologies') that co-exist in any social or cultural space, and the subjective perceptions, preferences, and evaluative predilections that characterise the way each of them views administrative justice;
- the specific cosmology with which a given model of administrative justice is associated, and the manner in which it influences how the model defines the ends a system of administrative justice should pursue, identifies specific processes as having the propensity to effectively deliver those ends, and justifies (or ignores) the trade-offs, costs, and potential for adverse outcomes inherent in the model; and
- the consequences the subjective biases and blind spots inherited from the underlying worldview have on the system's form, function and output.

The Analytical Scheme: Administrative Justice in (Cultural) Context

GGCT's analytical framework builds on a taxonomy that uses two dimensions to classify social relations, contexts and forms of organisation. These dimensions are usually represented in GGCT as perpendicular axes in a two-dimensional space. The vertical axis, called 'grid' in Douglas's work, represents social regulation; that is to say, the control rules, roles and prescriptions exercise over social life. The horizontal axis, 'group', represents social integration; that is, the extent to which behaviour is shaped by the sense of the value and importance of being part of a larger collective entity.

In prior work (Arvind et al. 2022), we have argued that in the context of administrative justice the grid dimension is best understood as representing the character of administrative justice in relation to how focused it is on following proper rules and processes as distinct from working out from first principles what would represent a substantively fair outcome in an individual case. At the bottom end, or 'low grid', administrative justice frameworks and the individuals tasked with delivering it can engage more fully with substantive principles, values and goals in determining whether the outcome reached in an individual case was a just one. At the top end, or 'high grid', they are more concerned with ensuring that the values, principles and goals embedded in the system were used in a way that met appropriate and recognised standards, and less so with whether the application of those principles and standards produced an outcome that might be considered 'just' outside the framework they provide.

Group, similarly, is best understood as representing the extent to which the polity or domain being administered is seen as a field of contestation with discordant interests in constant conflict as opposed to a field of underlying concord where there is a real and realisable common good that will benefit all parts of the polity. At the left end, or 'low group', discord is real and simmers because competing interests are always in tension, and administrative justice's concern is to manage the contestation that inevitably characterises the conduct of public business in a discordant polity. To the extent that concord can be said to exist at all, it exists only as the coincidence of particular interests aligning on particular issues or decisions. At the right end, or 'high group', concord is real and emerges from a deeper well of shared interests. High group conceptions do not deny the reality of contestation, but regard it as representing instances where a person's private interests clash with interests that they too possess as a member of a polity: if industrialists' private interest as polluters clashes with the public interest in a clean environment, that is

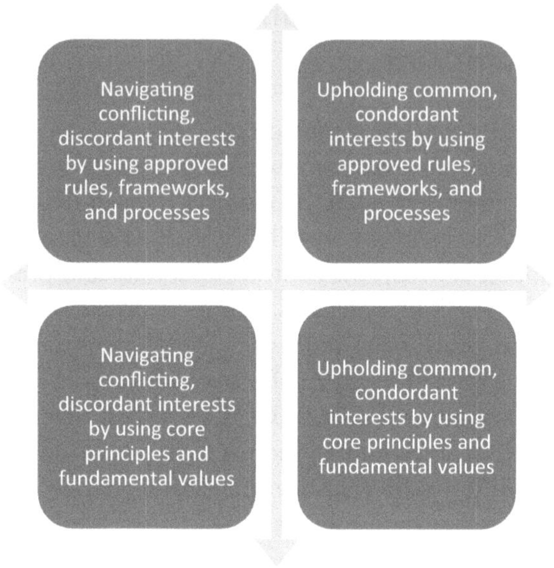

Fig. 6.1 Four thought styles of administrative justice

an interest that affects not just others but also the industrialists themselves. Administrative justice, in this conception, provides a vehicle for reconciling such conflicts by identifying and upholding the shared, concordant interest that lies beneath the surface of the apparent conflict.

Putting these two dimensions together, we can classify thought styles of administrative justice in terms of four quadrants, summarised in Fig. 6.1.

The Positive Diagonal and Models of Administrative Justice

In GGCT, these four quadrants are often described as lying on two diagonals. The upper right and lower left quadrants are linked by the 'positive diagonal'. This is not just because the diagonal has a positive slope, but, perhaps more importantly, because the thought styles associated with the bottom left and top rights have in common a positive, affirming attitude to authority and power (Douglas 1996: 46, 176–178). The upper left and lower right quadrants, on the other hand, comprise the 'negative diagonal', named for its negative slope as well as because it is not interested in holding power (Douglas 1996: 44, 178–181). In the remainder of this section, we discuss the two thought styles aligning along the positive diagonal before turning, in the next section, to the negative diagonal.

The Upper Right Quadrant: Shared Interests and Approved Frameworks

Douglas frequently described the upper right quadrant as 'hierarchical' or as involving a 'complex collective' (Douglas 1996: 175): a form of social ordering that is both tightly integrated (in the sense of being built on a strong sense of shared interests) and tightly regulated (in the sense of being governed by a strong cross-hatch of rules, norms, and practices having binding or suasive force). Administrative justice in this quadrant is built on a cosmology that sees society as characterised by common, concordant interests, which administrators can identify and respond to by drawing on their professional expertise as administrators, regulators or domain experts. The emphasis on expertise means that social ordering in this quadrant has a top-down character and a focus on rules and processes produced through expertise; but the potentially exclusionary effects of a top-down ordering are mitigated by a clear sense of shared interests common to all. There may be disagreements as to the fairness of an individual outcome, and people may feel hard done by when their private interests receive what they believe to be inadequate consideration. However, the appropriate response to these outcomes is to ensure that the system has in fact correctly deployed its expertise to identify and give effect to deeper shared interests.

Embracing Adler's systems perspective, we can say that, of the six models of administrative justice so far discussed, three fit within this quadrant: bureaucratic rationality, professional treatment and managerialism. Bureaucratic rationality focuses on applying rules to an accurate understanding of a person's circumstances, while managerialism focuses on clearly defined standards such as efficiency and measurable performance indicators, all of which are characteristic of a thought style that emphasises the role in administrative justice of concordant interests, expertise and recognised standards. For similar reasons, so does professional treatment, which emphasises the role of professional knowledge, expertise and standards.

The Lower Left Quadrant: Divergent Interests and Core Values

The lower left quadrant, which Douglas described as 'individualist', sits at the opposite end of the spectrum from the central community: a form of social ordering which is both weakly integrated (in that it lacks a strong sense of a common community with shared goals and commitments) and weakly regulated (in that it is unwilling to give a central place in its structures to a distinctive bureaucratic rationality, although it is not suspicious of authority per se). Here, interests are seen as fundamentally in conflict and lacking any deeper concord—a conflict that necessarily poses a fundamental challenge to administrative justice. At the same time, the commitment of this thought style to substantive values rather than formal criteria embedded in bureaucratic rationality leads it to the view that administrative justice's approach to dealing with conflict must lie in embedding within it certain core principles or norms of general application. These operate as rules of 'fair competition' between competing interests, or (to use a different analogy) like the rules of the road that manage conflicts between the interests of different road users by establishing principles of priority applicable to different situations. Mere expertise is inadequate unless anchored by norms and, indeed, may be counterproductive to administrative justice if it leads to the emergence of a distinctive bureaucratic rationality that rejects these norms.

Different models of administrative justice lying within this quadrant may emphasise different norms, but all share a common focus on the importance to administrative justice of upholding core substantive norms (and not merely procedures) anchored to demotic perspectives (and not merely grounded in expertise), and on preventing administrative agencies from developing distinctive bureaucratic rationalities at variance with these core norms. Of the six models discussed above, this too encompasses three: the model of 'moral judgement', the 'consumerist' and 'market' models. As Adler highlighted, 'moral judgement' aims at conflict resolution by providing a person seeking administrative justice with the opportunity to assert rights, and it seeks its legitimacy in the underpinning value of fairness—all of which reflect norms of general application and are phrased in terms that resonate with demotic perspectives of justice. 'Consumerism' is similarly grounded: as Adler pointed out, its use of devices such as citizen's charters expressly seeks to insulate its approach to administrative justice from slipping into bureaucratic rationality, embedding instead a commitment to recognising and upholding certain core expectations that users of public services have. Markets are similar: here, the laws of demand and supply are used to counter the emergence of bureaucratic rationality and keep the administration focused on meeting standards expected by the consumer.

The Negative Diagonal: A Missing Dimension in Administrative Justice Models?

The two thought styles on the positive diagonal, discussed in the previous section, between them exhaust all six models of administrative justice discussed by Adler. It is not surprising that Adler conceives of models of administrative justice lying along the positive diagonal, since his operational understanding of the concept foreground arguments for acceptability of outcomes of the exercise of administrative power. The negative diagonal, on the other hand, is, as Douglas puts it, 'the diagonal of withdrawal and protest' (Douglas 1996: 44). While an emphasis on models of administrative justice is not entirely absent either from top left or bottom right perspectives, we would not necessarily expect the same emphasis on articulating positive models of administrative justice that we see with the positive diagonal. Nonetheless, as we show in the remainder of this section, there is nevertheless value in reflecting on the implications of these two thought styles for administrative justice. As Harlow and Rawlings have argued, the contemporary 'poles' of administrative law thought have recently come under challenge from more critical populist perspectives (Harlow and Rawlings 2023). Understanding the force of critique and the kind of responses that they might potentially generate could be seen as part of a project of engaging with populist challenges to the dominant models of administrative justice.

The Upper Left Quadrant: Divergent Interests and Approved Frameworks

Douglas described the upper left quadrant as 'fatalist' or (and perhaps more accurately) 'isolate': a form of social ordering which is weakly integrated in that it lacks a strong sense of common community and shared goals, but at the same time is strongly regulated in that it leaves significant scope for the emergence of a cross-hatch of binding rules, norms and practices. Like the upper right quadrant, social ordering in this quadrant has a top-down character and focuses on processes instituted by a competent authority. Unlike the upper right quadrant, here the potential for exclusion or marginalisation inherent in a top-down ordering remain unmitigated. There is neither a clear sense of interests that everyone shares, nor is there a sense of a polity whose common good can be easily identified.

None of the six models of administrative justice identified by Adler conform to this quadrant. Yet as Nonet and Selznick have recognised, there may be conditions under which a more top-down system of decision-making based on the arbitrary exercise of authority may be justified to deny claimants benefits to which they would otherwise be entitled—if only due to the lack of viable alternatives. Nonet and Selznick's analysis speaks to difficulties of making just decisions under conditions of austerity in which increased demands on the state are met with abundant power but scarce resources:

> Confronted with pressing issues of justice or public welfare, the government may seek to avoid commitments and resist demands. New claims are given low priority or brushed aside as illegitimate. Through neglect, the state controls the rise of expectations. It does so partly out of awareness of genuine limits to political and administrative capacity and partly out of fear that frustrated expectations will undermine the foundations of political allegiance and public peace. (Nonet and Selznick [1978] 2011: 37)

In such conditions, there is a mismatch (or gap) between the sorts of arguments for the acceptability of outcomes of the sort that align on the positive diagonal and what the state can deliver in terms of administrative justice. Street-level bureaucrats may attempt to paper over the cracks by taking on a role as 'gatekeepers' to processes that may in themselves still be justified in positive terms (Lipsky 1980).

Alternatively, administrative procedures may instead rely on devices, such as lotteries, which are explicit in their arbitrariness in terms of *outcomes* but which adhere (or claim to adhere) to particular ideals of fairness in terms of *process* (Adler 2003: 335). Making decisions about the allocation of public resources through chance is clearly negative, in the sense that it represents an abandonment of faith in the capacity of rules, expertise or participation to contribute to good decision-making. Yet, at the same time, lotteries might, in the face of such an abandonment, be attractive to public agencies as a form of decision-making. This is both because lotteries are transparent about the arbitrariness of outcomes, and because decisions over outcomes are made without regard to personal circumstances or characteristics. And as Halliday and Scott (2010) have noted, lotteries have been used for this purpose in immigration and educational sectors, precisely for this reason.

Nonetheless—and here we offer a provocation for further inquiry—we should perhaps not associate the upper left quadrant solely with sortilege as a form of decision-making. There may also be merit in associating the upper left quadrant with an underlying embrace of arbitrariness in the design of administrative systems—beyond the proper operation of the rules, frameworks and processes themselves. If, as Harlow and Rawlings (2023) have claimed, the populist turn in political discourse involves a rejection of pluralism as well as elitism, in favour of direct linkages between politicians and 'the real people', then we might expect such a politics to favour administrative systems that embrace more personalised styles of form and authority in administrative systems, along with a rejection of bureaucratically rational decision-making, in favour of direct and personalised messaging, as well as a general and basic disdain for procedural values in favour of 'getting things done' (Harlow and Rawlings 2023).

We are not suggesting that trends towards a more populist politics, and towards administrative forms and processes conducive to such a style of politics, are inevitable or irreversible. Our provocation is simply that we can see in some strands of populist doctrine a tendency towards styles of government that emphasise the power-conferring function of rules, frameworks and processes, while minimising the role of devices for 'structuring, checking and confining' of executive discretion (Davis 1969). Far from improving standards of administrative justice, such devices may be seen as an obstacle to asserting the interests of 'the real people', where these are resisted by other interests.

The Lower Right Quadrant: Shared Interests and Core Values

The lower right quadrant was described by Douglas in her early work as 'egalitarian', but in her later work she adopted the less politically charged term 'enclavist': a form of social ordering that is tightly integrated, sharing with the upper right quadrant a sense of common community and shared interests, but also weakly regulated, sharing with the lower left quadrant a preference for generally applicable principles and norms over bureaucratic rationality. Thought styles in this quadrant tend to value simplicity and relationality, and to be wary of the tendency to authoritarianism inherent in top-down institutional arrangements. Administrative justice is accordingly built on a cosmology that sees society as characterised by shared interests and goals, but unlike the upper right quadrant it sees demotic norms and aspirations as a better instantiation of these shared interests than technocratic expertise, and it accordingly assigns a higher priority to actions like citizen empowerment (Lodge and Stirton 2010: 361–362). Indeed, dissatisfaction with the top-down hierarchism of the top right quadrant is frequently a major factor driving affiliation with this quadrant (Douglas 1996: 114–115, 176).

In the wider literature on public administration, it is arguably Robert Dahl's theory of polyarchy that presents the fullest account of a style of administration aligned with this quadrant. Dahl formulated polyarchy ('control of leaders') in opposition to hierarchy ('control by leaders') as a way of accounting for social configurations that made it possible for non-leaders to 'exercise a relatively high degree of control over leaders' (Dahl 1984: 227), and his work discusses in considerable detail the types of institutions and commitments that are necessary to sustain polyarchy.

Equally, in broader public law scholarship, we find—while not embracing the framework of GGCT—an emphasis on deliberation and consensus within decision-making that is certainly characteristic, we suggest, of the lower right quadrant's thought style. Patrick McAuslan, for example, in his seminal *The Ideologies of Planning Law*, identifies a third model of planning law, in contrast to the more established private property and good public administration models. This model:

> … sees law as the provider of rights of participation in the land use planning process not by virtue of the ownership of property but by virtue of the more abstract principles of democracy and justice. These in turn come down to the argument that all who are likely to be affected by or who have, for whatever reason, an interest or concern in a proposed development of land or change in the environment should have the right of participation in the decision on that proposal just because they might be affected or are interested. (McAuslan 1980: 5)

While McAuslan's work focuses on land-use planning, the consensus and deliberation perspective is central to the work of the so-called Sheffield School of Public Law that was influential in the 1980s. In one of his earliest articles, Tony Prosser (1982) builds on the work of Habermas and others to argue that the *participation* (in the sense of the parties affected by a decision taking part in a discussion free from domination with an equal 'say' in the decision) and *accountability* (the requirement that justifications in the form of reasons for action must be given by those exercising public power) can and should serve as key organising concepts of a critical public law.

A key underlying assumption here, with the writing of the Sheffield School authors, as with McAuslan, is that administrative justice is at best imperfectly characterised as a *lis inter partes* between the administration and the person that is the subject of some administrative action (such as a grant or refusal of planning permission). J. D. B. Mitchell (1966, 135) invoked the maxim of Portalis: *Juger l'administration c'est aussi administrer.* As used by Mitchell, this phrase signifies not only that any legal decision has the potential to interfere with administrative processes. Mitchell also intended to underscore the idea that judging administrative matters inevitably involved subtle judgement about where the public interest lies. The point is put more affirmatively by Nonet and Selznick who (characterising one of the guiding assumptions of 'responsive law') argue:

> If the legal order is to lend affirmative authority to purpose, the focus of legal analysis must be the social patterns and institutional arrangements that frustrate the achievement of legal ends, not the aggrieved individual per se. (Nonet and Selznick [1978] 2011: 106)

In other words, characteristic of this particular thought style is the denial, or at least weakening, of the dividing line between the making of policy and the judging of an administrative dispute. This requires in turn a style of administrative justice that is open and inclusive, because administrative disputes involve multi-dimensional considerations about how to use the endowment of the community (whether financial, or land, or otherwise) in the manner settled on by the community itself. A just administrative decision, on this account, is one around which broad consensus can be reached, after listening to the arguments publicly put forward, and subjected to critical questioning, by all the affected parties.

While there is an undoubted emphasis on procedure within the deliberation and participation style of administrative justice, it is in its substantive dimension that this style is at its most radical. Prosser, taking his inspiration from Habermas, makes the point that a public law of the sort he proposes would preclude outcomes that are stabilised by force, and would thus tend towards substantive as well as procedural justice (Prosser 1982: 11). Drilling down to the specific concerns of administrative justice, McAuslan similarly sees this approach as extending beyond the purely procedural:

> Substantive aspects take in what may be called the alternative society; not just more lay input into the existing governmental system but new structures and processes of government which deliberately and significantly alter the balance between the governed and the governors; greater attention paid to social community and ecological factors which assume or are geared to reproducing the same kind of society that exists at present. The wider aspect of the ideology has the effect of putting it almost into the position of an ideology of opposition to existing government structures, process and policies… (McAuslan 1980: 6)

Distilling the core propositions about the operational question and decision legitimacy narrative, as we have done above, we can see in deliberation and consensus that the key operational question is a slightly more complex one to formulate: it would be something like, 'Where does the consensus lie?' And the legitimacy narrative around the decision becomes, 'You were afforded a meaningful opportunity to participate in the decision, and were given a reasoned justification for it'. Moving towards characteristic modes of redress, we can see some similarity with the consumerist style in that there is an emphasis on voice; however, the kind of voice that is envisaged by deliberation and consensus goes beyond the opportunity to express a preference. Voice, in the deliberation and consensus style, means the opportunity of involvement, rather than merely input in the making of decisions. It also is a remedy by all those whose interests are affected, as in McAuslan's example of all those who might be affected by a development or land-use case, rather than just the property owner.

Experiences of Administrative Justice

In the section above, we used GGCT to compare and classify different normative models of administrative justice in the sense of 'those qualities of a system that provide arguments for the acceptability of its outcomes'. Yet, Adler, by emphasising in his treatment of administrative justice various forms of remedy and mechanisms of accountability, draws our attention to the fact that people's empirical experiences of administrative justice may feel very different to their own aspirations for administrative justice. In the remainder of this section, we explore the implications of this in more detail, using the framework of GGCT again.

User Experiences of Administrative Justice

Despite the fact that, in terms of design, much of the world of public administration may fall within the upper right, bottom right and bottom left quadrants, there is reason to believe that, when it comes to empirical experiences of administrative justice systems, individuals may associate it more with the upper left quadrant whereby they feel excluded or marginalised, 'bypassed by authority and power' (Douglas 1996: 69). It is not hard to see why. There may be something profoundly unattractive to the modern liberal mind about the idea of the state's ends being at variance with the polity's: as Nonet and Selznick (1978) pointed out, in the modern era administration is seen as a way of making law more responsive to wider social needs. Yet one should be cautious of succumbing to presentism. Administration does not inevitably produce responsive law: as Nonet and Selznick also showed, in the eras of repressive and autonomous law administration made law less responsive to wider social needs. This arguably remains true in the present day in at least some contexts. In the UK, it is explicitly true of colonial governments. As the House of Lords emphasised in *Bancoult (No 2)*, and as constitutional historians have argued, the constitutional order of the UK itself continues to be influenced by principles inherited from the Tudor era (Endicott 2015).

More generally, administrative institutions, like any other institution, have a natural propensity to being insulated from demotic thought styles and, absent institutions that effectively bring administrative justice back into contact with these thought styles, there is no guarantee that administrative justice practices will in fact meet the aspirations of individuals and groups in the relevant community, however much it may conform to its own internal standards.

Operator Experiences of Administrative Justice

While the above argument considers the experience of citizens or users of administrative systems, we might also consider the experiences of those tasked with operating the system. There are good reasons why the upper left quadrant is likely to play a greater role in the operators' experiences of administrative justice too. Policy is hotly contested in many polities today, and the goals administrators pursue as well as the ideas and principles those goals reflect can change radically with a change of government. Here, the policies that the executive pursues at a particular point of time may simply reflect a temporary truce or compromise between interest groups, rather than the deeper substantive values or expertise-driven pathways to shared goals that the positive diagonal presupposes; and administrators may consequently find themselves having to pursue goals or implement policies they regard as unjust or inadvisable because they clash either with their own values or with what they have learned through their expertise.

As Lo has shown in his study of Norwegian municipal government, administrative officials feel a 'moral and professional obligation' to work towards what they perceive to be the common good, even where that sits uneasily with the law's normative framework (Lo 2021). Where systems of administrative justice deny them this opportunity, the result is that administrative decision-makers lose faith in the ability of their rules and procedures to produce the right outcome (Hertogh 2010: 215; Halliday 2004: 60). As Hertogh has shown, such a process, if sustained over time, can produce a situation in which administrative officials find themselves alienated from the rules and systems they are tasked with applying.

'Alienation' as a concept has been the subject of complex theorisation in the social sciences, but we use it here in the somewhat simpler sense in which it was introduced by Simmel. To Simmel, alienation was a product of the ascendency of objective culture—things created by humans, such as law, science, and so on—over subjective culture—more personal aspects of human life, such as values, feelings, and beliefs. Simmel argued that the steady shrinkage of the domain of subjective culture, and the expansion of objective culture, made it ever harder for individuals to identify with the cultural objects that constituted objective culture. Alienation was the result of this, a sense of meaninglessness in which cultural products cease to be meaningful to humans, and a sense of powerlessness, involving a loss of agency and creativity (Simmel [1907] 1978: 454ff). As empirical work has shown, it is precisely these two dimensions that characterise the sense of policy alienation administrative officials face in such environments (see, e.g., Tummers et al. 2009), and they highlight the real risk that systems that are perceived by their designers as furthering a particular model of administrative justice end up being perceived very differently by the individuals tasked with delivering them. As a result, the upper left quadrant draws our attention to the alienating effect systems of administrative justice might have on the administrative officials tasked with administering them.

Conclusion

A short chapter such as this can at most point to the rich potential in the use of GGCT as one tool in the box of administrative justice theorists. It takes from Adler the importance of a focus on administrative justice *systems* and modes of redress—indeed it could be argued that it is this focus that distinguishes administrative justice scholarship from the broader canons of public administration and administrative law. But equally, it highlights how too narrow a focus on arguments for the *acceptability* of administrative decisions about individual circumstances risks overlooking those thought styles of administrative justice that align along the negative diagonal of withdrawal and protest, and which provide a basis for critique, rejection and transformation of administrative systems and their justificatory claims. Such critical perspectives play a particularly important role where the gap between the demands on administrative systems and their potential to meet such demands are most hard-pressed. These are the conditions under which both top left populism and radical demands for participatory justice are most likely to make themselves heard. Administrative justice scholars, practitioners and system designers ignore such perspectives at their peril.

References

Adler, Michael. (2003). A Socio-Legal Approach to Administrative Justice. *Law and Policy,* 25(4), 323–352.

Adler, Michael. (2006). Fairness in Context. *Journal of Law and Society*, *33*(4), 615–638.

Arvind, T. T., Halliday, Simon., and Stirton, Lindsay. (2022). Judicial Review and Administrative Justice. In M. Hertogh et al. (eds.), *Oxford Handbook of Administrative Justice.* Oxford: Oxford University Press.

Cane, Peter. (2009). *Administrative Tribunals and Adjudication.* Oxford: Hart Publishing.

Craven, Richard. (2023). Managing Dissonance: Bureaucratic Justice and Public Procurement. *Regulation and Governance, 17*, 215–233.

Dahl, Robert. (1984). Polyarchy, Pluralism, and Scale. *Scandinavian Political Studies, 7*(4), 225–240.

Davis. (1969). *Discretionary Justice: A Preliminary Inquiry.* Baton Rouge: Louisiana State University Press.

Douglas, Mary. (1982). Introduction to Grid-Group Analysis. In Mary Douglas (ed.), *Essays in the Sociology of Perception.* Abingdon: Routledge and Kegan Paul.

Douglas, Mary. (1996). *Thought Styles: Critical Essays on Good Taste*. London: Sage Publications.

Endicott, Timothy. (2015). Was *Entick v Carrington* a Landmark? In Adam Tomkins and Paul Scott (eds.), *Entick v Carrington: 250 Years of the Rule of Law*. Oxford: Hart Publishing.

Halliday, Simon (2004) *Judicial Review and Compliance with Administrative Law.* Oxford: Hart Publishing.

Halliday, Simon and Scott, Colin. (2010). A Cultural Analysis of Administrative Justice. In Michael Adler (ed.), *Administrative Justice in Context*. Oxford: Hart Publishing.

Harlow, Carol and Rawlings, Rick. (2023). Populism and Administrative Law. In Eoin Carolan, J. N. E. Varahus and Sarah Fulham-McQuillan (eds.), *The Making and Remaking of Public Law*. Oxford, Hart Publishing.

Hertogh, Marc. (2010). Through the Eyes of Bureaucrats: How Front-Line Officials Understand Administrative Justice. In Michael Adler (ed.), *Administrative Justice in Context*. Oxford: Hart Publishing.

Kirkham, Richard. (2022). The Ombud as Chameleon: A Story of Adaptation to Different Administrative Cultures. In Marc Hertogh, Richard Kirkham, Robert

Thomas and Joe Tomlinson (eds.), *The Oxford Handbook of Administrative Justice*. Oxford: Oxford University Press.

Lipsky, Michael. (1980). *Street-Level Bureaucracy: The Dilemmas of the Individual in Public Services*. New York: Russel Sage Foundation.

Lo, Christian. (2021). *When Politics Meets Bureauacracy: Rules, Norms, Conformity and Cheating*. Manchester: Manchester University Press.

Lodge, Martin, and Stirton, Lindsay. (2010). Accountability in the Regulatory State. In Robert Baldwin, Martin Cave, and Martin Lodge (eds.), *The Oxford Handbook of Regulation*. Oxford: Oxford University Press.

Mashaw, Jerry. (1983). *Bureaucratic Justice: Managing Social Security Disability Claims*. New Haven: Yale University Press.

McAuslan. (1980). *The Ideologies of Planning Law*. Oxford: Pergamon.

Mitchell, J. D. B. (1966). The State of Public Law in the UK. *International and Comparative Law Quarterly, 15*(1), 133–149.

Nonet, Philippe, and Selznick, Philip. ([1978] 2011). *Law and Society in Transition: Towards Responsive Law*. London: Routledge.

Prosser, Tony. (1982). Towards a Critical Public Law. *Journal of Law and Society*, 9(1), 1–18.

Sainsbury, Roy. (2008). Administrative Justice, Discretion and the Welfare to Work Project. *Journal of Social Welfare and Family Law*, *30*(4), 323–338.

Simmel, Georg. ([1907] 1978). *The Philosophy of Money*. Tom Bottomore and David Frisby trans. London: Routledge.

Stirton, Lindsay and Lodge, Martin. (2001). Transparency Mechanisms: Building Publicness into Public Services. *Journal of Law and Society*, *28*(4), 471–489.

Tummers, Lars, Bekkers, Victor, and Steijn, Bram. (2009). Policy Alienation of Public Professionals. *Public Management Review*, *11*(5), 685–706.

7

The Political Vulnerability of the American Administrative State

Robert A. Kagan

Introduction

Reflecting Michael Adler's insightful scholarship,[1] sociolegal research on administrative justice has focused primarily on how governmental bureaucracies have implemented social benefit and service programs, enforced regulations, and dealt with immigration cases. Scholars have analyzed variation in agencies' modes of case-handling, how organizational dynamics affect the fairness of bureaucratic decision-making, and more (Adler 2010; Hertogh et al. 2022). The stability and public-regarding posture of the administrative state as a whole, however, has been taken for granted, at least in democratic nations. Yet in recent decades, conservative political movements in Europe and the United States have challenged the administrative state's stability and its traditions of nonpartisan law-implementation and promotion of the general welfare.

This essay has been stimulated by the stated intent of President Donald Trump's 2017–2021 administration to "deconstruct" the federal regulatory state in the United States, and by the even more serious threat to that

[1] The author thanks Michael Adler for drawing me into the administrative justice scholarly community, as well as for his sterling example and warm friendship.

R. A. Kagan (✉)
Department of Political Science and School of Law, University of California, Berkeley, CA, USA
e-mail: rak@berkeley.edu

S. Cowan and S. Halliday (eds.), *Socio-Legal Generation*, Palgrave Socio-Legal Studies,
https://doi.org/10.1007/978-3-031-67244-6_7

state posed by the possibility of Trump's re-election in 2024. "I will totally obliterate the Deep State," Trump proclaimed at a campaign event on June 13, 2023, hours after his arraignment on federal charges of obstruction of justice and of unlawful retention and handling of classified national security documents (Swan et al. 2023a)—charges that reflect the former president's repeated disrespect for institutional norms and laws. On another front, a strengthened conservative majority on the U.S. Supreme Court, responding to the ideas of a well-funded, anti-statist legal movement, has struck down four major federal agency regulations, empowering lower federal courts to follow their lead in future cases.

The regulatory-welfare state has been widely regarded as an essential, valued feature of modern democratic governance. We might ask, therefore, is it actually vulnerable to political efforts to "deconstruct" it? What might create and intensify such vulnerabilities, and why? This essay examines those questions by treating the American experience as a case study in the politics of the administrative state, attempting to view that experience in comparative perspective. The discussion will focus on (1) the features of the U.S. political system that have made its administrative-regulatory state particularly vulnerable to efforts to weaken it; (2) recent political and legal developments that have intensified the threat of such weakening; and (3) the significant institutional and cultural sources of resistance to that threat.

Two preliminary points: First, what would "deconstructing" an administrative state mean? Trump and his supporters have not provided any definition. But for the purposes of this essay, we can speculate that it might have two dimensions, substantive and procedural. The substantive dimension would entail eliminating politically controversial regulatory, welfare, or law-enforcement programs, or drastically shrinking their funding—that is, making cuts much more drastic than the "reforms" typically demanded by conservative political parties. The procedural dimension would entail repudiating or disregarding the normative traditions of the administrative state, such as insulation of day-to-day administrative and law-enforcement decision-makers from partisan political interference, adherence to the rule of law, and adherence to the canons of administrative law that promote public-regarding, evidence-based policy-making. Erosion of such norms, of course, would enable a chief executive to fire administrative and law-enforcement officials at will and use the powers and resources of government to benefit only himself and his supporters and to disadvantage his critics.

Second, in their multi-national analysis of "how democracies die," political scientists Steven Levitsky and Daniel Ziblatt (2018) observe while the first steps down that fateful path often have been taken by a charismatic, demagogic political outsider—such as Mussolini and Hitler and Hugo Chavez—he typically has obtained *control* of government power only via the acquiescence or support of an established political party. In this essay, therefore, attention will be paid less to the sources of voter support for Donald Trump and more to the role of the Republican Party and its major funders in paving the way for Trump's 2016–2020 presidency, his possible re-election in 2024, and his antagonism toward the administrative state.

The American Administrative State: Some Historically-Based Vulnerabilities

In the United States, administrative governance was slow to develop, especially in comparison to European nations in which the establishment of strong, centralized royal bureaucracies preceded the development of democracy (Shefter 1994). The young nation's political culture, forged in a revolt against a distant colonial monarchy, emphasized individualism and local self-government, along with a populist distrust of concentrated governmental power. In his comparative analysis of political cultures, Seymour Martin Lipset (1991: 21) wrote that "America began and continues as the most antistatist, legalistic, and [individual] rights-oriented nation." The rights articulated in the United States and most state constitutions, however, are "negative rights," restricting the power of governments to infringe on individuals' liberties—not "positive rights," such as those that obligate governments to provide everyone basic levels of sustenance, shelter, and health care.[2]

The Anti-statist Legacy

Through much of the nineteenth century, governance in the United States was dominated not by bureaucrats in Washington or state capitals but by decentralized political parties and by locally selected judges (Skowronek 1982; Fukuyama 2014; Kagan 2019, Ch. 3). In the last hundred years, however, anti-statist attitudes have coexisted with a competing strain in the national political culture—attitudes that favor nationwide governmental programs to regulate dangerous technologies, heedless business practices, racial discrimination, environmental degradation, and to provide financial

[2] The major exceptions are provisions in many state constitutions, enacted in the late nineteenth or early twentieth century, that guarantee a system of free public education.

aid and services for impoverished families. Anti-statist sentiment failed to block the establishment of many federal governmental regulatory and social welfare bureaucracies, especially during President Franklin Roosevelt's administration, as it addressed the economic crisis of the 1930s depression, and in the 1964–1972 period, when large Democratic Congressional majorities responded to social movements for civil rights, environmental protection, and anti-poverty measures. But even in those eras, anti-statist politicians often compelled Congress to limit the coverage, accessibility, and generosity of social benefit programs, especially as compared to those created by modern governments in Western Europe and Canada (Kagan 2019, Ch. 8). Compared to citizens in other rich democracies, Americans have remained more reluctant to accept the high tax burdens required for generous cradle-to-grave health and welfare coverage. The United States taxes its citizens less[3] and spends less on social benefits as a percentage of GDP than comparably rich countries (Wilensky 2002; Alesina and Glaeser 2004).[4] Overall, America's strong strain of anti-statist sentiment suggests that under some political conditions, the U.S. administrative state may be especially vulnerable to all-out political assault.

The Federal Bureaucracy: Political Responsiveness vs Professionalism

In the early nineteenth century, competing political parties built electoral support through webs of patronage. Elected executives staffed administrative positions via a job-granting "spoils system" ("to the electoral victor, belong the spoils") (Fukuyama 2014). The federal government did not create a merit-based civil service system until the enactment of the Pendleton Act in 1883, and even then did so incompletely (Mashaw 2012). Thus, after an electoral change in the political party occupying the White House, the newly elected

[3] According to OECD data, in 2015, taxes in the United States (federal, state, and local combined) equaled 26.4% of GDP, while the OECD average was over 34%. German taxes were over 36% of GDP and in France, 45% (Porter, 2017).

[4] Jacob Hacker (2002) showed that in 1995, public social welfare expenditures in the United States equalled only 17.1 percent of GDP (as compared to 35–37% in Scandinavian countries, and 25–30% in Germany, the Netherlands, Italy, and the U.K.). However, *private* expenditures for the same purposes (often subsidized through tax deductions) were much higher in the United States, amounting to 8.3% of GDP, which narrows the U.S.–Western European difference in total social provision somewhat. See also Howard (2007) and Tach and Edin (2017).

president can replace the top several tiers of leadership[5] in most federal agencies, with considerable emphasis on the appointees' ideological alignment with the president. For each such political appointment, the president must gain the approval of the Senate, but even senators from the opposing political party usually defer to an elected president's choices.

That legacy of the spoils system could be defended on grounds that powerful administrative agencies *should* be fully responsive to the appointing president ("the people's choice"). In that view, electoral responsiveness should take precedence over politically neutral administrative professionalism. That precedence sometimes is desirable. But, regularizing post-election, partisan shuffling of top agency policymakers and administrators, as the U.S. has done, would enable a freshly elected president who is hostile to administrative governance to replace the top stratum of administrative agency officials, including those who may be the most experienced and committed to their agency's mission, with appointees who are committed to drastic cuts in the agency's level of energy and in its role in governance. Even short of that, as partisan party polarization has increased in the last thirty years, political trust in the "executive branch" has declined by 20% (Brady and Kent 2022: 45).

A Constitutional Vulnerability

In the last decades of the nineteenth century and the beginning of the twentieth century, popular objections to the many risks and harms generated by rapid industrialization, commercialization, and urbanization led governments at all levels to create new administrative agencies—local departments of public health; state commissions to regulate workplace safety, insurance companies, and other businesses "affected with a public interest" (Novak 2017; Friedman 1973: 396–405); and federal agencies to regulate railroads, meat packers, and canneries. In response, business interests, preaching the gospel of free markets and economic liberty, challenged in court many of these regimes and many regulations they promulgated. In the *Lochner* case, the U.S. Supreme Court held that the post-Civil War 14th Amendment's "due process" clause barred "unreasonable" restrictions on "freedom of contract."[6] Invoking that principle, the Court struck down many state laws designed to protect workers' safety and health and their rights to organize labor unions. The Court invalidated some federal regulations on grounds that

[5] Cabinet secretaries and their subordinates at the Deputy Secretary, Under Secretary, and Assistant Secretary levels, all with the advice and consent of the Senate. These subordinates number at least 10 for each department, in some departments 30 or more.

[6] Lochner v New York, 198 U.S 45 (1905)

business practices such as manufacturing, mining, labor relations and retail sales were local matters, beyond Congress's constitutional power to regulate "interstate commerce."

Nevertheless, the administrative state, state and federal, continued to grow. And as it did, conservative constitutional theorists continued to claim that administrative bodies were becoming an unauthorized fourth branch of government that exercised legislative (that is, policymaking) powers that the Constitution vested only in Congress, and adjudicatory powers that the Constitution explicitly vested in courts. In the 1930s, President Franklin Roosevelt and a Democratic Congress enacted a wave of statutes creating new regulatory programs, new agencies to administer them, and nationwide social benefit programs for retired and unemployed workers and for poor families. But a conservative 5:4 majority on the Supreme Court held several of those "New Deal" laws unconstitutional. Most strikingly, in 1935, in the *Schechter Poultry* case, the Court unanimously held that the National Industrial Recovery Act—a keynote New Deal effort to stabilize a devastating downward wage-price spiral—violated the Constitution. First, the Court's opinion said, Congress, by authorizing the regulation of prices and wages in a local market (for chickens), had gone well beyond its constitutional powers to regulate interstate commerce. Second, the Court opinion asserted that Congress had unlawfully delegated broad legislative powers to a government agency, the National Recovery Administration, as well as to private advisory panels, all without providing sufficiently specific statutory guidance.[7]

The Court having pointed a gun at the New Deal, Roosevelt pointed one at the Court. The president asked Congress to enact a law expanding the number of justices, which would enable him to appoint more pro-New Deal Democrats. One conservative justice then backed off, joining the more progressive justices in voting to uphold a reenacted Congressional labor law. Another conservative justice resigned, enabling Roosevelt to appoint a New Deal Democrat. In short order, a new politically-progressive Supreme Court majority discarded older precedents, adopted a very broad interpretation of the Commerce Clause, and abandoned both the *Schechter* case's "nondelegation doctrine" and *Lochner*'s interpretation of the 14th Amendment. The "Roosevelt" Court, in effect, bestowed Constitutional legitimacy on the federal administrative-regulatory state (Kagan et al. 2013: 204–207). A post-World War II Administrative Procedure Act, which established procedural standards for policymaking and adjudication by federal agencies, seemingly

[7] *Schechter Poultry Corp. v. United States*, 295 US 495 (1935).

cemented that legitimation, as did further elaboration of that act's procedural requirements by the federal courts in the 1960s and '70s (Kagan et al. 2013: 209–211).

The federal administrative state expanded much further in the 1960s and '70s, as Congress enacted landmark civil rights, environmental, worker safety, and consumer protection laws, each with new enforcement agencies; and new national health insurance programs covering the elderly (Medicare) and the poor (Medicaid); and more generous benefit programs for the poor families and disabled workers. The constitutionality of all these laws was upheld or not challenged. Business appeals to the courts were mostly about whether agency rules had been made in conformity with the 1946 Administrative Procedure Act. In the 1984 *Chevron* case, the Supreme Court held that if there was any ambiguity about whether an agency-issued rule or decision was within the scope of the regulatory statute enacted by Congress, the courts should defer to the administrative agency and its expert judgment. But in recent years, as will be discussed later, conservative legal scholars and judges have renewed the arguments about the constitutionality and authority of the federal administrative state—arguments that seemingly had been laid to rest in the late 1930s and early 1940s.

Three Other Distinctive Features of American Government

The clash between President Roosevelt and the Supreme Court highlights another distinctive feature of American government: the *political selection of judges*. In most American states, judges are elected. In others, they are appointed by elected governors. Federal judges at all levels are appointed by the president, subject to approval by the Senate. This can make the selection of judges a field for intense partisan conflict, as has occurred with increasing intensity in the last 35 years. Consequently, as we shall see, presidents and allied senators who are determined to shrink and weaken the national administrative state can appoint anti-statist U.S. Supreme Court justices (and other federal judges) primed to sustain Constitutional challenges to both the statutes that define the missions of federal agencies and the regulations those agencies promulgate.

Second, the system of *open primary elections* that was created by both the Democratic and Republican parties in the late 1960s and early 1970s has weakened the ability of established party leaders to control the nomination process. Party "primaries" enable charismatic or well-funded political outsiders to challenge and sometimes defeat long-time office-holders. On one hand, the grueling, expensive state-by-state presidential primary elections historically have prevented candidates without prior office-holding experience and support of at least some established party leaders to win the party's nomination. Yet, the open primary system is precisely what enabled an inexperienced outsider candidate like Donald J. Trump, hostile or indifferent to the traditions and norms of the administrative state, to win his party's nomination in 2020—and again in 2024.

Third, in the United States, the bulk of the increasingly large amounts of money spent to advance political candidates' electoral chances is raised from private donors—directly, or through political action groups, or through the political parties. While millions of moderate-income partisans contribute to the candidate or party of their choice, this system of *private campaign finance* gives very large donors and coalitions of such donors a disproportionate and significant influence on candidate selection and success. As discussed in the next section, the private campaign finance system, together with the open party primary election system, has enabled certain extraordinarily wealthy, anti-statist donors and their organizations to play a major role in pushing the Republican Party toward a more intensely partisan, aggressive stance. And in conjunction with America's system of partisan selection of judges, donor-funded organizations have imbued young conservative lawyers with anti-statist legal ideas, and effectively advocated their eventual appointment to the Supreme Court and lower federal courts (Hollis-Brusky 2015).

A Changing Republican Party Paves the Way

World War II and its aftermath was an era of business-government cooperation. Both "big business" and the Republican Party accepted a larger central government role for funding scientific and technological research, promoting economic stability and growth, financing large infrastructure projects, and much more (Hacker and Pierson 2016). President Dwight Eisenhower, 1952–1960, a moderate Republican, recognized the popularity of the Democrats' New Deal social security programs, and, facing the Cold War's pressure for military spending, did not seek to reverse the steeply progressive income tax laws that had been adopted to fund the World War II effort. In the 1960s and early 1970s, as noted earlier, Democratic Congresses expanded social benefit programs and enacted a wave of new regulatory statutes and new regulatory agencies. Republican legislators proposed reforms designed to make particular regulations more economically efficient, but did not reject regulatory programs on principle. The administrative state's legitimacy, and its ever-growing role in American governance, seemed secure. Developments in party politics, however, would soon bring changes to the Republican Party—changes that would pave a path to power for Donald Trump and for high court judges who would pose serious threats to the federal administrative state that was constructed during the Roosevelt Administration, World War II, and the 1960–1980 period.

Racial Realignment

When Lyndon Johnson pushed through Congress the federal Civil Rights Act (1964) and the Voting Rights Act (1965), he predicted those laws, which at long last would forbid racial discrimination nationwide, would also end the Democratic Party's century-long dominance in all the ex-Confederate states. Sure enough, by the late 1970s, those states had become the Republicans' new electorally solid base. White southern and border state voters who flocked to the Republican Party prominently included white evangelical "Christian nationalists," who believed, then and now, that they are being discriminated against by federal civil rights, social welfare, and immigration laws and policies, crafted by irreligious liberal elites (Greenhouse 2023). Republican Party leaders eagerly sought the support of conservative Christian leaders in Southern and border states who denounced "the secular, sexually liberated, science based, 'big government' ethos" that they felt liberal elites had imposed upon their way of life (Woodard 2011: 278).

Intensification of Anti-statist Politics

At the same time, financial and other business elites, another key Republican constituency, were moving toward the right on regulatory and tax policy. In 1980, Ronald Reagan was elected president, having campaigned against "over-regulation" and having proclaimed "government is the problem, not the solution." His electoral success pushed ever more Republicans to that posture. Meanwhile, a network of extremely wealthy, libertarian businessmen had embarked on a long-term campaign that year by year drew the Republican Party toward a more implacably ideological anti-regulatory, anti-taxation posture (Hacker and Pierson 2016). The conservative donors developed sophisticated systems for channeling unprecedentedly large amounts of untraceable "dark money" to Republican candidates and to organizations committed to their anti-statist agenda (Mayer 2016). Year after year, as shown by economists Emmanuel Saenz and Gabriel Zucman (2019), well-funded conservative lobbyists and their Congressional allies chipped away at the tax laws and their enforcement, enabling the very wealthy to shield income and increases in their wealth from taxation and capture a giant share of the nation's income—thereby exacerbating the growing inequality between America's waxing super-rich and its economically-waning working classes.

The Conservative Legal Movement

A cluster of anti-statist donors also sought to move the federal judiciary to the political right. They created and funded the Federalist Society, which fostered legal theories that conservative lawyers could use to challenge the Supreme Court rulings that had legitimated the regulatory-administrative state. The Federalist Society also built a political network that placed ideological adherents in the U.S. Department of Justice and on the federal courts (Teles 2008; Hollis-Brusky 2015). Reagan's Attorney General, Edwin Meese, had instructed U.S. Attorneys to employ in their legal briefs an "original intent" mode of Constitutional interpretation—an interpretive approach that promised to restrict or even upend the liberal "Warren Court" rulings of the 1950s and '60 s (Heinzerling 2022). "Originalism" became a Federalist Society litmus test for endorsing Republican appointments to the Supreme Court. Starting the mid-1990s, the Court's 5:4 majority steadily moved to the right in both its Constitutional and statutory rulings, overruling or evading rights-protecting precedents (Burbank and Farhang 2017; Kagan 2019: 268–7, 281–83).

The Denigration of Science

The "Progressive" activists who advocated the creation of administrative agencies in the late nineteenth century valorized science as a basis for effective policy-making and for legitimating administrative authority (Tushnet 2022). Pasteur's germ theory stimulated the creation of public departments of health and guided the regulation of drinking water, the canning of foods, and more. Environmental science underpins and guides contemporary environmental regulation. Polls show that in recent decades, Americans' confidence in science, almost alone among a list of political and nonpolitical institutions, has remained high (Brady and Kent 2022: 46–47)—but not among committed Republicans and self-identified conservatives (Oreskes and Conway 2022). In 2020, 88% of Democrats agreed with scientific findings that climate change was a major threat to Americans' well-being, but only 31% of Republicans shared those views.[8]

That partisan polarization in attitudes toward science, according to political scientists Naomi Oreskes and Eric Conway (2022), also can be traced back to wealthy, anti-government activists and donors and to Ronald Reagan's presidency. Reagan rejected a science-based treaty with Canada to reduce pollution from coal-fired power plants, stating that the science was insufficient to justify it. That set a politically attractive precedent for Republican politicians: fighting popular regulatory proposals indirectly by rejecting or questioning "science that illuminated any problem that invited (or worse, seemed to demand) government action" (Oreskes and Conway 2022: 110). On the basis of numerous studies and examples, Oreskes and Conway conclude that among "political conservatives ... contemporary distrust of science is collateral damage, a spillover effect of distrust in government" (id, at 101).[9] Similar collateral damage, of course, is Republicans' reduced faith in the governmental administrators whose authority and arguments are based, in significant measure, on their and their agency's evidence-based expertise.

Toward Plutocratic Populism

Republican politicians' culture also changed. In the early 1990s, Congressman Newt Gingrich encouraged fellow Republican politicians to treat politics as warfare. He publicly characterized Democrats not as well-meaning people with whom Republicans disagreed but as "pathetic" or "sick," "unpatriotic" and "immoral" (Levitsky and Ziblatt 2018). This antagonistic, hyper-partisan vision was disseminated by conservative talk radio hosts and by Rupert Murdoch's "Fox News" cable television station, "instigating and intensifying tribalism among both rank-and-file Republicans and politicians who compete for conservative media attention" (Hacker and Pierson 2019). Conservative Republicans' anti-liberal propaganda also helped

---

[8] Comparing the politics of regulation in the United States and in Europe, David Vogel (2012) observed that by the early twenty-first century in the United States, "Each claim about a new risk is likely to be challenged by a counter-narrative contending that it was misinformed" (264). During the 2012 election campaign, Republican candidates and prominent conservative politicians and conservative television commentators denounced global warming, or the human contribution to it, as a hoax.

[9] McCright and Dunlap (2010) emphasize that American conservatives reject only "impact" science findings, concerned with harms to the environment or human health, but not "production" science that supports investment in business and industry. See also Oreskes and Conway (2022, fn 15) for further studies. They add, citing O'Brien and Noy (2020) and Veldman (2019): "As the Republican Party has become identified with conservative religiosity – in particular, evangelical Protestantism – religious and political skepticism of science have become mutually constitutive and self-reinforcing."

energize grass roots anti-statist movements, such as the Tea Party groups that arose in passionate opposition to Democratic President Barack Obama's 2009 Affordable Care Act, a law which made health insurance more widely available. More recently, Fox News has reinforced the widening partisan divide by creating an "alternative factual" world for its listeners, one that demonizes Democrats and any Republican who departs from the party line.

By 2016, the combination of angry populist voters and targeted spending by wealthy plutocrats had come to dominate Republican primary elections, purging the party of moderates. Political scientists Jacob Hacker and Paul Pierson (2020) refer to the Republican Party's melding of populism and tax-cutting for wealthy "plutocrats" as plutocratic populism. Here are excerpts from one of their papers (2019: 6), summarizing their 2020 book's arguments:

> As the GOP aligned with …[the plutocrats], it turned its back on the economic concerns of the middle class….. Instead, the party made tax cuts for the wealthiest Americans and corporations the centerpiece—indeed, almost the entirety—of its economic platform. It became ever more aggressive in criticizing government spending programs of all kinds. … The Republican Party also adopted increasingly radical [negative]views of government regulation. …. None of [these] policy positions … has strong popular support. On the contrary, they are, for the most part, massively unpopular. (Hacker and Pierson 2018; Willamson 2017)
>
> Daniel Ziblatt (2017) has observed, ….if economic resources are vastly unequal, and a conservative party is politically aligned with the small circle of winners, something besides economics must be offered as a rationale for voting conservative. … And in modern politics, the list of candidates … is short and grim: nationalism; sectional loyalties; racial, ethnic, religious or cultural divisions; demonization of government and political elites; and fear of immigrants …
>
> [Thus] the Republican Party maintained political support from an electoral base drawn more and more from the white working class—and more and more through the manufacture and exploitation of tribalism, the demonization of political opponents, and increasingly shrill appeals to racial, ethnic and cultural loyalties… [It] was only a matter of time before a candidate no one thought could win would discover that calling immigrants "rapists" was a fast track to the Republican nomination.

That candidate, of course, was Donald Trump, who embodied a populist disrespect for the norms of democratic government and administrative integrity—and also was amenable to giving the plutocrats the massive tax cuts they wanted.

The Trump Administration

The Assault on the Administrative-Regulatory State

Donald Trump came into office in 2017 with full-throated bluster against the imagined "deep state"—rhetoric that reflected the paranoid conspiracy theories of his far-right supporters. Republicans' business-world constituency may have been pleased by Trump's promise to cut regulations "by 75%, maybe more." He issued an executive order instructing executive branch agencies to repeal two regulations for every new one they proposed (Coglianese et al. 2021). Trump's appointees to lead major departments and agencies included a number of wealthy, conservative campaign donors, as well as lobbyists and lawyers who had a record of actively opposing laws and regulations disliked by the industries they now would be in charge of regulating. Some Trump nominees had previously called for the elimination of the very agency they were appointed to head, or for radical limits on its authority (Lewis 2018). Trump Administration officials moved rapidly to repeal regulations that had been issued during the preceding Obama administration, to abandon existing prosecutions of regulatory violations, and to purge their organizations of regulatory experts and scientists (Davenport 2018; Protess and Silver-Greenberg 2017; Cowley and Silver-Greenberg 2017; Goodnough and Zarntke 2017). Throughout his term, Trump frequently fired, attempted to fire, or publicly denigrated administrators who were intent on adhering to laws, regulations, or long entrenched norms rather than acceding to the president's transgressive demands (Levitsky and Ziblatt (2018: 177–178).[10] And for four years, the Trump Administration prevented career agency officials from issuing important new regulations that they had been developing before Trump took office.

Many more Trump Administration initiatives, however, failed or stalled. Overall, Trump and his appointees dented the administrative-regulatory state and led many of its dedicated civil servants to retire. But they did not "dismantle" it. An academic study found that the Trump Administration

[10] Late in his term, Trump issued a sweeping executive order removing civil service protection for career office-holders whose work involves policy-making (CREW 2020). It was too late to implement the order, and President Biden repealed it, but if Trump had been re-elected in 2020, it would have significantly magnified his power to squelch agency efforts to faithfully implement or improve the nation's regulatory and social welfare laws and regulations.

had promulgated almost as many "economically significant" *pro-regulatory* regulations as significant *deregulatory* ones (Coglianese et al. 2019). Even when it had a Republican majority in both houses of Congress, the Trump Administration failed to fulfill its much heralded promise to repeal Obama's Affordable Care Act, or repeal any major regulatory statute, or make major cuts in funding for huge social spending programs such as Social Security and Medicare. For his populist base, Trump had provided pleasing anti-elite bluster and constant lies that his asserted cuts in regulation had liberated markets. For his plutocrat supporters, however, he and Congressional Republicans actually delivered a large prize: a huge tax-reduction law that especially favored the very rich.

Repulsing the Trump Administrations Assault

By and large, therefore, the federal administrative-regulatory state withstood the Trump Administration's promised dismantling. Why and how? First of all, most of it was not attacked. Of the innumerable provisions in the thousands of statutes and implementing regulations administered by federal government, the overwhelming majority do not elicit partisan political criticism. Every day, those laws continued to guide the actions of government food safety inspectors, social services agency officials, auditors of government-funded infrastructure projects, managers of the national forests, scientists in the National Weather Bureau, and many more. But what about the laws and regulations that the Trump Administration did vow to repeal or amend? To a remarkable extent, those efforts failed, due primarily to two modes of resistance.

(i) Adversarial Legalism[11]

Virtually every anti-regulatory Trump Administration initiative triggered a lawsuit or appeal that challenged its legality. Most prominently, the cases were filed by attorney generals from politically Democratic states and by liberal advocacy organizations such as the American Civil Liberties Union and the Environmental Defense Fund. In an overwhelming majority of those cases, the federal courts ruled in the challengers' favor. The judges—in many

---

[11] "Adversarial legalism" is my conceptual label for litigation and judicial decision-making as a mode of political action, policy implementation, administrative accountability, and dispute settlement—a mode that is much more prominent in the United States than in other rich democracies (Kagan 2019).

cases, even judges appointed by Trump—held that the Trump Administration initiatives were inconsistent with the underlying regulatory statutes; or blatantly lacked scientific or other evidentiary support; or violated important procedural tenets of administrative law (Sanger-Katz 2019; Institute for Policy Integrity 2019).[12] Sometimes, the agency in question tried to remedy the defect, and in some cases eventually succeeded, although the court case often delayed deregulatory change until near the end of Trump's term. Sometimes, the agency didn't even try again.

(ii) Path Dependence

As of the beginning of the twenty-first century, the major laws, institutions, and legal practices that constitute the federal administrative-regulatory state had been entrenched for several decades, generating what social scientists call change-resistant "path dependency" (Pierson 1996). That is, many businesses, activist organizations, and members of the public had adapted to, relied on, or benefited from those laws, institutions, and practices, and hence are inclined to fight against efforts to weaken them. The lawsuits and appeals by liberal lawyers and advocacy groups mentioned above reflect that dynamic. Path dependency also often plays out in elections and public protests. By the end of the 1990s, conservative opponents of the administrative-regulatory state had already learned a hard political lesson: because of the many veto points in the American policy-making and legislative process, plus the depth of public support for major environmental, health and safety, civil rights, and social welfare policies,[13] it has rarely been possible for Republicans to repeal or substantially weaken important regulatory or social welfare statutes and regulations (Burbank and Farhang 2017). During the 2000–2020 period, Republican Congressional leaders did not even try to repeal any major regulatory statute, other than the 2009 Obama-era Affordable Health Care Act, or even to amend any such statute, save for some parts of the 2010 Dodd-Frank Act, which was designed to stabilize the financial services industry.

[12] As of the end of 2019, according to the Institute of Policy Integrity at N.Y.U. School of Law (2019), in 35 out of the 36 court cases involving environmental policy (and in 64 of 68 cases involving all kinds of regulations), the judges ruled against the Trump Administration, or else the Administration, seeing the handwriting on the courthouse wall, withdrew its initiative.

[13] "Public support" may exclude "conservative Republicans." For example, an April 2019 Yale University survey of registered voters found that excluding "conservative Republicans" (but including "moderate Republicans" and "independents"), a strong majority believe that global warming is happening, is caused mostly by human activities, and is very worrisome.

The Supreme Court and the Administrative-Regulatory State

The Supreme Court, with its life-tenured justices, was less subject to the political pressures of path dependency. By the time Trump took office in early 2017, the wealthy anti-statist activists who had launched the conservative legal movement, working through the Federalist Society and the Republican Senate leadership, had already made major strides in populating the federal courts with ideologically aligned judges. During the Obama administration, Senate Republicans had turned their "advice and consent" role in judicial appointments into a hyper-partisan resistance mechanism, sharply reducing Obama's ability to appoint Democratic judges to open judicial positions. And in an unprecedented violation of Constitutional norms, Senate Republican leaders had refused for the eight month balance of the president's term to even consider Obama's nominee for a new opening on the Supreme Court. Consequently, Trump inherited an opening on the Court that had been blatantly "stolen" from the Democrats, enabling him to immediately make an appointment that increased the Court's conservative majority. Subsequently, Trump was able to make two more Supreme Court appointments plus scores of appointments to the depleted lower federal courts. His judicial appointments all had been selected by the Office of the President's Counsel, which was staffed by affiliates of the Federalist Society, dedicated to picking judges who were reliably anti-statist, pro-business, anti-abortion, and "originalist" in interpreting the Constitution.

A 2017 Trump appointment to the Supreme Court, Court of Appeals judge Neil Gorsuch, had written a concurring opinion in which, as summarized by a legal journalist and a law professor (Bazelon and Posner 2017):

> he attacked *Chevron* deference, writing that the rule "certainly seems to have added prodigious new powers to an already titanic administrative state." Remarkably, Judge Gorsuch argued that *Chevron* — one of the most frequently cited cases in the legal canon — is illegitimate in part because it is out of step with (you guessed it) *Schechter Poultry*. Never mind that the Supreme Court hasn't since relied on its 1935 attempt to scuttle the New Deal.

The *Chevron* doctrine, as noted above, said that in reviewing whether an agency-promulgated regulation was consistent with the Congressional statute the agency was implementing, judges should defer to that agency's expert judgment in that regard, unless the statute *clearly* does not authorize the regulation. By 2022, according to administrative law scholar Lisa Heinzerling (2022), the Republican Supreme Court majority was using that "unless" clause aggressively, repeatedly finding the statute "clearly" precludes the regulation in question—and thereby was blocking implementation of methodically prepared Obama-era regulatory measures.

Moreover, by resurrecting a rarely used "major questions doctrine," the Trump-expanded conservative majority created an additional way to invalidate administrative regulations promulgated by Democratic administrations. When an agency's regulation addresses an issue of "major national significance," the Court held, it must be supported by very clear Congressional authorization—an idea that has strong echoes of the long-discarded *Schecter Poultry* case's "non-delegation" doctrine. Wielding that flexible concept, the Republican majority has already struck down three important Biden Administration regulations.[14] In the aftermath of these decisions, Heinzerling (2022) reports:

> Agencies' specific policy choices about immigration, telecommunications, antitrust, student debt relief, climate change disclosures, diagnostic medical devices, insurance coverage of contraceptives, nuclear waste storage, and discrimination based on gender identity and sexual orientation—to name a few—have all been ... [challenged in lower federal courts]as unlawful because the relevant issues are too important and the statutory language less than crystalline.

In the current era of closely divided Congresses and partisan gridlock, it is extraordinarily difficult for Congress to enact a clarifying statute. Thus, the near-death of *Chevron* deference and the manipulable "major questions doctrine" mean that each time conservative judges invalidate an important administrative rule, the federal government's efforts to address a major social problem may totally stall. Thus, with many anti-statist Republican judges entrenched in the federal judiciary for life, the conservative legal movement, even if unable so far to "deconstruct" the American administrative-regulatory state, has already hampered its expansion and improvement, and probably will continue to do so for some time.

[14] One regulation, promulgated by the Centers for Disease Control and Prevention, had imposed a nationwide moratorium on evictions of financially needy tenants in counties experiencing substantial or high levels of COVID-19 transmission. *Alabama Association of Realtors v. DHS (2022).* The second, issued by the Occupational Health and Safety Administration, was designed to control the spread of COVID by requiring business firms operating large workplaces to require all on-site employees to be vaccinated or be tested daily. *National Federation of Independent Businesses v. Department of Labor (2022).* The third was an Obama Administration regulation requiring electric power plants throughout the nation to make large reductions in emissions of greenhouse gases: *West Virginia v. EPA (2023).*

Conclusion: The Future

"It is difficult to predict, especially the future," is a Danish folk saying, although it's often attributed to Neils Bohr, to American baseball player Yogi Berra, and to many others. They all are right about that. So at the time this essay is written, August 2023, it is impossible to be confident that Donald Trump will not be re-elected in November 2024, despite having been twice impeached for abuses of power and four times indicted for criminal conduct, including offenses connected to his attempts to prevent the transfer of power after losing the 2020 election. Regardless of what transpires, speculating about a second Trump Administration might reveal ways in which Trump—or some future president who has similar authoritarian, anti-statist impulses—could go about dismantling, weakening, or corrupting America's federal administrative state.

First, a second-term President Trump would probably be more disciplined in his political appointments to top agency positions, ensuring that his appointees would above all else be personally loyal and obedient to him, yet perhaps more competent than his first-term cabinet appointees.[15]

Second, a restored-to-power President Trump would almost certainly revive his unexecuted first-term executive order that reclassified hundreds of experienced leadership and policy analyst positions as "political appointments," unprotected by the civil service laws that prevent arbitrary dismissal. Trump could use such appointments to purge "liberals" from the Department of Justice, the FBI, and the Foreign Service, and to replace experienced administrators, scientists, and subject-matter experts in the Environmental Protection Administration and in any other agency at which the president might take offense.[16]

Third, Trump might well use the administrative powers of the presidency and federal agencies' law enforcement powers in blatantly political ways to punish bureaucrats, politicians, business corporations, and social groups who had voted against him, or who criticize him, while favoring those who support him.

---

[15] A journalistic investigation reported in mid-2023 that well-funded conservative organizations were already building lists of candidates selected for their commitment to Trump and "for their animus against the system," while already "preparing for legal challenges …." (Swan 2022a).

[16] A July 2023 investigative report by New York Times reporters concluded: "Mr. Trump and his associates have a broader goal: to alter the balance of power by increasing the president's authority over every part of the federal government that now operates, by either law or tradition, with any measure of independence from political interference by the White House, according to a review of his campaign policy proposals and interviews with people close to him" (Swan et al. 2023b).

Fourth, whether or not Trump again is president, the conservative Supreme Court justices might continue to feel few constraints on their anti-administrative state impulses. In a series of recent cases, law professor Lisa Heinzerling (2022: np) has observed, those justices seemed to be edging toward the "unitary executive" theory, an idea that gained prominence among conservative lawyers in the Reagan and the George W. Bush administrations. Article 2 of the 1789 Constitution begins "The executive power shall be vested in a President of the United States ..." The conservative lawyers take that to mean, according to Heinzerling, that "the president controls government personnel and decisions all the way down—and that it is unconstitutional for Congress to provide otherwise... This means that the president can tell the EPA head, for example, exactly at what level to set the national air quality standards." The unitary executive theory seems also to have found its way into Trump's circle of advisors. A July 2023 investigative report concluded: "Mr. Trump and his associates have a broader goal: to alter the balance of power by increasing the president's authority over every part of the federal government that now operates, by either law or tradition, with any measure of independence from political interference by the White House, according to a review of his campaign policy proposals and interviews with people close to him" (Swan et al. 2023b). A Supreme Court ruling endorsing the unitary executive theory would empower Trump to take action to achieve that "broader goal"—and to "deconstruct" selective parts of administrative-regulatory state.

Here it is necessary to reassert that this this subsection, as indicated at its outset, sets forth only some speculative scenarios, each of which depends on a cascade of legal and political contingencies that may well turn out differently. The scenarios do suggest, however, that the creation of a simultaneously populist and plutocratic anti-statist Republican party in the United States, together with a federal judiciary staffed with many ideologically sympathetic judges, does at least threaten the far-from-perfect but reasonably public-regarding and professional American administrative-regulatory state—a set of institutions that have been at the heart of American governance in the last 70 years.

It is also necessary to note that the American administrative state retains sources of political and cultural support that reduce that threat. The United States is a closely divided polity. Democratic candidates for president have won the popular vote in seven of the last eight elections. If we shift the political scenarios and imagine that Democrats win the presidency and a Congressional majority in 2024, they could continue the Biden Administrations efforts to strengthen the administrative-regulatory state. They might also find ways of maneuvering through some of the impediments the Supreme Court has started to erect. Political scientists who study the expansion and contraction of judicial power have found that national high courts have often become more powerful in periods of partisan division (Kapiszewski et al. 2013). But when partisan judges get too far out of favor with popular and legislative majorities (as during the New Deal in the United States), legislative leaders and the chief executive usually take action to limit or dilute the judges' power, or the threat of those restrictions impels the judges to retreat (Dahl 1957; Whittington 2008; Epstein et al. 2001).

More generally, alongside anti-statism, there is an enduring pro-government strain in American political culture. It is rooted, the historian Lawrence Friedman (1985) has written, in the technologically and organizationally sophisticated nature of environmentally advanced societies, which make it evident that governments have the capacity to devise and implement programs to prevent serious risks of harm. They also now have the taxing power and collective resources to provide financial help and medical care for the most unfortunate. In consequence, Friedman observed, in the course of the twentieth century, a new norm became prevalent, displacing the fatalism that characterized much of society throughout human history: because government *can* provide those protections and benefits, it has an *obligation* to do so. Thus in the aftermath of highly publicized disasters like massive petroleum spills, toxic chemical leaks, and food poisonings, politically overwhelming demands arise from civil society, urging government action to prevent a recurrence. Amidst economically devastating events like hurricanes and floods, the 2008 subprime mortgage bubble collapse, and the business shutdowns and layoffs of the 2020–2022 COVID pandemic, intense political pressures arise for government financial aid. Almost uniformly, elected political leaders scramble to respond, proposing new laws, regulatory reforms, loan guarantees for rebuilding, stimulus payments for the whole economy, and more.

That is how the American regulatory state was assembled: crisis by crisis, statute by statute, agency by agency. That is why it almost surely will persist. Because many things inevitably will go horribly wrong, political pressures to improve and expand the activist administrative-regulatory state will arise, and more often than not will prevail, at least in part. The multiple crises that will be generated by climate change will only intensify the demands on government to mobilize expertise, finance preventive and relief efforts, and compel compliance with fundamental norms. If life-tenured anti-statist Supreme Court justices too often block pressing demands for regulation and government aid, Congress and the president may well change the Court, as in the case of its conservative predecessor that, for a while, blocked New Deal regulation in the 1930s. Conservative backlashes against the administrative-regulatory state may recur as well, but like the Trump Administration in the 2017–2020 period, it is more likely that they will merely delay the further expansion of the administrative-regulatory state than to deconstruct it.

References

Adler, Michael. (2010). *Administrative Justice in Context.* Oxford, UK: Oxford University Press,

Alesina, Alberto and Glaeser, Edward. (2004). *Fighting Poverty In the US and Europe: A World of Difference.* Oxford, UK: Oxford University Press.

Bazelon, Emily and Posner, Eric. (2017). The Government Gorsuch Wants to Undo. *New York Times, Review Section,* April 1, 2017. https://www.nytimes.com/2017/04/01/sunday-review/the-government-gorsuch-wants-to-undo.html

Brady, Henry and Kent, Thomas. (2022). Fifty Years of Declining Confidence & Increasing Polarization in Trust in American Institutions. *Daedalus*: Fall 2022, pp. 43–66.

Burbank, Stephen and Farhang, Sean. (2017). *Rights and Retrenchment: The Counterrevolution Against Federal Litigation.* New York: Cambridge University Press.

Coglianese, Cary, Sarin, Natasha and Shapiro, Stuart. (2019). *Deregulatory Deceptions: Reviewing the Trump Administration's Claims About Regulatory Reform.* Penn Program on Regulation, University of Pennsylvania, November 1, 2020 https://scholarship.law.upenn.edu/faculty_scholarship/2229/.

Cowley, Stacy and Silver-Greenberg, Jessica. (2017). Consumer Regulator to Step Down from Office He Opened. *New York Times*, November 16, 2017, p. B4.

CREW. (2020). *Reforming Executive Branch Ethics.* Citizens for Responsibility and Ethics in Washington, December 2, 2020. https://www.citizensforethics.org/wp-content/uploads/2020/11/Section-4-Reforming-Executive-Branch-Ethics.pdf.

Dahl, Robert. (1957). Decisionmaking in a Democracy: The Supreme Court as a National Policy Maker. *Journal of Public Law, 6*, 279.

Davenport, Coral. (2018). In the Trump Administration, Science Is Unwelcome. So Is Advice. *New York Times*, June 9, 2018.

Epstein, Lee, Knight, Jack and Svetsova, Olga. (2001). The Role of Constitutional Courts in the Establishment and Maintenance of Democratic Systems of Government. *Law & Society Review, 35*, 117–163.

Friedman, Lawrence M. (1973). *A History of American Law.* New York: Simon & Schuster.

Friedman, Lawrence M. (1985). *Total Justice.* New York: Russell Sage Foundation

Friedman, Lawrence M. (2016). *American Amnesia: How the War on Government Led Us to Forget What Made America Prosper.* New York: Simon & Schuster.

Friedman, Lawrence M. (2018). The Dog That Almost Barked: What the ACA Repeal Fight Says about the Resilience of the American Welfare State. *Journal of Health Policy, Politics and Law, 43*(4), 551–577.

Fukuyama, Francis. (2014). *Political Order and Political Decay: From the Industrial Revolution to the Globalization of Democracy.* New York: Farrar, Straus and Giroux.

Goodnough, Abby and Zarntke, Kate. (2017). Under Trump, Rethinking How Doctors Charge. *New York Times,* November 12, pp. A1, 13.

Greenhouse, Linda. (2023). Victimhood and Vengeance. *New York Review of Books,* February 9, 2023. https://www.nybooks.com/articles/2023/02/09/victimhood-and-vengeance-the-flag-and-the-cross/.

Hacker, Jacob. (2002). *The Divided Welfare State: The Battle Over Public and Private Social Benefits in the United States.* Cambridge University Press, New York, NY.

Hacker, Jacob and Pierson, Paul. (2016). *American Amnesia: How the War on Government Led Us to Forget What Made America Prosper*. New York: Simon & Schuster.

Hacker, Jacob and Pierson, Paul. (2019). Plutocrats with Pitchforks: The Distinctive Politics of Right-Wing Populism in the United States. Paper presented at the Annual Meeting of the American Political Science Association, August 2019. https://www.law.berkeley.edu/wp-content/uploads/2019/09/Hacker_Pierson_APSA_2019.pdf.

Hacker, Jacob and Pierson, Paul. (2020). *Let Them Eat Tweets: How the Right Rules in an Age of Extreme Inequality.* New York: Liveright Publishing, division of W.W. Norton.

Heinzerling, Lisa. (2022). How Government Ends. *Boston Review*, September 22, 2022. https://www.bostonreview.net/articles/how-government-ends/.

Hertogh, Marc, Kirkham, Richard, Thomas, Robert and Tomlinson, Joe (eds.). (2022). *The Oxford Handbook of Administrative Justice.* New York: Oxford University Press.

Hollis-Brusky, Amanda. (2015). *Ideas with Consequences: The Federalist Society and the Conservative Counterrevolution.* New York: Oxford University Press.

Howard, Christopher. (2007). *The Welfare State Nobody Knows.*Princeton, NJ: Princeton University Press.

Institute for Policy Integrity. (2019). *Roundup: Trump-Era Deregulation in the Courts.* New York: New York University Law School, January 14, 2019.

Kagan, Robert A. (2013). A Consequential Court: The U.S. Supreme Court in the Twentieth Century. In Diana Kapiszewski, Gordon Silverstein and Robert A. Kagan (eds.), *Consequential Courts: Judicial Roles in Global Perspective.* Cambridge University Press.

Kagan, Robert A. (2019). *Adversarial Legalism: The American Way of Law*, 2nd ed. Cambridge, MA: Harvard University Press.

Kapiszewski, Diana, Silverstein, Gordon and Kagan, Robert A. (eds.). (2013). *Consequential Courts: Judicial Roles in Global Perspective.* Cambridge University Press.

Levitsky, Steven and Ziblatt, Daniel. (2018). *How Democracies Die*. New York: Broadway Books.
Lipset, Seymour Martin. (1991) *Continental Divide: The Values and Institutions of the United States and Canada*. New York: Routledge.
Mashaw, Jerry. (2012). *Creating the Administrative Constitution; The Lost One Hundred Years of American Administrative Law*. New Haven: Yale University Press.
Mayer, Jane. (2016). *Dark Money: The Hidden History of the Billionaires Behind the Rise of the Radical Right*. New York: Anchor Books.
McCright, Aaron and Dunlap, Riley. (2010). Anti-Reflexivity: The American Conservative Movement's Success in Undermining Climate Science and Policy. *Theory, Culture & Society, 27*, 100–133.
Novak, William. (2017). Putting the 'Public' in Public Administration; The Rise of the Public Utility Idea. In Nicholas Parillo (ed.), *Administrative Law from the Inside Out: Essays on Themes in the Work of Jerry L. Mashaw*. New York: Cambridge University Press.
O'Brien, Timothy and Noy, Shiri. (2020). Political Identity and Confidence in Science and Religion in the United States. *Sociology of Religion: A Quarterly Review, 81*, 439-461.
Oreskes, Naomi and Conway, Eric. (2022). From Anti-Government to Anti-Science: Why Conservatives Have Turned Against Science. *Daedalus*, Fall 2022, pp. 98–123.
Oreskes, Naomi and Conway, Eric. (2010). *Merchants of Doubt: How a Handful of Scientists Obscured the Truth on Issues from Tobacco Smoke to Global Warming*. New York: Bloomsbury Publishing.
Pierson, Paul. (1996). The New Politics of the Welfare State. *World Politics, 48*, 143–179.
Protess, Ben and Silver-Greenberg, Jessica. (2017). Trump Era Is Taming a Watchdog for Banks. *New York Times*, November 16, 2017, pp. B1, 4.
Saenz, Emmanuel and Zucman, Gabriel. (2019). *The Triumph of Injustice: How the Rich Dodge Taxes and How to Make Them Pay*. New York: W.W. Norton.
Sanger-Katz, Margot. (2019). Struggling to Follow the Rules About Rules. *New York Times*, January 23, p. A18.
Skowronek, Stephen. (1982). *Building a New American State: The Expansion of National Administrative Capacities, 1877–1920*. New York: Cambridge University Press.
Swan, Jonathan. (2022). A Radical Plan for Trump's Second Term. *Axios*, July 22, 2022. https://www.axios.com/2022/07/22/trump-2025-radical-plan-second-term.
Swan, Jonathan, Savage, Charlie and Haberman, Maggie. (2023a). The Radical Strategy Behind Trump's Promise to 'Go After' Biden. *New York Times*, June 15, 1923.
Swan, Jonathan, Savage, Charlie and Haberman, Maggie. (2023b). Trump and Allies Forge Plans to Increase Presidential Power in 2025. New York Times, July 17, 2023.

Tach, Laura and Edin, Kathryn. (2017). The Social Safety Net after Welfare Reform: Recent Developments and Consequences for Household Dynamics. *Annual Review of Sociology*, *43*, 541–561.
Teles, Steven. (2008). *The Rise of the Conservative Legal Movement*. Princeton, NJ: Princeton University Press.
Veldman, Robin. (2019). *The Gospel of Climate Skepticism: Why Evangelical Christians Oppose Climate Action.* Berkeley: University of California Press.
Vogel, David. (2012). *The Politics of Precaution: Regulating Health, Safety and Environmental Risks in Europe and the United States.* Princeton, NJ: Princeton University Press.
Whittington, Keith. (2008). *Political Foundations of Judicial Supremacy: The Presidency, the Supreme Court, and Constitutional Leadership in U.S. History*. Princeton, NJ: Princeton University Press.
Wilensky, Harold. (2002). *Rich Democracies: Political Economy, Public Policy, and Performance*. Berkeley, CA: University of California Press
Williamson, Vanessa A. (2017). *Read My Lips: Why Americans Are Proud to Pay Taxes.* Princeton, NJ: Princeton University Press.
Woodard, Colin. (2011). *American Nations; A History of the Eleven Rival Regional Cultures of North America.* New York, Penguin Books.
Ziblatt, Daniel. (2017). *Conservative Political Parties and the Birth of Modern Democracy in Europe*. Cambridge University Press.

8

Rights and Obligations in Social Security

Gráinne McKeever

Introduction

2023 marks the 75th anniversary of the creation of the social security system, designed to tackle the evil of 'want' through cash-transfers to individuals facing unemployment, ill health or bereavement and to support the well-being of children and families. Establishing the system was not simple and its creation represents an extraordinary achievement of politics and of bureaucracy. The detail of this is perhaps not well known but is remarkable enough to have been publicly documented by the DWP Director General Neil Couling, who has current responsibility for setting up Universal Credit, acknowledging the meticulous process that built the foundations of our social security system (Couling 2023). The popularity of the system today, however, does not adequately reflect either its achievements or its potential. The politics of helping the poor has mutated back to its pre-welfare state origins of 'fairness' to the 'taxpayer,' manifesting in an increasingly complex system that is as likely to alienate as to support those who need to rely on it (Harris 2013). The never-ending legal complexities that arise for those navigating through the volumes of governing regulations may be one of the reasons why

My thanks to Sharon Cowan, Jackie Gulland, Simon Halliday and Mark Simpson for their comments on earlier drafts of this chapter.

G. McKeever (✉)
Ulster University School of Law, Belfast, Northern Ireland, UK
e-mail: g.mckeever@ulster.ac.uk

S. Cowan and S. Halliday (eds.), *Socio-Legal Generation*, Palgrave Socio-Legal Studies,
https://doi.org/10.1007/978-3-031-67244-6_8

there is a relatively small field of social security lawyers and why there is a reason for them to be indebted to Michael Adler's research. It is unlikely that Adler would categorise himself as a social security lawyer and yet his research should be read by all of those who do and who are concerned with social rights, obligations, proportionality and adjudicative processes.

This chapter reviews the research contribution of Adler to our understanding of the core dimensions of social security law and policy that can frame the lawyer's arguments on the state's duties towards its citizens. This journey takes us through Adler's prescient analyses of the rights and obligations of citizens in the context of their entitlement to social security benefits. It reviews the effect of increasingly punitive social security policies as demonstrated by Adler's research on sanctions, which is also evidenced in penalties for social security fraud. It uses Adler's research to highlight the barriers to challenging social security decision-making, examining the oversight and adjudication processes that apply and which often frustrate access to justice. Finally, the chapter follows Adler's lead in identifying priority issues for the future of social security that his lifetime of research points to.

Rights and Obligations

Twenty years ago, Adler identified the overall goals of social security as being the provision of income support, the reduction of inequality and the promotion of social integration, a characterisation based on his analysis of the shifting aims of social security over the life span of the welfare state (Adler 2001). By that point in time, his research had examined in detail the history of social security, beginning with the Beveridgian scheme of universal contributory benefits that would insure individuals against common social risks such as unemployment or ill health, supplemented by means-tested social assistance for exceptional circumstances such as support for children born outside of marriage. As Adler notes, "[t]he aim was to prevent want (or poverty) by providing a decent level of income as of right and without resort to a means test" (Adler 2008: 96). This insurance-oriented scheme relied heavily on the early mid-twentieth-century plan for full employment, which itself was based on the fact that "[p]olicy makers assumed that everyone would prefer work to unemployment" (Adler 2008: 97). In turn, waged work was seen as a predominantly male occupation, with women's economic security built on marriage security provided by their working husbands. By the 1960s, the plan for means-tested benefits to become redundant was found wanting as unemployment rose and the profile of households moved away from the nuclear family model of two parents/one breadwinner, to include greater numbers of (predominantly female) single parent households, ineligible for insurance-based benefits and reliant on means-tested support. The swing from social insurance to social assistance was further entrenched by Labour government policy to create a new supplementary benefit which "institutionalised a two-tier structure of social security provisions, comprising unemployment insurance for those who met the contribution conditions for 12 months and supplementary benefit for those who did not" (Adler 2008: 97; 2004).

Adler's research also examines a related shift of policy emphasis in the 1960s, namely the introduction of earnings-related supplements for flat-rate, non-taxable unemployment and sickness benefits (Adler 2008). This created the seemingly unintended consequence that claimants could find themselves better off on benefits than in work, raising government concerns that this financial incentive would override any socially based incentives to return to work. The purpose of social security returned once more to its problematic origin of providing a level of support that would not displace the need to work, neatly articulated by Grover:

> At the centre of social security policy for working age people is a perceived policy contradiction; that if the needs of people who are not in waged work are relieved, they will be disincentivised from taking waged work when it is available or incentivised to leave work for unemployment. (Grover 2020: 2)

To off-set this 'unemployment trap,' benefit levels were kept low while a wage stop was imposed to limit the amount of social assistance to a level that a worker could have expected to earn if they were in work. As Adler explains, however, "the government was, in due course, persuaded that it was wrong for the social security system to pay benefits at less than subsistence level during periods of high unemployment, the wage stop was used less and less and it was eventually abolished in 1975" (Adler 2008: 98).

From the 1980s, a consistent policy development in social security flowed primarily from the trajectory set by the Thatcher administration, defined by Adler as "reducing so-called welfare dependency, restricting benefit eligibility and closely policing the job-seeking behaviour of the unemployed" (Adler 2013: 230; see also Bochel and Defty 2007). Successive administrations increased the conditionality requirements for out of work benefits and expanded the profile of claimants subject to them to include the sick and disabled under the Welfare Reform Act 2007 (Grover and Piggott 2010; Patrick 2011; Larkin 2011) and lone parents (Andersen 2020) and drug users (Harris 2010) under the Welfare Reform Act 2009. The stricter benefits regime was matched with an increase in sanctions and an 'obsession' with social security fraud, creating a stigmatised perception of people on benefits (Adler 2013: 232). Although stigma in social security was not new, Adler charts its increase, culminating in the Blair/Brown government's "excessively authoritarian policies and practice," including the often pointless activation measures during a period of high unemployment (Adler 2013: 232; see also Lundy 2000; Fitzpatrick 2024). The corresponding incentives included tax credits to help the low paid by subsidising their wages, which came "at the expense of benefits for those out of work" (Adler 2004: 92). Despite being intended to reduce the stigma of means-tested benefits, the effect was to relegate 'social security' to mean means-tested welfare (IFG and SSAC 2022). Tax credits rather than benefits became a new form of social protection for a set of risks (primarily low pay and the costs of childcare) and to manage the unintended and perverse consequences of social assistance, such as the poverty and unemployment traps, low take-up of means-tested benefits and the disincentive to save (Adler 2004).

While social security has always been a combination of help and control, the 1980s–2000s saw it become increasingly contractual. Such a contractual relationship ought to be "a relationship of exchange between individual (legal) rights and collective (legal) duties," but it provides limited protections for claimants (Adler 1997: 392). The first limitation, as defined by Adler, is that individual rights are seen as being matched by specific duty bearers having responsibility to deliver and protect those rights, whilst general duties (for example, to protect someone from poverty) may have no specific right attached for individuals (Adler 1997: 393). The second limitation flows from this, namely the imbalance between claimant rights and government responsibilities. Drawing on Marshall's vision of a welfare state as "a state in which citizens enjoy extensive civil rights, extensive political rights and extensive social rights," Adler interrogates the discrepancy that demands duties while withholding rights from citizens (Adler 2018: 66). Plant's analysis of citizenship in social security is that it has oscillated between citizenship as status and citizenship as achievement (Plant 1999). In Adler's analysis, the contractual model of social security which expanded under the Labour administration from 1997 "called into question the idea of an unconditional right to benefit [and] … made [the government's] preference for a reciprocity-based notion rather than a status-based notion of citizenship clear" (Adler 2008: 113). In order to fulfil its side of the reciprocity bargain, Plant argued that government would need to be the employer of last resort to ensure there would be work available for all required obtain it, but he also predicted—correctly—that this would be too expensive and not something the government would do (Plant 1999). The notable absence of extended state duties justifies Adler's conclusion that citizenship as reciprocity is the dominant approach, which includes not just work-based contributions for insurance benefits but fulfilment of work-related obligations for assistance benefits (Adler 2008; Dwyer 2008). This expansion comes at a cost to claimants, where punitive policies are directed towards enforcement of these duties. The rights/obligations dilemma thus leads directly to Adler's work on social security sanctions.

Punitive Policies

As with the development of conditionality for out of work benefits, Adler analyses the simultaneous development of sanctions—a financial penalty alongside a suspension of benefit payments—that are applied when conditionality is deemed to have been breached. His research sets the scene by looking at why benefit sanctions are not a matter of public concern despite clear problems with their impact, scale and effectiveness. The narrative (predominantly by government) of social security claimants—and the poor more generally—as underserving and feckless has deep foundations, and although it has been consistently challenged it has never been effectively dismantled (Fraser 1973; Timmins 2017; Jensen and Tyler 2015; Patrick 2016). Perhaps, the most obvious reason for this failure is that it does not suit many political agendas to do so, particularly where the costs of maintaining support are seen as unpopular among the electorate, where a chicken-and-egg relationship between popular opinion and public policy can cloud political discourse. Even where political ideologies differ between those that see individuals as responsible for their own circumstances and those that attribute poverty to structural factors beyond an individual's control, there is still an underpinning theme of making support conditional on the individual's efforts to help relieve themselves of their benefit 'dependency,' as well as being the route by which they can access their entitlements. This consistent political narrative can be read clearly through the legislative expansion of conditionality underpinned by sanctions that have become progressively more punitive.

Adler's 2018 book on sanctions reflects on the corresponding public perceptions on the deservingness of social security claimants from 1993 to 2013 noting the high—and highly inaccurate—estimation by the public of social security fraud (Adler 2018). In line with the trajectory of conditionality, the fight against fraud has been intensified by successive administrations, with a disproportionate focus on low level fraud (McKeever 1999a; 2012). The predictable result has been to reinforce notions of 'deserving' and 'undeserving' claimants, and to disguise the real issue of perverse motivations within the benefit system with the Robin Hood myth which sees taxpayers as givers and the poor as takers (Cook 1989; McKeever 1999b). For example, the most common fraud in Universal Credit—the primary income replacement benefit for working age claimants—is misrepresenting earnings, while the third most common is failure to declare a partner contributing to household income (DWP 2022). The National Audit Office has refused to qualify DWP's accounts for the last 35 years because of levels of fraud and error, but this relates to underpayment as well as overpayment, and to claimant and departmental error as well as fraud (DWP 2023a). Clearly, however, fraud is a public problem, but while these frauds are not condoned, they have long been identified as 'need' based (NAO 2008), and while the need to address them is not disputed, the proportionality of the response may be questioned. In 1998, the Labour government undertook to review the rules which are broken most frequently to see if they placed an unfair burden on honesty, commissioning Lord Grabiner to examine the issue of benefit fraud in the informal economy (McKeever 1999b). Grabiner identified that common frauds involved rules which were most vulnerable to abuse—including the earnings disregard and the reduction in overall benefit income when single claimants formed familial partnerships—but concluded that it would be too costly to change these rules ((HM Treasury 2000). The government accepted this recommendation, pushing the cost of maintaining this perversity on to claimants and punishing them for succumbing to the inbuilt fraud incentives.

Punishment was built on an increased determination to create a culture of resistance to fraud among the public and those administering social security benefits, summed up by a dual-approach of legislation, setting out a ramped-up framework for the detection, prosecution and punishment of fraud (McKeever 1999a), and a media campaign to banish the idea that some frauds are condonable (McKeever 1999b). The sanction regime for fraud that was established under the Social Security Fraud Act 1997 became progressively punitive under successive Acts, from the Social Security Fraud Act 2001, to the Welfare Reform Act 2007, the Welfare Reform Act 2009 and the Welfare Reform Act 2012 (McKeever 2011). Fraud policy was therefore driven by the need to make it more difficult to commit fraud and more punitive towards those who did, rather than on eradicating perversity and making the system fairer for claimants. The increasingly harsh response to fraud evidenced in the legislation feeds into the idea that fraud is rife, which in turn feeds the public suspicion about the integrity of claimants. It is an effective deflection from more substantive discussions about how to determine issues of eligibility and has the cumulative effect of clouding all claimants with suspicion (McKeever 2009).

The political vulnerability of social security claimants meant that there was considerable success with this approach and led Adler to conclude that "if the public has been led to believe that fiddling is extensive, then using sanctions may seem justified" (Adler 2018: 17). Indeed, the intolerance towards benefit claimants is evidenced across the social security system, including the increase in conditionality to 'activate' them (Watts et al. 2018). Adler's research, however, is rigorous in deconstructing that justification, beginning with the disproportionality inherent in the sanctions regime as it applies to claimants deemed to have breached the conditions of their benefit. Sanctions are most common for missing or being late for an interview with a work coach: the Public Law Project reports that between February 2021 and January 2022, this accounted for 99% of the reasons given for a sanction decision (Selman 2022). This results in claimants losing 100% of their income (after housing costs, and if they have no children or other top-ups), with the duration of sanction based on the nature and frequency of sanctionable behaviour. This steeply scaled process ranges from an additional seven days without benefit from the date of compliance for a Work-Focused Interview requirement, to the most extreme sanction of 182 days for a third failure within a year of failing to apply for or to accept paid work (Adler 2024). Adler challenges the proportionality of the response to the actions that led to the sanction and highlights how, even on the argument that sanctions are required to ensure claimants actively seek and secure work, the evidence—including DWP's own (DWP 2023b)—shows "negative impacts for job quality and stability in the longer term, along with increased transitions to non-employment or economic inactivity" (Adler 2024: 17; Webster 2023).

Adler also compares the treatment of sanctioned claimants to citizens who are punished via court fines for breaches of civil or criminal law. The inferior treatment of social security claimants is evidenced from the application of a penalty in advance of a claimant being able to challenge the determination of breach, while for court fines, the adjudication on guilt precedes the issue of punishment. Challenging a decision to sanction requires a claimant to first go through an internal review process known as mandatory reconsideration (MR) (SSAC 2016). Only when this process completes can a post-hoc tribunal hearing be progressed for a claimant to challenge the retrospective application of a sanction. This process is argued by Adler to be in breach of Bingham's eight principles that comprise the rule of law (Bingham 2010), including access to justice, since the claimant may have to endure a sanction during the often lengthy period of getting a tribunal hearing. Adler also queries the compliance with the principle of respect for fundamental rights, which relies on Article 6 ECHR (the right to a fair trial) which may be breached by the "attenuated arrangements for challenging the imposition of a sanction" involving MR as a prerequisite to being able to access an independent tribunal (Adler 2018: 133; see also Tipping 2020).

A policy that fails to adhere to the rule of law, that fails on its own terms and that is disproportionate in scale and impact is in need of either reform or abolition. Adler proposes a range of ways in which the policy failures might be addressed, including alternative punishments such as community service; not applying sanctions to claimants most at risk of harm from their effects such as lone parents, homeless or disabled people; reducing their severity; applying them only to serious breaches; providing a hearing before sanctioning; and letting claimants appeal directly to tribunal without the additional hurdle of mandatory reconsideration. He also distinguishes between failures that might cause or prolong unemployment (such as voluntarily leaving a job or refusing to apply for a suitable job) and those that are unlikely to do so (such as not applying for a clearly unsuitable job, or being late for an appointment with the work coach). While such measures and operational distinctions would be an improvement, Adler ultimately concludes that the abolition of sanctions may be the best way forward:

> Although it is entirely reasonable that benefits should be subject to conditions and that the conditions need to be met before the benefit is paid, there is a strong case to be made that it is not really necessary to go any further than this. (Adler 2024: 21)

It is incumbent on the state to ensure that conditions of benefit entitlement are lawful and not unduly onerous. The sanctions regime—whether it relates to social security fraud or benefit conditionality—exemplifies the problem with focusing on claimant responsibilities while ignoring the state's duty to protect claimant rights. The reality, however, is that sanctions remain firmly fixed as part of the social security landscape and so Adler's research on the systems of administrative justice that frame social security decision-making and adjudication becomes critical.

Challenging Decision-Making

Adler defines the administrative justice system as "[t]he principles that can be used to evaluate the justice inherent in administrative decision-making," encompassing both internal procedures and external accountability (Adler

2003: 323). His conceptualisation of administrative justice draws on related concepts of justice, in particular that of procedural and social justice (Adler 2003; 2018). Social justice—defined by Miller as how "the good and bad things in life should be distributed among the members of a human society" (Miller 1999: 1)—provides a way for evaluating social, economic and fiscal policy and is a concern of government departments responsible for devising programmes of taxation and public expenditure (Adler 2010). The primary outcomes of administrative procedures in social security are to confer whichever entitlements and impose whatever obligations that are determined by these programmes, and so the purpose of procedural justice in making these decisions is to ensure that "individuals are treated in a manner that reflects what is due to them in light of their personal characteristics and circumstances" (Adler 2010: 132). Procedural justice is therefore an important component of social justice and of how administrative agencies should treat people. Administrative justice is also intended to be preventative and remedial as well as procedural:

> individual forms of dispute resolution within administrative justice serve the dual purpose of justice with accountability – individual citizens holding public bodies and their decision-makers to account for their actions – and consequentially improving public administration. (McKeever 2020)

Adler's analysis of accountability in administrative justice recognises this, taking a bottom-up as well as a top-down perspective, focusing on both internal accountabilities, based on departmental decision-making processes, and external accountability, delivered through tribunals and oversight bodies, charting the pendulum swings in government commitment to each (Adler 2012).

Oversight and Adjudication

A significant body of Adler's research focuses on critiquing and developing models of administrative justice (see Adler 2006b; 2010; 2022a), flowing from his analysis of Mashaw's models of bureaucratic justice (Mashaw 1983). In brief, Adler's conclusion is that Mashaw does not recognise the role that external forms of accountability play in achieving administrative justice, and in Adler's re-worked models that rename and add to Mashaw's models, a legal model replaces Mashaw's model of moral judgement to represent the one most likely to be prioritised by lawyers, court and tribunal personnel and organisations representing clients' interests (Adler 2006). A detailed analysis of this research is taken up by Arvind et al. in this volume (see Chapter 6), but it is fair to say that Adler faced significant critique of the models he developed (see Sainsbury 2008; Halliday 2004; Cane 2009). While Adler has defended his analysis (Adler 2010), perhaps the most significant defence comes from Mashaw himself. At one level, Mashaw notes that Adler's critique of *Bureaucratic Justice*'s failure to take account of external oversight mechanisms is "quite beside the point of that book's overall argument," given that the purpose of the modelling was to reorient discussion away from external oversight and towards an internal critique (Mashaw 2022: 393). What he also acknowledges, however, is that "[Adler's] inclusion of that dimension in his models points towards an obvious truth that [*Bureaucratic Justice*]'s models ignore: acceptability of the 'justice' of an administrative system does turn in part on its modes of external accountability" (Mashaw 2022: 393). Adler's ability to connect the internal and external mechanisms of administrative justice as an end-to-end process is therefore a critical contribution to our understanding of administrative justice generally and social security specifically.

Adler reviews the rise and fall of administrative justice policy in the UK, the peak of which was the creation of the Administrative Justice and Tribunals Council (AJTC), an advisory body established under the Tribunals, Courts and Enforcement Act 2007 to keep the administrative justice system under review (Adler 2012; 2022a). The AJTC proposed a strategic programme to improve decision-making and reduce appeals, but its recommendations were largely ignored by government and it was ultimately abolished in 2013 as part of a large-scale 'bonfire of the quangos' (Adler 2012). Successor bodies have had even more limited power and influence, and so scrutiny of decision-making in social security has instead fallen to National Audit Office and Parliamentary Committee inquiries, with reports highly critical of the poor quality of decision-making, but with little obvious outcome in improving this position (Adler 2022a).

The power of front-line decision-makers would seem to contribute to both cause and effect of the questionable quality and consistency of decisions. Charting the development of social security adjudication, Adler analyses how the power transfer from adjudication officers—bureaucrats with judicial responsibility who had statutory powers to make decisions on entitlement independent of the Minister—to Personal Advisers attached to Jobcentres—street level bureaucrats with significant discretionary powers and acting in the name of the Secretary of State—has overridden the protections of the legal model of administrative justice. This shift incorporated the abolition of the position of Chief Adjudication Officer who had a statutory responsibility for monitoring and reporting on adjudication standards (Adler 2006a: 974). In its place, quality assurance now relies on claimants requesting internal review of the decision—the mandatory process which prioritises the civil service-oriented bureaucratic model of administrative justice—and subsequently making a further application to an independent tribunal if mandatory reconsideration (MR) is unsuccessful.

In 2006, citing research from Genn (1994) and Baldwin et al. (1992), Adler argued "there are considerable limits to the effectiveness of tribunals as a check on administrative decision-making that are due both to the fact that many potential appellants assume that the original decision is 'correct,' or that it will be very difficult to get it changed, and to short-comings in the tribunals themselves" (Adler 2006: 973). The effect of MR would certainly seem to have entrenched this reaction where the process itself appears to drive down the volume of appeals. Thomas and Tomlinson have highlighted the dramatic drop in appeals following the introduction of MR, and argued that "[a]dministrative review has largely weakened the ability of people to secure redress" (Thomas and Tomlinson 2019). Drawing on research by Halliday and Cowan (2003), Adler highlights the likelihood of this being linked to claimant fatigue which deters individuals from challenging adverse decisions (Adler 2022a; see also Pleasence et al. 2012). This would be less concerning if MR lived up to its potential for swift and efficient correction of errors, but the quality assurance process here seems limited while the need for independent appeal becomes more vital. Part of the difficulty is that success rates for MR are low: Adler cites a 17% success rate for the 1.5 million reconsiderations undertaken from 2013 to 2017, which contrasts sharply with the tribunal success rate of 40–65% in the same time period (Adler 2022a: 628). If it were the case that there was learning derived from this then perhaps the process would seem less futile but Thomas demonstrates that the organisational learning loop is missing and so the capacity to improve decision-making or review based on tribunal outcomes is virtually non-existent (Thomas 2015). The problem loop therefore remains—a poor quality first instance decision may be reinforced rather than corrected by a poor quality second instance decision, which may—for tenacious claimants—ultimately be corrected by an independent tribunal but with no consequential improvement to poor quality first or second instance decision-making.

The tribunal process itself is described by Thomas and Tomlinson as "complex, drawn-out, and inefficient" (Thomas and Tomlinson 2019: 541). Although it is intended to be more 'user friendly' than the court system, the illusion of informality, accessibility and efficiency in a hearing is too often shattered by barriers to participation that permeate the lived experience of tribunal users, particularly where they are unrepresented (McKeever 2013). Those barriers may be reduced by tribunal members who, through an inquisitorial approach, help the user to participate effectively. Adler's research, however, speaks to the problems with the increased judicialisation of tribunals and the impact of this on an inquisitorial or enabling approach. His concerns date back to his research on supplementary benefit tribunals, when judicialising tribunals for means-tested benefits became an empirical as well as theoretical focus (Adler and Bradley 1976; Adler 2001; 2006b). These changes culminated in reforms under the Social Security Act 1998 which provided for single judge tribunals—the legally qualified member—to be joined by the non-legally qualified panel members "only as necessary" (Adler 2001: 139). The specialist skills of these lay members, such as medical knowledge and experience of living with disability, were intended to draw out the reality of an appellant's circumstances. Their absence was therefore seen to "undermine the inquisitorial principle that [the tribunal system] sought to establish as one of its distinguishing features in the wider civil justice system" (Wikeley 2000: 476). Further drift was identified in Adler's critique of the incorporation of tribunals within HM Courts Service, raising further concerns that tribunals would be more likely to succumb to the dominance of court culture (Adler 2012). These concerns are evidenced through the continuing judicialisation of tribunals which did not signify increased judicial oversight for social security decision-making; instead, the "greater use of administrative review has gone hand-in-hand with a correspondingly smaller role for the judicial control of front-line administrative decisions" (Thomas and Tomlinson 2019: 538). Consequently, "[m]any of the legitimising qualities of tribunals have effectively been jettisoned for little in return" (Thomas and Tomlinson 2019: 556). The processes of both administrative review and tribunal appeal remain problematic, as research by the Public Law Project on the experiences of challenging sanction decisions bears out: "a combination of significant practical barriers and a lack of trust in the system mean that sanctioned claimants currently do not have an effective or accessible route to challenge sanction decisions" (Selman 2022: 6).

What we are left with is a political narrative about workshy and underserving claimants. Departmental decision-makers now act on behalf of the Secretary of State rather than the judiciary and a sanction effectively labels the claimant as the most workshy and therefore least deserving of all claimants, most of whom are already under a cloud of suspected fraud. These claimants, above anyone else, need protection from the politics of welfare, by a system that ought to be concerned only with a neutral application of the rules. But, since the rules themselves embed the scrounger narrative and punish failures that make no difference to employability, alongside those that might, even that ambition seems too much. The best that can be said of the current state of administrative justice as a means of protecting citizen entitlements is that it looks weak.

Future Directions

Given the significance of Adler's research on analysing the social security landscape to date, it is no surprise that he has also led the call for a future research agenda for social welfare law, policy and practice (Adler 2022b). He is clear that a 'more of the same' approach to research cannot be recommended because the social and political environment, and nature of social welfare in the UK, have changed profoundly in recent years, not least due to the effects of the financial crisis from 2008, Brexit from 2012 and Covid from 2019. Aside from the agenda set by those responding to his challenge, there is an agenda that remains critical within the work he has already done, circling back to the very problem that his research helps to unpick, namely identifying the purpose of social security.

It is clear from Adler's research that the purpose of social security should, at a minimum, be to prevent poverty. For this to be delivered, benefits should be set at no less than subsistence level, moving away from the penury brought forward since the 1980s and reasserted under the Coalition and Conservative governments, recognising—as Adler notes governments in the past have done—that it is wrong to pay benefits at less than subsistence level when sustaining adequate income through work is not possible. The means by which this purpose should be achieved relate also to the conditions of entitlement which form part of the state's contract with its citizens. The state can make justifiable demands on citizens, but the scale of justification should be matched by substantive, enforceable rights. Authoritarian approaches skew the balance but for social security to be effective in preventing rather than entrenching poverty, the focus on claimant support should not elide with any type of punishment since this adds no value to protecting the integrity of social security or in achieving its purpose (Watts and Fitzpatrick 2018).

Adler's conclusion on the 'feebleness' of legal protection for socio-economic rights is entirely accurate (Adler 2018: 112), and so to deliver on its purpose of preventing poverty, specific duties must attach to the state, aligned with specific rights that the citizen can enforce. Adler argues that the European Social Charter, which is already part of the UK's legal framework and enshrines the rights to social security and social assistance, could—and arguably should—be the vehicle to deliver this (Adler 2018; Boyle and Flegg 2022; Simpson et al. 2023), but even before reaching this dizzy height of rights protection, those rights that have been promised through social security legislation need to be more accessible (McKeever and Simpson 2024). Barriers that inhibit access to administrative and legal challenges to bureaucratic decision-making have no place in delivering the primary purpose of social security, which must be considered as an end-to-end process from application to decision and any onward appeal. Internal processes and external adjudication must therefore comply with the rule of law and ensure that smooth access to social security benefits is delivered as a core function of the administrative justice system.

Overall, however, Adler's research urges us to lift our eyes higher, beyond the core function of poverty prevention. His focus on rights protection centres the ambition for a social security system that acknowledges individual claimants as citizens, entitled to the same respect and rights that those beyond the system can enjoy. Punishments proportionate to the nature of the offence and due process rights to challenge these decisions are one example. Effective support for lone parents and disabled people as a necessary corrective to the push into a discriminatory and insecure workplace is another, as is recognising the value of contributions by citizens unable to engage in waged work. And access to sufficient income as the essential element of reciprocal citizenship underpins all this. In short, Adler advocates for social citizenship through which claimants can access the social rights that Marshall saw the social security system as capable of delivering (Marshall and Bottomore 1992; Fitzpatrick et al. 2019).

Conclusion

The lifetime of research by Michael Adler has not just been devoted to social security law, but so much of it connects to his insights here. Key to this has been his contribution to the discipline of socio-legal studies, through which he has created an eco-system where social security lawyers have found a unique place to flourish, supported by Adler's mentorship and his ability to challenge ideas and methods. Adler's own academic path through social security law and policy has been informed by his work with those whom it affects, including as a lay member of the Social Security Appeal Tribunal and working to create support for citizens' rights (Adler 2006b). The need to understand how social security works is rooted in his belief that government should treat its citizens—and non-citizens—fairly and that this is a hallmark of good government (Adler 2006b). His work evidences all of this.

Taking the history of social security as a way to understand how the vagaries of politics can impact on those dependent on state support, Adler articulates the problems with creeping conditionality that betray the government's duty on how it should treat its citizens. The punitive responses to those who fail to meet often onerous conditions is not merely unnecessary and disproportionate, but economically devastating and destabilising for claimants in both the short and long term. The need for accountability in administrative decision-making is underpinned by social and procedural justice and demands that both internal practices and external processes can deliver the benefits that citizens are entitled to. Whether the delivery models can succeed depends on the adjudicative integrity of administrative justice, from claim to contestation, and while a judicial process can deliver individualised justice, the barriers to reaching this outcome and the system failure to learn from it means that the rights and responsibilities of claimants remain out of kilter. That we know all of this is down to decades of Adler's research, through which he continues to set an agenda while encouraging, supporting and promoting the work of others who have learned from and contributed to his thinking. For that, social security lawyers in particular are very grateful.

References

Adler, M., and Bradley, A. (1976). *Justice, Discretion and Poverty: Supplementary Benefit Appeal Tribunals in Britain.* London: Professional Books.

Adler, M. (1997). Decision-Making and Appeals in Social Security: In Need of Reform? *The Political Quarterly* 388.

Adler, M. (2001). Substantive Justice & Procedural Fairness in Social Security: The UK Experience. In P. Robson and A. Kjønstad (eds.), *Poverty and the Law.* London: Hart.

Adler, M. (2003). A Socio-Legal Approach to Administrative Justice. *Law and Policy* 323.

Adler, M. (2004). Combining Welfare-to-Work Measures with Tax Credits: A New Hybrid Approach to Social Security in the United Kingdom. *International Social Security Review* 87.

Alder, M. (2006a). Tribunal Reform: Proportionate Dispute Resolution and the Pursuit of Administrative Justice. *Modern Law Review* 958.

Adler, M. (2006b). Fairness in Context. *Journal of Law and Society* 615.

Adler, M. (2008). *The Justice Implications of 'Activation Policies' in the UK.* Centre for European Research, University of Gothenburg.

Adler, M. (2010). Understanding and Analysing Administrative Justice. In M. Adler (ed.), *Administrative Justice in Context*. London: Hart.
Adler, M. (2012). The Rise and Fall of Administrative Justice—A Cautionary Tale. *Socio-Legal Review* 28.
Adler, M. (2013). Conditionality, Sanctions and the Effective Absence of Redress in the British "New Deal" Programs. In E. Brodkin and G. Marston (eds.), *Work and the Welfare State: The Politics and Management of Policy Change*. Washington, DC: Georgetown University Press and Copenhagen, DJØF.
Adler, M. (2018). *Cruel, Inhuman or Degrading Treatment? Benefit Sanctions in the UK*. Basingstoke: Palgrave Pivot.
Adler, M. (2022a). The Future of Administrative Justice. In M. Hertogh, R. Kirkham, R. Thomas, and J. Tomlinson (eds.), *The Oxford Handbook of Administrative Justice.* Oxford: OUP.
Adler, M. (2022b). *A Research Agenda for Social Welfare Law, Policy and Practice* (ed.). Cheltenham: Edward Elgar Publishing.
Adler, M. (2024). Do Benefit Sanctions Have a Future? *Journal of Social Security Law.*
Andersen, K. (2020). Universal Credit, Gender and Unpaid Childcare: Mothers' Accounts of the New Welfare Conditionality Regime. *Critical Social Policy* 430.
Baldwin, J., Wikeley, N., and Young, R. (1992). *Judging Social Security: The Adjudication of Claims for Benefit in Britain.* Oxford: Clarendon Press.
Bingham, T. (2010). *The Rule of Law.* London: Allen Lane.
Bochel, H., and Defty, A. (2007). MPs' Attitudes to Welfare: A New Consensus? *Journal of Social Policy* 1.
Boyle, K., and Flegg, A. (2022). *The Right to Social Security in the UK—An Explainer.* London: Nuffield Foundation.
Cane, P. (2009). *Administrative Tribunals and Adjudication.* Oxford: Hart.
Cook, D. (1989). *Rich Law, Poor Law Differential Response to Tax and Supplementary Benefit.* Milton Keynes: Open University Press.
Couling, N. (2023). As Someone in the Midst of Implementing #UniversalCredit, a Few Observations on the Implementation of the Post-war Social Security System. @NeilCouling, 5 June 2023.
DWP. (2022). *Fighting Fraud in the Welfare System*, CP 679.
DWP. (2023a). *Annual Report and Accounts 2022–23 for the Year Ended 31 March 2023*, HC1455.
DWP. (2023b). *The Impact of Benefit Sanctions on Employment Outcomes—Draft Report (2023).* Available at https://www.gov.uk/government/publications/the-impact-of-benefit-sanctions-on-employment-outcomes-draft-report.
Dwyer, P. (2008). The Conditional Welfare State. In M. Powell (ed.), *Modernising the Welfare State.* Bristol: Policy Press.
Fitzpatrick, C., McKeever, G., and Simpson, M. (2019). Conditionality, Discretion and TH Marshall's 'Right to Welfare'. *Journal of Social Welfare and Family Law* 445.

Fitzpatrick, C. (2024). "Poor Citizens": Social Welfare and the Encouragement of Work. In H. Carr, E. Kirton-Darling, J. Meers, and M. F. Salcedo Repolês (eds.), *Research Handbook on Social Welfare Law*. Cheltenham: Edward Elgar Publishing.

Fraser, D. (1973). *The Evolution of the British Welfare State: A History of Social Policy Since the Industrial Revolution*. London: Macmillan Press.

Genn, H. (1994). Tribunal Review of Administrative Decision-Making. In G. Richardson and H. Genn (eds.), *Administrative Law and Government Action*. Oxford: Clarendon Press.

Grover, C. (2020). The Household Benefit Cap: Understanding the Restriction of Benefit Income in Britain. *Journal of Social Policy* 1.

Grover, C., and Piggott, L. (2010). 'From Incapacity to ESA: Social Sorting, Sickness and Impairment, and Social Security. *Policy Studies* 265.

Halliday, S., and Cowan, D. (2003). *The Appeal of Internal Review: Administrative Justice and the (Non)Emergence of Disputes*. Oxford: Hart.

Halliday, S. (2004). *Judicial Review and Compliance with Administrative Law*. Oxford: Hart.

Harris, N. (2010). Conditional Rights, Benefit Reform, and Drug Users: Reducing Dependency? *Journal of Law and Society* 233.

Harris, N. (2013). *Law in a Complex State*. Oxford: Hart.

HM Treasury. (2000). *The Informal Economy: A Report by Lord Grabiner Q.C.* London: TSO.

IFG and SSAC. (2022). *Jobs and Benefits: The Covid-19 Challenge—A Joint Report by the Institute for Government and Social Security Advisory Committee*. London: DWP.

Jensen, T., and Tyler, I. (2015). Benefit Broods: The Cultural and Political Crafting of Anti-welfare Commonsense. *Critical Social Policy* 470.

Larkin, P. (2011). Incapacity, the Labour Market and Social Security: Coercion into "Positive" Citizenship. *Modern Law Review* 385.

Lundy, L. (2000). From Welfare to Work? Social Security and Unemployment. In N. Harris (ed.), *Social Security Law in Context*. Oxford: OUP.

Marshall, T. H., and Bottomore, T. (1992). *Citizenship and Social Class*. London: Pluto.

Mashaw, J. L. (1983). *Bureaucratic Justice*. New Haven and London: Yale University Press.

Mashaw, J. L. (2022). Models of Administrative Justice. In M. Hertogh, R. Kirkham, R. Thomas, and J. Tomlinson (eds.), *The Oxford Handbook of Administrative Justice*. Oxford: OUP.

McKeever, G. (1999a). Detecting, Prosecuting and Punishing Benefit Fraud: The Social Security (Administration) Fraud Act 1997. *Modern Law Review* 261.

McKeever, G. (1999b). Fighting Fraud: An Evaluation of the Government's Social Security Fraud Strategy. *Journal of Social Welfare and Family Law* 357.

McKeever, G. (2009). Balancing Rights and Responsibilities: The Case of Social Security Fraud. *Journal of Social Security Law* 139.

McKeever, G. (2011). *Memorandum Submitted to the Public Bill Committee on the Welfare Reform Bill*, in Public Bill Committee Written Evidence (Bill154) 2010–2012, (WR52). London: TSO.
McKeever, G. (2012). Social Citizenship and Social Security Fraud in the UK and Australia. *Social Policy and Administration* 465.
McKeever, G. (2013). A Ladder of Legal Participation for Tribunal Users. *Public Law* 575.
McKeever, G. (2020). Comparing Courts and Tribunals Through the Lens of Legal Participation. *Civil Justice Quarterly* 217.
McKeever, G., and Simpson, M. (2024). Welfare Rights in Theory and Practice. In H. Carr, E. Kirton-Darling, J. Meers, and M. F. Salcedo Repolês (eds.), *Research Handbook on Social Welfare Law*. Cheltenham: Edward Elgar Publishing.
Miller, D. (1999). *Principles of Social Justice*. Harvard: Harvard University Press.
NAO. (2008). *Progress in Tackling Benefit Fraud* HC 102. London: TSO.
Patrick, R. (2011). Disabling or Enabling: The Extension of Work-Related Conditionality to Disabled People. *Social Policy and Society* 309.
Patrick, R. (2016). Living with and Responding to the 'Scrounger' Narrative in the UK: Exploring Everyday Strategies of Acceptance, Resistance and Deflection. *Journal of Poverty and Social Justice* 245.
Plant, R. (1999). Supply Side Citizenship? *Journal of Social Security Law* 124.
Pleasence, P., Balmer, N. J., and Sandefur, R. L. (2012). *Paths to Justice: A Past, Present and Future Roadmap*. Centre for Empirical Legal Studies, UCL.
SSAC. (2016). *Occasional Paper 18: Decision Making and Mandatory Reconsideration*. London: DWP.
Sainsbury, R. (2008). Administrative Justice, Discretion and the 'Welfare to Work' Project. *Journal of Social Welfare and Family Law* 323.
Selman, C. (2022). *Benefit Sanctions: A Presumption of Guilt*. London: Public Law Project.
Simpson, M., McKeever, G., and Fitzpatrick, C. (2023). Legal Protection Against Destitution in the UK: The Case for a Right to a Subsistence Minimum. *Modern Law Review* 465.
Timmins, N. (2017). *The Five Giants: A Biography of the Welfare State*. London: Harper Collins.
Tipping, J. (2020). Employment and Support Allowance: Mandatory Reconsideration and Appeals Come Full Circle. *Journal of Social Welfare and Family Law* 516.
Thomas, R. (2015). Administrative Justice, Better Decisions, and Organisational Learning. *Public Law* 111.
Thomas, R. and Tomlinson, J. (2019). A Different Tale of Judicial Power: Administrative Review as a Problematic Response to the Judicialisation of Tribunals. *Public Law* 537.
Watts, B. and Fitzpatrick, S. (2018). *Welfare Conditionality*. London: Routledge.
Watts, B., Fitzpatrick, S., and Johnsen, S. (2018). Controlling Homeless People? Power, Interventionism and Legitimacy. *Journal of Social Policy* 235.

Webster, D. (2023). *Commentary on the DWP Draft Report*. London: Child Poverty Action Group.

Wikeley, N. (2000). Burying Bell: Managing the Judicialisation of Social Security Tribunals. *Modern Law Review* 475.

9

Law, Begging and Pragmatic Decency

Sara Stendahl

Introduction

Extreme inequality is troublesome, for society (Wilkinson and Pickett 2011, cited in Adler 2019: 90). Or, to quote Michael Adler, "*Extreme inequalities undermine solidarity and have many undesirable consequences*" (Adler 2019: 90). In a world of haves and have-nots, the existence of street begging is one example of extreme inequality; another extreme is the existence of the super-rich (Adler 2019). In Sweden, the recurrence of begging has coincided with a growth in economic inequality at large; at both ends of the scale, extreme positions have become more common (Oxfam 2022, cited in Europaportalen 2024; Kallifatides and Sjöberg 2023; Cervenka 2022). Legal and political developments have led to local decisions to ban begging and the present Prime Minister leads a party that, pre-election, promised criminalisation on a national level. To understand this development, unimaginable 20 years ago, there is a need for context but also, I sense, a need for ethics and normative fellowship. Context is, in this paper, mainly drawn from history, whilst I lean on the work of Onora O'Neill and Avashi Margalit to create some ethical building blocks (O'Neill 1996; Margalit 1996). Independently from each other, O'Neil and Margalit provide useful concepts of justice and decency. It is in the work of Michael Adler that I have found normative

S. Stendahl (✉)
The Department of Law, The School of Business, Economics and Law, Gothenburg University, Gothenburg, Sweden
e-mail: sara.stendahl@law.gu.se

S. Cowan and S. Halliday (eds.), *Socio-Legal Generation*, Palgrave Socio-Legal Studies, https://doi.org/10.1007/978-3-031-67244-6_9

kinship; a common stance from which to view the world. The work of Adler provides, alongside some comparative thoughts, also arguments for poverty to be battled (Adler 2019),[1] for the need to conceptualise the denial of basic social entitlements as degrading treatment (Adler 2018), for viewing begging as a social question (Adler et al. 2011) and for the relevance of mirroring the provocation induced by extreme poverty with the provocation of extreme wealth (Adler 2019). All of these positions reflect a standpoint in the face of social injustice that I find essential (if not existential) at a time in history when the collective European, societal, response to the "social question" seems to be under renegotiation.

The act of begging has been a provocative phenomenon almost regardless of what time period is studied (see the historical overview below in section 5). At present, in Sweden, begging is again on the political agenda resulting in political positioning and calls for legal responses. In this heated setting, the Supreme Administrative Court decided that there was a need for new case law [precedent] and in December 2018, a judgment was given that allowed for the local banning of begging (below referred to as the "Vellinge-verdict"). Drawing on some of the themes of Adler's work, this chapter will describe the development leading up to this judgment, and its aftermath. The chapter asks: How has the legal response to begging, as a social question and /or as a question of public order, developed over time? Why does the legal response to begging remain an inflamed question in 2023? The chapter is structured as follows. Below, after a section on terminology (2), follows a section providing some background facts (3) and a presentation of the concept of "pragmatic decency" (4). In section 5, the historical development of the regulation of begging in Sweden is described, followed by a section on recent legal developments (6). Finally, the practices thus described are discussed in a concluding section (7).

Terminology

A Short Note on Terminology: in analytical terms, begging is in the present paper approached as a means to obtain transfer of resources called for by social need as a means for self- or family support. The act involves at minimum two individuals, the person begging (asking for money or goods) and the individual being asked to give. In addition, begging is in this paper restricted to an act carried out between strangers, located in public space and

[1] Michael Adler initiated and was the prime organiser of a highly successful 2017 workshop on the social minimum held at the Oniati International Institute for the Sociology of Law, an initiative that resulted in a collection of texts published in Kotkas. Leijten and Pennings 2019.

with no (or symbolic) transfer of physical goods or services in return for the gift transferred. Describing begging in this manner follows the often-used Lee and Farrell definition determining begging as being "a public request for money, food or other goods with little or nothing of value given in return to the potential donor" (Barret and Farrell 2003).

Whilst this analytical definition of begging also includes what is described as the everyday meaning of "begging" in Sweden in 2023, it could be that it disguises the present ethnic aspect. The visual of begging at present includes a number of traditional and very old signifiers that are linked to "street begging": a cup, maybe a written sign, passive, silent, sitting, occupying a small space, dressed in poor clothing. In Sweden, in 2023, beggars are also signalling a "foreign" identity: Roma from Eastern Europe. In the 1990s, a person begging would typically be an ethnic Swede with addiction and/or psychiatric problems asking for coins outside the liquor store, and whilst it is unclear whether everyday language of 2023 would still consider such an individual as a "beggar" or such an act as "begging", it would be included in the analytical definition.

Begging is not criminalised in Sweden. The response from society to "ban" begging is not the same as criminalising. There are no regulations on begging to be found in the penal code. Still, banning is a distinct legal response legitimising a perception of "begging" as a disturbing, unwanted, behaviour that provides for authorities to control it and for this purpose also to issue individual fines. In Sweden, it is only possible to issue local bans. During the period 1964–2018, there was no local banning of begging in Sweden. There is no formal source that keeps an updated account of how many of the 290 Swedish municipalities that at present have either issued a local ban or are in the process of doing so, but according to a survey performed in January 2019 (after the Vellinge-verdict), 26 municipalities declared a political ambition to ban begging (Dagens Samhälle 2019). In October 2022, the number of municipalities that had actually issued a ban was 15 (Dagens Nyheter 2022). The local debate on this issue is often intense and a decision to ban can also be turned to its opposite as local political majorities shift over time.

When the Supreme Administrative Court in 2018 discussed the meaning and definition of "begging", it evaded the problem by somehow indicating "you know it when you see it". The Court, as a means of presenting its argument, asks in the judgment if the municipality has been as distinct as is needed when formulating its ordinance. And it responds, by stating that "it is not obvious how a distinction shall be made between passive collection of money and other collection of money – 'collection of money in money boxes or in a similar way' – that the municipality regulates through a system of permits". The Court continues "However, the Supreme Administrative Court is of the opinion that by using the word 'begging' in the ordinance, sufficient clarity is achieved" (HFDs dom Mål nr 2149–18: 9).

Begging in Sweden: The Background

In Sweden, the four founding principles that form government are regulated through a written constitution. The principles are: the principle of the sovereignty of the people; parliamentarism; local self-governance; and constitutional monarchy. For this paper, it is important to understand the principle of local self-governance. Whilst Sweden is what sometimes is described as a *one unity state,* it is at the same time marked by a high degree of self-governance in the 290 local municipalities.

Municipalities have local governments elected through public elections, they have a right to taxation and core delegated responsibilities in such sectors as social welfare, healthcare, law and order, education, etc. The principle of local self-governance has deep historical roots (formalised in 1863 through the first local government ordinance). It is defended with reference to democratic legitimacy and the need to guarantee local responsibility and influence.

Whilst the legislation on public order that is used to ban begging in the twenty-first century does not mention any specific group, it is a fact that in modern times, as well as in historic times, there is a Roma aspect present at the very core of the topic of begging (Hansson 2023; Johnson 2016). The stark majority of individuals who are begging in Sweden today are EU citizens of Roma origin, mainly from Romania and Bulgaria (Hansson, 2023; Wagman et al. 2019; Ekendahl et al. 2018; Ciulinaru 2017). Thus, they are individuals legally present in Sweden but also "foreign" and "Roma". It is hard to know if the act of begging had been considered less a matter of disorder and more a social matter, if the begging had been carried out by mainly non-foreign, non-Roma, people.

The expansion of the European Union during 2004 and 2007 resulted in 12 new member states of which several were relatively poor and some had a large minority of Roma, a minority that has fared badly in most European states for centuries, not least in east European states such as Romania, Bulgaria and Slovakia. Present day motions in favour of regulating begging have been present since 2010 and are distinctly a response to the increase of poor EU citizens, often Roma, who are begging in public areas, typically outside grocery stores.[2] All EU citizens have a right to travel freely in Europe during a three-month period as tourists. If you wish to stay longer, you should find work or find other financial means to cope including a sickness insurance. However, there is no registration of entry and even if this had been the case, there are no limits to have a renewed three-month period as a tourist, if you return to your home country in between. Thus, EU citizens are not expelled (Lambertz 2014).

There are different critical voices in the debate on begging arguing the moral standpoint not to give to beggars, and these are also the voices in favour of regulation and banning. Reoccurring themes used to strengthen such arguments are: (1) begging is a symptom of trafficking (poor people are used by organised criminals and the money given feeds organised crime; (2) begging as "swindle" (those begging are not really poor but have cars and houses at home, in their home countries); (3) beggars are poor but foreign and their own country should support them (and thus refrain from exporting social problems within Europe).[3] In local political debates, it is mainly the first argument that is voiced with emphasis, thus a decision to ban begging is described as a humane act to save people from the risk of trafficking. In 2015, between 4000 and 6000 destitute EU citizens were living in Sweden, and whilst it is hard to find facts on the exact number, it is estimated that the figures have stayed about the same, although with a decline during the years of the Covid-19 pandemic (Swärd 2015). I have found no figures that estimate the decline in presence of Roma migrants during Covid-19, but the pandemic is used as one explanation for the, at the time parallel, decline in presence of beggars.

Developments after the 2018 Vellinge-verdict led to the establishment of local decisions where begging was banned in a number municipalities ruled by right-wing/conservative political majorities. Begging as a political question remains an initiative mainly driven by the Sweden Democrats and the Conservative party. As a visible phenomenon, begging decreased overall after 2019, but rather than being an effect of the Vellinge-verdict, the main explanations for this, found in printed media, are the Covid pandemic that made travelling harder and the fact that it has become less common that people

[2] The timeline is similar to developments in the UK, although it is not clear if the causes overlap. In a report from 2011 Adler, Bromley and Rosie write "...the apparent growth of street begging in Britain represents a return to practices which were common in previous centuries but which the welfare state appeared, until quite recently, to have eliminated". The quote could just as well have been a description of the situation in Sweden at that time (Adler et al. 2011: 2).

[3] If these standpoints are compared to the findings in the 2011 UK report, there are overlaps but also differences. That there exists a perception of fake beggars is similar, but otherwise the Swedish context seems to be more marked by the fact that those who beg are both foreign and Roma (Adler et al. 2011: 8).

use coins and cash for payment.[4] Still, begging has remained on the political agenda. In the 2022 national elections, the Conservative Party promised to criminalise begging on national level.[5] In the same 2022 elections, the Sweden Democrats promised to work for the possibility to deny citizenship and expel foreigners who have an "indecent, dishonorable, life-style" (Sverigedemokraterna 2022; Tidöavtalet 2022), a promise that reconnects to a rarely used piece of legislation, abolished in 1981, that itself was reminiscence of the 1885 Vagrancy Act (see below).

After the elections in 2022, the so-called "Tidö agreement" made it possible for a slim right-wing conservative minority to form a Government, given the support of the Sweden Democrats. In this political landscape, the question of begging has stayed topical (Tidö-avtalet 2022; Regeringsdeklaration 2022). The Tidö agreement is a 62 pages long text that in some detail outlines a political agreement between four of the political parties with seats in the Swedish Parliament. The agreement outlines the conditions that form the basis for a majority to appoint the head of the Conservative Party as Prime Minister and his Cabinet the Government of Sweden. Of these four parties, the Sweden Democrats got most votes in the election, but it is not a party included in the Government. The Conservative party and the Sweden Democrats have followed up on their promises and argue for criminalisation and a national ban on begging. The Tidö agreement includes a paragraph stating that a Governmental Committee (not yet appointed) shall investigate the prerequisites for such policies. The agreement spells out that the Government Committee shall formulate a proposal for a national ban, whatever its other conclusions (Tidö-avtalet 2022 p. 27). In an individual private Parliaments member's motion, a member of the Conservative party has proposed a national ban on begging (Lifvenhage 2023). At time of writing, the motion is being considered by the Committee on Justice but the linked committee reports have not yet been made public. However, an actual proposition to legislate on a national ban on begging would threaten to break the government coalition as two of the elected Parliament members of the Liberal party (included in the minority government) have declared that they will oppose such legislation.

[4] The importance of "spare change" is identified in the British report as maybe the most important factor affecting the decision to give to beggars or not (Adler et al. 2011 p. 25).

[5] The fact that different perceptions of how to understand and act in relation to begging fall quite clearly in a traditional right/left political divide seems to be similar in Sweden and the UK (Adler et al. 2011 p. 8). It is also a fact that political parties to the right (in Sweden) have a problem attracting female voters and that the gap between how men and women vote increases (SCB 2021). The British report identifies gender as one parameter that affects attitudes to begging (ibid.).

Apart from EU citizens with a Roma descent, there are also national Swedish Roma who have a history that can be traced back 500 years. The Swedish Roma is today recognised as a national minority. As late as the nineteenth and twentieth centuries, Swedish municipalities actively tried to ensure that families identified as "gypsies" or "travellers" did not settle down within their borders (Ericsson 2017: 38; Tervonen 2010). Roma families could sometimes be allowed to stay, but only for a limited period and then they were forced to move on. Children of (Swedish) Roma descent were not allowed to go to school. This public policy was sometimes reinforced by collective violence carried out by the local population to force those of Roma descent to leave. In such processes, locals who gave residence to Roma could also be punished, formally in terms of fines or informally by the local population through threats of violence and repercussion (Ericsson 2017: 38 f.). When such violence was reported, there is evidence that indicates that the Police reacted late and leniently (Ericsson 2017). During the years 1914–1954, Swedish law stated that all "foreign gypsies" should be refused entry at the border (Ericsson 2017: 53 ff; 62). Thus, the treatment of the Swedish Roma minority has been marked by a very long history of systematic exclusion, harsh assimilation policies, prejudice, racism and violence reflecting a culture of deep structural injustice. Whilst the present "begging question" is distinctly linked to the presence of foreign Roma in Sweden, and their situation in their home countries Romania and Bulgaria, the Swedish legacy when it comes to Roma discrimination is also part of the context. Whilst the situation for Swedish Roma has improved, distinctly, the question of Roma discrimination is not resolved nor to be described as past history.

"Pragmatic Decency"

I have previously argued that Sweden, in practice, as municipalities face ultimate social need, is marked by a normative pattern (Christensen 1996) that can be described as "pragmatic decency" (Stendahl and Swedrup 2019).The concept refers to a pattern of norms linked to pragmatism (methods of problem-solving at local level that are based less on principle and more on results) and decency used to indicate an important but basic, maybe even minimalistic, quality of interaction between public entities and individuals, to make possible co-living in societies that aspire to be more than civilised. The proposal is based on a notion of decency ideally framed by Onora O'Neill's definitions of obligations of justice (rejection of injury) and obligations of virtue (rejection of indifference and neglect) and the work of Avishai Margalit who makes a distinction between a decent society (in which institutions do not humiliate people) and a civilised society in which people do not humiliate each other (O'Neill 1996; Margalit 1996).

O'Neill writes on the topic of scope, and explores different ideas in human history that determine with whom we share resources. She asks: "Who counts?", and shows how this question has divided writings on ethics and justice for centuries. There are two typical responses, one described as more particularist and another described as more universalist. The particularist response to the question about scope drives towards anchoring ethical values in the traditions and practices of distinct communities. A universalist response is more inclusive and defines the domain of ethical consideration as including, for instance, all human beings or all living beings, or maybe all beings with certain characteristics (as soul, reason, personhood, consciousness). O'Neill's question, "who counts?", is a philosophical question but it has strong links to law (often the instrument chosen to draw limits).

When proposing that the concept of "pragmatic decency" is useful as an analytical tool to understand the local practices of Swedish municipalities, the proposal was based on the identification of a "legally framed practice that is pragmatic and driven by a capacity to handle problems (not solve them)" (Stendahl and Swedrup 2019: 65). We argued then that "[t]here seems to be some level of minimal decency that must be upheld in society also for those who do not meet the qualifications. Some kind of moral agreement, that in no municipality should anyone have to freeze to death, or starve, or be denied treatment if seriously ill. The content of this 'minimum' is not laid down in law or practice, and thus it is not transparent" (Stendahl and Swedrup 2019: 65). We called this pattern "pragmatic decency" and argued that it had a trajectory that could be traced far back, that it was universalistic in scope and that it was based on values that corresponded to fundamental human rights norms.

The scope determined by pragmatic decency can perhaps be described, in principle, as less fixed and rather delimited by a constructive, ongoing, process aimed at determining who is within the domain of our ethical consideration at each time and place. In practice, this delimitation of scope is more universalist than particularist in character. Still, it might also be a normative pattern that is distinctly challenged by the influx of destitute Roma EU citizens (Hansson 2023).

Regulating Begging—A Historical Overview Covering the Seventeenth to the Twentieth Centuries[6]

What follows is an overview describing how law, over time, has been used as a response to begging in Sweden. The purpose of this exposé is to describe how society over centuries has dealt with begging as a sign of both destitute need and provocative disturbance. The findings form an important backdrop to my analyses of the present situation and my interest in elaborating on *pragmatic decency* as a normative pattern guiding local social policies.

The act of begging has been approached as a societal dilemma since the seventeenth century and this is as far back as we will follow its regulatory history. During the Reformation (1527–1600), a previously predominantly Catholic Sweden turned Lutheran protestant. The Reformation marks not only the end of the Catholic era in Sweden but is also described as the end of the Middle Ages. In the Middle Ages, before 1600, the response to begging was marked by the religious narratives of the old Church Fathers that protected a right to survival. Begging for survival was not banned, and the person begging was not (at least not by statute) considered bad or reprehensible. In contrast, at least in theory, the beggar filled a function in society providing the more fortunate with opportunities to act in the spirit of God.

The Reformation and the shift to Protestantism became part of a development that made the societal perception of begging and beggars more harsh, as the value of daily work was emphasised. The overarching responsibility for the poor became the responsibility of the state/the monarch (Koefoed 2017). It should be emphasised that although the state (the monarch) took over responsibility, in Sweden, the church became part of the state and continued in practice, to have a crucial role in taking care of the poor and sick. This remains visible also today as the main NGOs active in the social field have a religious (protestant) foundation. Also, in Lutheran Protestantism, it was a charitable duty to give to the poor, but the importance of daily work and that fact that salvation was not described as reached by giving alms changed the idea of how to relate to the poor (Koefoed 2017: 256). Presented below are, in chronologically order, some of the main regulations of relevance when discussing the development of law and begging.

The Act of 1642 [*1642 års tiggareordning*] that related to begging underlined the continued responsibility of the local parish and community to care

[6] I am in this section of the chapter at large indebted to the work of historians (often specialising in the history of law and/or religion).

for their own poor, including the sick and disabled. Begging outside your parish was prohibited. Families had to provide for their own family members. Sick people without relatives got healthcare from state hospitals. In 1664, an Act was issued that made it compulsory to "serve" [*1664 års allmänna legostadga*]. This statute was in force from 1664 to 1885 and meant that all able-bodied had an obligation to serve. It was unlawful not to be in work. Those able, and not in work, were during this period increasingly viewed as idle, lazy, immoral, indecent. Individuals not working were at risk of being put in forced labour (Johnsson 2016). The poor and able-bodied remained the responsibility of the local parish. However, begging was not uncommon and often described as "the only option" (Koefoed 2017). In 1686, an Act was issued that again emphasised the local responsibility towards the poor [*1686 års kyrkolag*]. Regulations became more detailed and formulated an obligation by local communities to establish a poorhouse in every parish (Koefoed 2017). Other means (apart from begging and poorhouses) to support for the poor included boarding out the provision of food and shelter or by other means securing that each farm gave provisions.

An Act operative between 1698 and 1847 [*1698 års förnyade tiggareordning*] laid down a restriction on begging, making it permissible only if an individual permit had been issued by the local congregation/parish. Begging was at this point perceived as a form of poverty-support (for those not able bodied). On a local level, begging would with time be phased out in favour of other collective solutions that were considered less shameful (also for the parish). Begging would, as time passed, be seen as a sign of inadequate poor relief. In 1763, came new regulations that specified the content of the responsibility of local actors to care for the poor [*1763 års förordning om ansvarsfördelning mellan staten och lokalsamhället*]. The poor were in this Act divided into three categories: the old and sick without relatives; the poor with contagious diseases to be cared for in hospitals; and orphans to be cared for in foster homes. Thus, poor relief in Sweden, at this point, did not include the able-bodied (who were compelled to serve). An ordinance in 1788 [*1788 års kungörelse om hemortsrätt*] stated (again) the principle that the local parish had to care for its own, but also the right to turn away people who came from elsewhere "for instance illegal itinerant beggars" (Koefoed 2017, citing Arner "Studier öfver svenska kyrkans ställning" pp. 4–17, in Markkola 2011: 109).

In 1811 [*1811 års provisoriska fattigvårdsförordning*], municipalities were given the right to tax citizens in order to pay for social care/poverty care. And whilst in 1818, the Act that made it compulsory to work became less strict, beggars were still at risk of being sent to forced labour and begging was treated much in the same way as stealing or vagrancy. 1826 brought a year of bad crops and the population fares badly. Many risked starvation and there was a general increase of poverty, vagrancy and begging. The Swedish King will during this year make statements emphasising the responsibility of local congregations to take care of "their own" poor in an effort to stop the increase of people going to Stockholm or other larger cities trying to find work and means for survival. By 1830, local bans on begging were quite common as congregations /parishes had created other collective responses providing for poor relief (like homes for the poor and other processes for how to share the burden of providing for the young, old and sick). At this time, there were 88 parishes that were shamed as "begging parishes" where permits to beg still were issued. The explanation given for this situation could be that the parish was really poor, that the inhabitants were greedy or that there were conflicts that made other collective arrangements impossible. Still, it seems as if begging could not be banned if no other poor relief was at hand (Johnsson 2016). In 1833, begging was legally identified as an activity that made a non-working position worse, more despicable [*Kungl. Maj:t den 29 juni 1833 förordning huru med försvarslöse borde hållas*].

By 1847, a total national ban on begging was issued through a Royal Ordinance [*1847 års fattigvårdförordning*]. Simultaneously, through the same legislation, the first coherent national social legislation on poverty was put in place and implemented (adopted six years earlier, in 1841). Financing was still a local matter (through a poor tax). There is at this point no "social rights" and no ideas on prevention in the law, but rather obligations on local communities to provide emergency help to the poor and destitute. The groups of deserving poor remained the same as in the Act from 1763.

The years 1867–1869 were a period where crops failed badly and starvation followed. The aftermath saw a continued, and increasing, flight of people who emigrated, and almost 1.5 million Swedes (a fifth of the population) eventually left Sweden with a peak from the mid-1880s to 1920, emigrating mainly to the USA.

This period of crisis and economic restraint affected also the legal situation of the poor. The 1870s seemed to be the beginning of a shift in how to perceive overall responsibility for the poor. Philanthropy (based on religious as well as secular values) increased, as did systems of mutual insurances. A short time later, in 1885, there was a new vagrancy Act [*Lagen den 12 juni 1885 angående lösdrivarares behandling*] replacing the 1664 Act that stipulated an obligation to serve. Still, a person living a vagrant life could also, after 1885, be sentenced to forced work, something which at this point was considered a treatment rather than as a punishment. Finally, at the end of this period, in 1964, a new Act on "antisocial asociality" [*Lag om samhällsfarlig asocialitet*] replaced the 1885 Vagrancy Act. The 1964 Act was rarely used and finally abolished in 1981.

In the late 1990s, a period marked by economic crisis as well as a major national reform of psychiatric care, there was an increase of visible poverty and begging, especially in the big cities. Those begging were Swedish citizens who had access to Swedish welfare, and begging was distinctly viewed as a social problem that needed social solutions (Beijer 1999).[7] The identified risk discussed was that begging could facilitate continued addiction practices, and thus, it was recommended not to give (out of care for those in need). This decision was eased by the fact that social need was cared for through the social services of a generous and comprehensive welfare state (Beijer 1999). There were, in the 1990s, no political propositions to institute bans on begging.

From the above chronological description of the regulation of begging in Sweden, a few things could be noted. Destitute poverty and poor people are dealt with as a local problem. The key argument is that local knowledge could best determine who is poor and who is lazy, and thus who is worthy of solidarity (the deserving poor). In most periods, begging has been rejected as an illegitimate social behaviour, but it has also been shameful for a society to have beggars (a visible sign of a lack of capacity to create collective social solutions). Historically, regulations governing the poor have been distinctly authoritarian, and violent (forced labour, etc.), and yet a national ban on begging was not issued until 1847 at a point in time when also the first coherent national social legislation on poverty was implemented. Early on, such "solutions" were local and came in the form of a forced labour, a poor house, auctioning out of orphans or others not able to support themselves. It was not only begging that was banned but also, in periods, and locally, the act of helping those not assessed to be the responsibility of the community (Meeuwisse and Swärd 2002). In more modern historical times, in the second half of the twentieth century, the act of begging, to the extent it was not considered extinct, was approached only as a social question. With this in mind, we end the historical overview and proceed to a more detailed account of how begging, to the surprise of many, returned as a matter of law in the twenty-first century.

---

[7] As in Sweden, it seems as if in the UK, street begging had in 2011 for some time been associated with practices of the past, a phenomenon eliminated by the welfare state (Adler et al. 2011: 1).

Regulating Begging—Developments in the Twenty-First Century

The legal reappearance of the begging as a matter of public order came about in May 2011 as a local initiative of the municipality of Sala, as the municipality decided to ban begging in public space. However, this initiative was later deemed to be in contradiction with the Act on Public Order by the County Administrative Board. In 2012, a notorious member of parliament from the Sweden Democrats wrote a motion proposing a national ban on begging that he distinctly directed against foreign, in his word, "professional", beggars (Ekeroth 2011). Then followed a number of years of political struggles between conservative municipalities and the state, where the municipalities tried to find ways to stop begging by Roma EU citizens. Until the Vellinge-judgement in 2018 (see below), all such efforts were pushed back, mainly with the argument that no municipality had been able to show that the begging in question constituted any real disturbance. In this debate, a 2014-case tried in a local public court became important, as it made a distinction between active and passive begging. Passive begging was according to the verdict in the 2014-case not disturbing (Södertälje Tingsrätt 2014).[8]

A few days before Christmas in 2018, the Swedish Supreme Administrative Court came to a decision in a high-profile case concerning begging. The two parties to the conflict were Vellinge, a small municipality in the south of Sweden, and the state, represented by the local County Administrative Board [Länstyrelsen i Skåne Län]. The case was registered inconspicuously as a case on "local ordinances on public order", but it was the "begging factor" of this conflict between different levels of public administrative bodies that caused intense media coverage and sharp political demarcations. In its decision, the Supreme Administrative Court decided in favour of Vellinge and declared that it was in accordance with Swedish law for a municipality to ban begging in defined areas. Whilst this decision was warmly welcomed by some, it was as intensely criticised by others. Thus, the case was resolved but the conflict between protagonists remained. Below, after a short summary, the core legal arguments of the case are described in some detail.

In the three instances of court procedure, the two parties developed their argument as follows: the County Administrative Board (representing state interests on a local level) emphasised that the right of municipalities to enact local ordinances on public order is conditional and that a municipality in

[8] The distinction made between passive and active (and sometimes aggressive begging) has been noted also in British studies. How the beggar is perceived is important for the begging person (Fitzpatrick and Kennedy 2000: 26 f.) for public perception and political reactions (see Adler et al. 2011: 8).

order to do so needs to show that locally decided restrictions (thus beyond those laid down in national law) are *really needed*. According to the County Administrative Board, the municipality had not been able to prove that the act of begging had caused disturbances to the public order of Vellinge. The County Administrative Board held on to this line of reasoning in all three trials as the matter processed through the legal system. The municipality responded by making emphasised reference to complaints communicated by members of the municipality summarised as testimonies on a systematic and continuing presence of beggars close to entrances of local stores, sometimes described as linked to public urinating and littering, disturbing not only to individuals but also to shop owners and commercial interests. According to the municipality in Vellinge, the universal understanding amongst its members (the inhabitants of Vellinge) was that begging was disturbing. The municipality also offered an argument based on proportionality: What had most protective value: the freedom of members of the municipality to collect money (begging) or the need to counteract begging? (in certain defined areas)?

Whilst the argument of the County Administrative Board was upheld in two instances, the Supreme Administrative Court decided in favour of the municipality. In contrast to previous court decisions, the Supreme Administrative Court did not interpret the emphasis on "real need" as a call for the municipality to show empirically proven facts of disturbance. The County Administrative Board had argued that in order to issue a local ordinance to ban begging, the municipality had to prove that there existed empirical reasons to do so in the form of actual disturbance. When the Supreme Administrative Court no longer interpreted the legal requirements of "real need" as linked to empirical facts, the case changed direction.

The Supreme Administrative Court framed the case as a balance of interest between the upholding of a local, open and far-reaching, right to issue ordinances on the one hand and national safeguards against the risk of too far-reaching regulations interfering with individual freedom on the other hand. It was emphasised by the Court that whilst there are no (or few) limits as to content and format, local ordinances have to serve a specific purpose and be proportional. The Court noted that all local ordinances have to be legal and appropriate. As the Court proceeded to discuss the specific circumstances of the Vellinge-case, the Court elaborates on three issues that require to be demonstrated: (i) the necessary link between a local ordinance and the aim to uphold "public order", (ii) the proportionality of any given measure and (iii) noting that it must be possible to apply and uphold the local ordinances. Thus, the scene is set and the court subsequently moved on to its assessment and the concluding arguments.

The first question the court approached is whether begging can be apprehended to be a disturbance and if/how such a standpoint or claim needs to be substantiated. If begging can be apprehended as a disturbance, the gateway criteria are met and we can proceed to an assessment of proportionality and operationalisation. In all previous instances, the case was determined already at this point, as begging was not, by the Courts, deemed to constitute a disturbance in Vellinge. However, the Supreme Administrative Court declared that there is no demand on municipalities to prove that an activity (as begging) has caused a disturbance in reality, or that the activity one wishes to regulate (collection of money in public) has been perceived as a disturbance by members of the municipality. It seems, therefore, as if the question, "What constitutes a disturbance?", is not perceived by the court as an empirical question. This conclusion makes unnecessary all arguments and facts that aim to prove actual disturbance or non-disturbance from the activity of begging in Vellinge. Thus, it seems as if the determination on what is a "disturbance" can in principle be answered in full by reference to ideological/political/normative arguments.

One could have expected a second part of this argument to have led to a testing of whether the specific activity "collection of money in public" meets general theoretical characteristics of what legally has constituted a disturbance (through studying legislation and previous case law). However, this is not the path chosen. Instead, the activity of collecting money is treated as a special case when it comes to local ordinances on law and order.

It is important for the Supreme Administrative Court that the specific action that is banned concerns collection of money, as the preparatory work to the Public Order Act specifically mentions collection of money and describes it as an activity that can be regulated by local ordinances. It should be noted that preparatory works, such as government bills and committee reports, are deemed essential legal sources used to interpret the law in Sweden. In addition, the Supreme Administrative Court makes a reference to the fact that the Swedish Association of Local Authorities and Regions [SKL] since 1995 suggested that municipalities should have a local ordinance that makes collection of money in public space an activity dependent on authorisation, a permit (SKR 1995). Many municipalities also have a standard clause on this, often, as in Vellinge, including two paragraphs. Paragraph 1 states: "For collection of money in collection boxes and the like, which do not form part of a public gathering or a public event subject to a permit, a permit is required from the police authority." Paragraph 2 states: "When the collection takes place in connection with the performance of street music a permission is not required" (Vellinge kommun 2023). In the local ordinances of Vellinge, the ban on begging is constructed through the addition of a third paragraph: "Passive collection of money (begging) is not allowed in those areas that are specified in appendix D in related documents below" (Vellinge kommun 2023).

That an activity needs a permit is of course not a reason to deny such permit. In order to deny an application for a permit regarding collection of money in public space, the police need to have sufficient reasons. This line of arguments takes us back to the meaning of "disturbance". When you apply for a permit, it is important to state the purpose of the collection. Whilst such facts could help the police to profile fake and cunning attempts to defraud people, denial on such grounds seems to have less to do with disturbance as such (and fraud is also regulated elsewhere). An application for a permit runs the risk of being denied if the activity risks getting in the way of other core activities, for instance, hindering entrance to stores, hindering traffic or hindering entrance to public transport.

Finally, the Court stated that Vellinge has the possibility to regulate begging in order to cope with what can be apprehended as a kind of disturbance, if this is done in a manner that does not conflict with the Public Order Act. As the banning is proposed to be in effect in certain defined public places, the Court is content and finds the ordinance to be within the ambit of the Public Order Act.

The developments surrounding the "Vellinge-case" did not go unnoticed amongst legal scholars in Sweden (Bremdahl and Kindström Dahlin 2018; 2019; Ahlin and Örenberg 2019; Mattsson 2019; Jivegård forthcoming). The core legal interest amongst legal scholars has been the constitutional issues related to the division of power between the state and the municipalities. The verdict was, however, also questioned as it did not elaborate on any of the potential Convention rights protected by the Council of Europe (neither civil nor social). After the Vellinge-verdict was delivered, the Civil Rights Defenders argued that there were aspects in the matter at hand that the Supreme Administrative Court had not dealt with and thus remained to be tried in court. The organisation argued that there were grounds to assess the decision to ban begging in Vellinge also in light of the Constitution and the European Convention on Human Rights (CRD 2019). In a prompt comment on the Lacatus case (see below), Professor Anna-Sara Lind urged the Supreme Administrative Court to elaborate on the human rights aspects of begging in any potentially upcoming case (Lind 2022). However, in April 2020, the Supreme Administrative Court decided to deny leave to appeal (HFD 2020).

After the ECtHR published its verdict in the case of Lacatus C. Suisse (in which the Court found that when the city of Geneva had fined and thereafter imprisoned a Roma person for begging, Switzerland had violated the ECHR Article 8 right to respect for private and family life), the legal discussion on begging in Sweden has continued to circle mainly around the question of whether or not the Vellinge-verdict is in line with the ECHR. The reasoning in the Lacatus case brought to the fore what Eddie Bamborough and Gijsbert Vonk describe the existence of a "safety net under the safety net" (Bambrough and Vonk 2021). The argument here is that the protection of human dignity, a common denominator of first and second generation human rights, creates a direct ECHR-protection against ultimate destitution (Mikkola 2010). This is an argument clearly in line with the approach taken by, for instance, Michael Adler in his 2018 book on benefit sanctions in the UK (Adler 2018). In failing welfare states, it seems as if the human rights argument is increasingly needed in order to create a "safety net under the safety net". In a Swedish context, this has been noted by Anna-Sara Lind in her comment on Lacatus C. Suisse (Lind 2022), but otherwise the core human rights argument used by, for instance, the organisation, the Civil Rights Defenders, has drawn more upon the Anglo-American argument, protecting begging as an act of speech (Article 11 of the ECHR) (Civil Rights Defenders [CRD] 2023). Thus, the dominant legal arguments in a Swedish setting, no matter whether pro or against the act of banning begging, have been surprisingly void of *social* aspects, thus an approach to begging as an expression of destitute poverty, and as such of common concern. In the legal debate following the verdict, such arguments have been almost as invisible as in the Vellinge-verdict itself. Apart from the different promises mentioned above and made as part of the election campaign of 2022, no other concrete legal developments have (so far) taken place in Sweden since 2018.

Concluding Thoughts: The Boundaries of Pragmatic Decency

There are legal "facts" in the field of "law and begging" that can be described and analysed in its black letter law logic. Still, it seems urgent to also explore perspectives that can provide a basis from which to analyse "law and begging" as a societal phenomenon. In this paper, a long historical perspective has been included in order to make more transparent what seems to be a recurring theme in the regulation of begging: the tension between approaching poverty (as materialised in begging) as a matter of social concern or as a matter of public order. Perhaps, the historical perspective might add some light on what, at present, seems to be a deep ethical conflict at the midst of the begging question: How far does our solidarity stretch and with whom do we share resources? In the above account of legal responses to begging over the past four centuries, some themes could be highlighted as indicating strong historic trajectories in the approach to begging.

First, begging has since the seventeenth century been dealt with by means of law and mainly as a matter of disturbance and "public order". The individual act of begging has been approached as a problematic, deviant behaviour, and law has been used as a tool to restrict or change such behaviour. This said, regulations restricting begging were for a long period of time, leading up to the 1980s, coordinated with social legislation, securing some societal response to need. For example, the first national ban on begging (issued in 1847) was not deemed possible until there was also a national legislation on poverty in place. On local level, the same interrelated perspective on demands for public order and a responsibility for safeguarding a bare social minimum existed.

Secondly, the act of begging has, as already noted, for the longest time been viewed as a problematic individual behaviour that reflects badly on the person active in begging. But, it has also been viewed as a symptom of local incapacity that shames the community. Historically, the presence of begging became a sign that local society had failed to create other more functional means of social response to poverty in the community.

Thirdly, there was a relatively short time period between 1980 and 2018 when begging was not identified as anything but a social problem. During this period, in the 1990s, street begging surprisingly reappeared as social phenomenon due to a mix of economic crisis and the implementation of a psychiatric care reform (that closed down many institutions). These developments challenged the welfare state but did not result in calls for banning but in demands for social reforms. By contrast, the fact the judges in the 2018 Vellinge-judgment avoided all elaboration on begging as a sign of social need, is, from a historical perspective, a remarkable sidestep in the long trajectory of how to understand begging.

Fourthly, begging has since the seventeenth century been dealt with as a problem to be resolved locally. The possibility for poor people to travel has in many periods been restricted, and those travelling, in spite of being poor, have been asked to "go home" to their own municipality/congregation/family for social support. The municipalities issuing local bans, supported by the 2018 ruling, might thus fall back on another strong theme present through history, which is to tell beggars to "go home", which in present times means home to Romania and Bulgaria. This is also the main political response forwarded as a solution to the social need of those begging.

The list above reflects recognisable traits in the Swedish legal responses to begging over centuries. Today, the question of begging is political dynamite because it falls distinctly in the clash between two ethical positions where solidarity and sense of community are at the core. There is not much common ground between a re-energised nationalistic "particularistic" position and an, at present, arguably, somewhat weakened socio-liberal "universalist" position. As the concept of citizenship is increasingly used as a boundary setting concept, the universal human rights argument has become politicised. The legal situation before the verdict in the Vellinge-case was that lower courts made the interpretation that it was not possible to issue local bans on begging, unless in the actual case, it had proved empirically disturbing. The verdict laid down an interpretation of law that made it possible for local municipalities to choose to issue bans on begging more on principle, regardless of whether the community faced any de facto disturbing practices. This situation has allowed for a diversification in policy on a local level on an ethically dividing question. With one exception, the municipalities that choose to issue local bans have all been governed by political majorities dominated by the right and the proposals have been pushed by either the Sweden Democrats or the Conservative Party. This development could have created a nimby situation (not in my backyard), had not the overall presence of begging deteriorated at a similar point in time.

I began this paper with a quote from Adler who linked the presence of extreme inequalities with the undermining of solidarity. From that perspective, it is worth noting that amongst the fifteen Swedish municipalities that have decided to issue local bans, we find Danderyd, Lidingö and Täby, the three municipalities that top the list of having "the wealthiest inhabitants in Sweden" (Swestat 2023). In welfare states, public institutions have been given a responsibility for the distribution and redistribution of wealth needed to secure social security for all. Thus, begging in welfare states gives rise to questions on the scope of public solidarity. In a Swedish context, those actually involved in begging will (largely) have no formal legal social rights that can be claimed in court (Stendahl 2014). However, the fact that a person does not have access to formal legal rights does not exclude the presence of a formal community responsibility to protect life and abstain from policies that amount to degrading treatment.

I have previously written on how law is used to determine who is included in the so-called universal welfare state (Stendahl 2016). It seems as if the legal response to begging is yet another example of an ongoing development where the welfare state is no longer expanding but chiselling out subsections amongst the have-nots. Legal responsibilities for those who have not earned social rights by staying in their "own" community or municipality decrease. There are no, or only minimal, legal responsibilities for the social wellbeing of poor foreigners who are living their lives in Sweden (Stendahl 2014). The decision by the Supreme Administrative Court in the Vellinge-case follows in step with this development as it acknowledges that a municipality has a right to protect its members from the sense of discomfort that they could feel face to face with a beggar who they do not count as someone with whom they feel ethically bound to share resources.

So far, the clash between the universalistic and particularistic standpoint on these issues has played out locally, but the present Government came to power on the promises that such policies should be national. My prediction is, given the Lacatus verdict of the ECtHR and the strong pattern of "pragmatic decency" reflected in local policies, that such a move forward would prove to be both legally and politically very troublesome for the Swedish Government. That said, I am aware that this might be a prediction coloured by wishful thinking.

In any case, it is clear that in the municipality of Vellinge, "pragmatic decency" came to a halt in the case of begging. This said, it should be noted that in more than sixty municipalities, such proposals have been turned down (Hansson 2023 p. 264). If the social aspects of begging are acknowledged, it is clear that banning and criminalisation is nothing but a means to move the provocation elsewhere, out of sight. But to denounce banning as a response to begging is not enough. Just as it was shameful for local communities to have no better collective response to destitute poverty than allowing begging in the nineteenth century, it is, or should be, shameful today. Acceptance does not respond to the ethical building blocks and normative kinship that I spoke of in the introduction, as I named O'Neill, Margalit and Adler. To acknowledge human suffering and destitution, a social question is a necessary step from which more constructive work can begin. The solution to begging, as a social question, spells solidarity and redistribution, access healthcare, a roof over one's head, work, social human rights and the acknowledgement of striving for inclusive justice and decency (Stendahl and Swedrup 2018). We cannot hope to find the specific legal and social constructs needed to meet the social question of the twenty-first century in history, but it is indeed urgent we dare propose concrete alternative routes to those formulated from a strict particularistic standpoint.

References

Adler, M., Bromley C., and Rosie, M. (2011). British Social Attitudes: The 17th Report. Sage Research Methods. https://doi.org/10.4135/9781849208635.

Adler, M. (2018). *Cruel, Inhuman or Degrading Treatment. Benefit Sanctions in the UK*. Cham: Palgrave Macmillan.

Adler, M. (2019). The Social Minimum in the Context of Inequality. In T. Kotkas, I. Leijten, and F. Pennings (red.), *Specifying and Securing a Social Minimum in the Battle Against Poverty*, pp 71–91. Oxford: Hart Publishing.

Ahlin, P., and Örnberg, Å. (2019). HFD 2018 ref 75: Tiggerdomen – Ännu en gång. In *FT,* s. 263–271.

Bambrough, E., and Vonk G. (2021). Case Note: ECLI:ECHR:2021:0119JUD001406516. EHRC updates, 2021 [downloaded 14–06–2023].

Beijer, U. (1999). Tiggeri – ett nygammalt fenomen. Forsknings och utvecklingsenheten, *FoU-rapport*, 29. Stockholm: Socialtjänstförvaltningen.

Bremdahl, P. and Kindström Dahlin, M., Normprövning och kommunal självstyrelse – med anledning av länsstyrelsernas beslut att upphäva Vellinge kommuns tiggeriförbud, *FT,* 2018, s. 185–207.

Bremdahl, P., and Kindström Dahlin, M. (2019). Kommunernas tolkningsutrymme: En kommentar till HFD 2018 ref 75 gällande förutsättningarna för att en kommun ska få reglera tiggeri genomlokala föreskrifter, *FT*, 2019, s. 113–118.

Cervenka, A. (2022). *Girig-Sverige, så blev folkhemmet ett paradis för de superrika* [Greedy-Sweden, How the People's Home Became a Paradise for the Super-Rich]. Stockholm: Natur och Kultur.

Ciulinaru, D. (2017). The Justification of Harsh Treatment of Homeless Romanian Migrants in Sweden. *Nordic Journal of Migration Research*, 7(4), 243–250.

Christensen, A. (1996). Skydd för etablerad position – ett normativt grundmönster. *TfR*, 04/1996, pp. 519–574.

Ferhatovic, M. (2022, October 27). Symbolfråga eller handlingskraft – här har det redan varit förbjudet att tigga i två år. *Dagens Nyheter*.

Dagens Samhälle. (2019). https://www.dagenssamhalle.se/styrning-och-beslut/kommunpolitik/har-ar-kommunerna-som-kan-infora-forbud/.

Ekendahl, M., Karlsson, P., and Minas, R. (2018). EU Citizens Begging and Sleeping Rough in Swedish Urban Areas: Social Work Perspectives on Problems and Target Groups. In *Nordic Social Work Research*, pp. 186–197. https://doi.org/10.1080/2156857X.2018.1518816.

Engberg, E. (2005). I fattiga omständigheter. Fattigvårdens former och understödstagare i Skellefteå socken under 1800-talet (diss.), *Department of Historical Studies*. Umeå University.

Ericsson, M. (2017). Såsom det brukas med tattare, Kollektivt våld mot familjer utpekade som tattare eller zigenare 1872–1955. *Historisk Tidskrift*, 137 (1), s. 37–63.

Fitzpatrick, S., and Kennedy, C. (2000). Getting by: Engaging with rough sleeping and The Big Issue in Glasgow and Edinburgh. Bristol: The Policy Press.

Hansson, E. (2023). *The Begging Question. Sweden's Social Responses to the Roma Destitute*. Lincoln: University of Nebraska Press.

Jivegård, D. G., PhD-project, "The Legal Production of the Disorderly" (Work in Progress, on file with author).

Johnson, T. (2016). *Vårt fredliga samhälle, Lösdriveri och försvarslöshet i Sverige under 1830–talet*, akademisk avhandling, Acta Universitatis Upsaliensis, nr 254, 2016.

Kallifatides, M., and Sjöberg, S. (2023). Alla får det inte bättre [Not everyone is better off], *Katalys*.

Koefoed, N. J. (2017). Social Responsibilities in the Protestant North. Denmark and Sweden. In Van Molle (ed.), *Charity and Welfare*. Leuven: Leuven University Press.

Kotkas, T., Leijten, I., and Pennings, F. (red.). (2019). *Specifying and Securing a Social Minimum in the Battle Against Poverty*. Oxford: Hart Publishing.

Lambertz, G. (2014). Begging, Human Rights and International Law. Institute for Cultural Diplomacy.

Barratt, L., and Farrall, C. (2003). Buddy, Can You Spare a Dime. *Urban Affairs Review, 38*(3), 299–234.

Lind, A.-S. (2022). Europadomstolens dom Lacatus C. Suisse, NR 14065/15, Dom av den 19 januari 2021(slutlig 19 april 2021). Prövning av tiggeriförbud i förhållande till Europakonventionen. I *FT*, pp. 461–470.

Margalit, A. (1996). *The Decent Society*. Cambridge, MA: Harvard University Press.

Mattsson, T. (2019). Domen om tiggeriförbudet och dess följder. *Blendow Lexnova Expertkommentar* (on file with author).

Meeuwisse, A., and Swärd, H. (2002). *Perspektiv på sociala problem*. Stockholm: Natur & Kultur.

Mikkola, M. (2010). *Social Human Rights of Europe*. Porvoo: Karelactio.

O'Neill, O. (1996). *A Constructive Account of Practical Reasoning. Towards Justice and Virtue*. Cambridge: Cambridge University Press.

Stendahl, S. (2014). Welfare State Borders: On Local Initiatives to Cater the Needs of Destitute EU Migrants in Swedish Cities. In W. van Oorschot, H. Peeters, and K. Boos (eds.), *Invisible Social Security, Essays in honour of Jos Berghman*, pp. 161–174. Lannoo Campus.

Stendahl, S. (2016). To Reside: To Live, Be Present, Belong. *European Journal of Social Security, 18*(2), 232–245.

Stendahl, S., and Swedrup, O. (2018). Social Human Rights as a Legal Strategy to Enhance EU Citizenship. In F. Pennings and M. Seeleib-Kaiser (eds.), *EU-Citizenship and Social Rights*, pp. 103–123. Cheltenham: Edward Elgar.

Stendahl, S., and Swedrup, O. (2019). A Social Minimum for Whom? Making a Case for a Normative Pattern of Pragmatic Decency. In T. Kotkas, I. Leijten, and F. Pennings (eds.), *The Battle Against Poverty: Specifying and Securing a Social Minimum*, pp. 47–67. Hart Publishing.

Sverigedemokraterna, Valmanifest (2022). https://sd.se/wp-content/uploads/2022/08/valmanifest.pdf. [2024–01–01].

Swärd, H. (2015). EU-medborgarna, tiggeriet och den synliga nöden – en kunskapsöversikt. *Socialmedicinsk tidskrift*. häfte 3. pp. 268–285.

Tervonen, M. (2010). *"Gypsies", "Travellers" and "Peasants": A study on Ethnic Boundry Drawing in Finland and Sweden ca 1860–1925* (diss.). Florence: European University Institute.

Tidöavtalet. (2022). [The Tidö-Agreement]. https://www.liberalerna.se/wp-content/uploads/tidoavtalet-overenskommelse-for-sverige-slutlig.pdf [2023–07–06].

Tuori, K. (2013). Law Beyond Law. In A. Numhauser-Henning and M. Rönnmar (eds.), *Normative Patterns and Legal Developments in the Social Dimension of the EU* . Oxford: Hart Publishing.

Wagman, Johansson, and Fristedt. (2019). Begging Abroad in Sweden; An Interview Study. *Scandinavian Journal of Occupational Therapy*. https://doi.org/10.1080/11038128.2018.1547790.

Public Records

National level

Regeringsförklaring [Declaration of Government] 2022, Protokoll 2022/23:10 Tisdagen den 18 oktober, at https://www.riksdagen.se/sv/dokument-och-lagar/dokument/protokoll/protokoll-20222310-tisdagen-den-18-oktober_ha0910/html/ [Accessed 2024–01–01].

Riksdagen Motion 2011/12:Sf344, "Förbud mot tiggeri", Ekeroth, K., at https://www.riksdagen.se/sv/dokument-och-lagar/dokument/motion/forbud-mot-tiggeri_gz02sf344/ [Accessed 2024–02–01].

Riksdagen Motion 2023/24:1436, "Förbud mot tiggeri," Lifvenhage, A-S., at https://www.riksdagen.se/sv/dokument-och-lagar/dokument/motion/tiggeriforbud_hb021436/ [Accessed 2024–02–01].

Justitieutskottet [Parliament Committee on Justice], utskottsbetänkande 2023/24:JuU16 [not yet published 2024–01–02].

Committee on Justice (Parliament), Committee Report 2023/24:JuU9 [not yet published 2024–01–02].

Local Level

Svenska kommunförbundet (SKR), "Lokala ordningsföreskrifter", cirkulär 1995:41, diarienummer 1995:0281, at https://skr.se/download/18.3859f07175024a45ec114f8/1602853360097/1995041.pdf [Accessed 2024–01–02].
Vellinge kommun, Lokala ordningsföreskrifter [The local public ordinance in Vellinge municipality], at https://vellinge.se/kommun-och-politik/kommunfakta/sa-styrs-vellinge/vellinge-styrdokument/lokala-ordningsforeskrifter/#:~:text=Ordningsföreskrifterna%20innehåller%20bestämmelser%20kring%20bland,ordningsföreskrifter%20som%20gäller%20i%20Vellinge [Accessed 2023–12–30].

Caselaw

The European Court of Human Rights, Lacatus v. Switzerland, nr 14065/15, at https://hudoc.echr.coe.int/app/conversion/pdf/?library=ECHR&id=003-6910043-9279633&filename=Judgment%20 [Accessed 2024–01–02].
HFD, Högsta Förvaltningsdomstolen [The Supreme Administrative Court], 2020–04–03, beslut i mål nr 5907–19. At https://crd.org/wp-content/uploads/2020/04/Beslut_HFD_2020-04-03.pdf [Accessed 2024–01–02].
HFD, Högsta förvaltningsdomstolen [The Supreme Administrative Court], the Velling-case, HFD 2018 ref. 75, mål 2149–18 at https://www.domstol.se/hogsta-forvaltningsdomstolen/avgoranden/2018/42000/ [Accessed 2024–01–02].
Södertälje Tingsrätt, 2014–02–21, dom mål nr 2014-B 266. (Not published).

Websites

Civil Rights defenders (CRD), Civil Rights Defenders överklagar dom om tiggerförbud, 12 augusti 2019, https://crd.org/sv/2019/08/12/civil-rights-defenders-overklagar-dom-om-tiggeriforbud/ [Accessed 2023–12–30].
Civil Rights Defenders (CRD), Yttrande angående fråga om fortsatt prövning i ärende 10477–17 NN ./. Vellinge kommun, 2019–01–24 at https://crd.org/wp-content/uploads/2017/09/Begäran-om-att-återuppta-laglighetsprövning-MASKAD.pdf [Accessed 2023–12–30].
Europaportalen 2024, https://www.europaportalen.se/2022/10/sverige-faller-drastiskt-i-jamlikhetsindex [Accessed 2024–01–01].
Statistikmyndigheten (SCB) [Statistics Sweden], Ökande gap mellan kvinnors och mäns partisympatier, at https://www.scb.se/hitta-statistik/artiklar/2021/okande-gap-mellan-kvinnors-och-mans-partisympatier/ [Accessed 2024–01–02].
SWESTAT, De rikaste kommunerna i Sverige i procent av riksmedelvärdet, at https://swestat.se/kommun-skattekraft-inv-med [Accessed 2023–07–06].

10

Administrative Justice and Austerity: The Case of Disputes About Adult Social Care

Jackie Gulland

Introduction

Michael Adler's work on administrative justice has had a profound effect on thinking and research on the topic internationally. He is also a renowned academic supervisor and mentor for early career scholars. He supervised my PhD on administrative justice and social care between 2003 and 2007. This chapter explores the issue twenty years on.

Social care in the UK is situated within a service which is driven by a combination of professional decision making, market forces and rationing of scarce resources. Whilst professional social workers assess people's needs for social care, a very high proportion of services is provided by private or third sector organisations. Resources are limited and are rationed by local authorities according to local priorities, based on risk. There are no absolute rights to social care although legislation provides people with rights to assessment. People seeking support for social care are, by definition, those who are disabled, older people and those with mental health challenges. Structural barriers make it more difficult for these people to be informed about their rights or to challenge decision making.

In the last twenty years, the world of social care has changed in key ways, including the effects of devolution, Brexit and the ongoing impacts of the Covid-19 pandemic. In this chapter, I will consider two key impacts: human

J. Gulland (✉)
University of Edinburgh, Edinburgh, Scotland, UK
e-mail: Jackie.Gulland@ed.ac.uk

S. Cowan and S. Halliday (eds.), *Socio-Legal Generation*, Palgrave Socio-Legal Studies,
https://doi.org/10.1007/978-3-031-67244-6_10

rights and austerity. Although the Human Rights Act was passed in 1998, understanding of and embedding of the principles of human rights have increased, particularly in the devolved nations. Other human rights instruments such as the United Nations Convention on the Rights of Persons with Disabilities have been ratified by the UK Government but are not enforceable in UK courts. Although access to resources was at the heart of disputes about access to services in the early 2000s, the financial crisis of 2008/9, austerity policies in the UK since 2010 and, more recently, deepening financial crisis since Covid-19 and increased demand brought about by an ageing population have meant that resources for social care are even more constrained than they were twenty years ago.

So where does this leave administrative justice in social care? In this chapter, I will explore whether the concept of administrative justice is helpful in understanding allocation of resources and disputes about social care in times of austerity.

Michael Adler has made a significant contribution to research on administrative justice and, in particular, in the role of redress mechanisms in achieving justice in social welfare. In this chapter, I will explore how the concept of administrative justice may be helpful in understanding access to social care services in the UK. Social care has been described as 'mainly invisible' (House of Lords 2022: 9), at least until it affects us personally. During the Covid-19 pandemic, social care became somewhat more visible as the crisis of deaths from Covid-19 in care homes and visiting rights for relatives hit some media headlines. However, it is often thought of as of minority interest to administrative justice scholars.

My own interest in this field grew originally from my work with disabled people's organisations in the 1990s, leading to an opportunity to pursue Masters and then PhD research with Michael Adler as my supervisor. I had worked for years in advice agencies and disability organisations, at the front line of advising people about their rights to social security, guiding them through the tribunal processes, about which Adler has written at length (Adler and Gulland 2003; Adler 2006, 2008). However, there seemed to be a gap when it came to social care. Local authorities had duties to assess people for social care services but potential service users had no rights to services and, it appeared, very few options for pursuing any disputes if they were refused services or if services were inadequate. The main mechanism for challenging decisions about social care was the local authority's internal complaints procedure. My PhD research enabled me to consider how this mechanism worked in enabling fair access to social care services (Gulland 2007). This chapter revisits that issue, twenty years.

To consider the value of an administrative justice approach to decision making and disputes in adult social care in the UK, this chapter provides an introduction to administrative justice. It then provides an overview of social care in the four nations of the UK and considers the various mechanisms for resolving disputes. The chapter continues by looking at how some key changes in social care in the last twenty years may affect our ability to assess the justice of these administrations, in particular, the effects of human rights thinking and austerity on social care resource allocation. The chapter concludes by returning to the concept of administrative justice and whether this can help us to understand justice in social care provision in times of intense pressures on resources.

Administrative Justice

Scholars are divided on the precise meaning of administrative justice (for extensive discussion, see Hertogh et al. 2022), but it is clear that Adler's contribution to the debate has been important. He argues that administrative justice has 'two dimensions': one that concerns initial decision making and another that concerns procedures to correct 'wrong' decisions (Adler 2022: 623). In his many works developing his concept of administrative justice, Adler draws explicitly on the work of Mashaw (1983) who defined administrative justice as 'those qualities of a decision process that provide arguments for the acceptability of its decisions' (p. 24). Adler's work is important because he has extended Mashaw's models to look not only at initial decision making but at the different modes of redress that can be associated with different models of justice. This inclusion of redress mechanisms has been one of Adler's key contributions to the administrative justice debate. This is not the place to critique Adler's extended models of justice. My purpose instead is to consider how his insights might help us to understand the nature of disputes about social care in the 2020s, in particular, in relation to redress mechanisms available.

Adler argues that we can distinguish between 'procedural' and 'substantive' justice (Adler 2010: 131), where procedural justice concerns the way in which decisions are made and substantive justice concerns the outcomes of those processes. Social care decision making happens when people are often at their most vulnerable and where outcomes can make life-changing differences to people's health and wellbeing. So, *how* those decisions are made may sometimes be as important as the results of those decisions.

To explore what this means for administrative justice in social care, the next section considers the legal and policy context of social care in the four nations of the UK, the current mechanisms for redress in each of the four nations and some recent proposals for change.

Social Care in the Four Nations of the UK

Social care is usually considered to mean provision of support for older people, disabled people, those with mental health challenges and unpaid carers. Such provision could include home-based support or residential care. More recently, policy rhetoric has moved away from discussing provision of services as the purpose of social care towards defining social care as a 'means to an end' in enabling people to realise their human rights and/or to enable wellbeing (Needham and Hall 2023: 24). In this chapter, my focus is on social care for adults although there are many overlaps between social care systems for adults and those which provide support to children and families, for example, where families have disabled children or where disabled people have children (Beresford and Slasberg 2023, 19). A distinctive element of social care in the UK is that funding and much organisation of social care is separate from health care, despite continuing policies to integrate the two. Beresford and Slasberg argue that what makes social care 'social' is that it is what 'supports or equips you to live in the social' (Beresford and Slasberg, 2023: 20). Legislative responsibility for social care provision and disputes is different in each of the four nations of England, Wales, Northern Ireland and Scotland. So, any assessment of social care and administrative justice requires a 'four nations' approach.

Despite extensive legislative responsibility for the state to provide social care services in certain circumstances, it is important to remember that most adult social care is provided by unpaid family carers (House of Lords 2022: 27). Unpaid care is often provided willingly but, where state care is inadequate or non-existent, it will usually be unpaid family members who provide support. Legislation in each of the four nations of the UK now provides recognition of unpaid carers as 'rights bearers' in their own right and provides powers and duties to provide for carers. However, there is little evidence that the existence of these rights has led to much in the way of support in practice (House of Lords 2022, Feeley 2021; Needham and Hall 2023; Stewart 2017). So, it is important to recognise that it is unpaid carers who provide the bulk of direct support to family members, rather than the state.

It is also important to remember that not all those who are in receipt of social care services are willing recipients. Social care also includes the state's power to impose 'services' where people are deemed to lack mental capacity or to be at risk to themselves or others. This is particularly the case in relation to mental health services and to residential accommodation, where, as Series reminds us 'the socio-legal landscape of care is haunted by its carceral past' (Series 2022: 1). This means that some disputes about social care concern deprivation of liberty or allegations of abuse or neglect and not just access to services. The law on deprivation of liberty, mental capacity, adult protection and regarding compulsory mental health measures is different in England and Wales, Scotland and Northern Ireland. There are also separate dispute mechanisms for these matters compared to disputes about allocation of resources. For the purposes of this chapter, I will not discuss compulsory care measures but it is important to remember that there are overlaps and grey areas between the compulsory and voluntary care arrangements, particularly where insufficient resources in the community lead to people ending up in institutional care or being subject to compulsory mental health measures (Series 2022: 212).

In England, Wales and Scotland social care funding and assessment of need is the responsibility of local authorities (or combined health and social care partnerships). In Northern Ireland, funding and assessment is the responsibility of the Department of Health. However, in all four nations, social care services are provided, increasingly since the 1990s, by private or third sector organisations. Legislation in the 1990s introduced the idea that the state (local authorities or joint health/social care boards) was responsible for assessing people's needs for services and for making decisions about funding, whether to fund in full or whether to require a financial contribution by the person in need. The provision of services was to be subject to market forces, initially through contracting with private or third sector organisations, where the local authority would commission and fund the service, whilst the day-to-day provision would come from these organisations. Since the 1990s, it has also been possible for authorities to provide personal budgets to those assessed as in need of services with which to purchase services directly. In practice, this policy of personalisation has brought its own problems (Tarrant 2020; Pearson and Ridley 2017; Pearson et al. 2018; Needham and Hall 2023). The combined result of the marketisation of social care services and direct payment arrangements is that direct provision of social care services by the state has become unusual. There is some variation between the four nations, with higher proportions of state provided care homes and home care services in Scotland, Wales and Northern Ireland, compared to England (Needham and Hall 2023: 62). Crucially, social care services are provided within limited budgets, where local authorities must make difficult decisions about priorities within their responsibilities. Linked to these limited budgets, in most cases, people have no statutory 'rights' to particular services or level of services.

Funding arrangements are different in each of the four nations, with both Scotland and Northern Ireland providing at least some home care without a means test, whilst means-testing all residential care. In Wales and England, all social care is means-tested. This means that media interest in care funding has often focused on the personal finances of those requiring care services, with ongoing concerns about how far people should be expected to use their savings or to sell their homes to pay for care. The media debate about care funding often obscures other issues of access to care in the first place or quality of services once provided. There has been discussion in all four nations since the 1990s on how best to reform funding for social care, but the issue of insufficient resources, at both individual and local authority level, remains at the heart of social care provision. For a summary of funding arrangements and policy proposals over the last twenty years or so, see Needham and Hall (2023).

To summarise, in relation to administrative justice, most decisions about assessments of need and funding of social care services are made by local authorities or joint health and social care partnerships, whilst most provision of care is by private or third sector organisations, or within the direct control of the care service user. This means that disputes and redress mechanisms are split between disputes about assessment and funding and disputes regarding quality of provision. Although these different kinds of redress may appear to be distinct, there are overlaps, particularly from the perspective of the person in need of care. My focus in this chapter will be on disputes regarding assessment and funding although I will also discuss briefly disputes about quality of services.

Social Care Redress Mechanisms

A recent House of Lords inquiry into social care found that 'Those who are assessed for their needs do not feel able to challenge the outcome of their assessment' (House of Lords 2022: 149). This contrasts strongly with a recent judicial review decision where it was stated that 'service users like the Claimant *can* access the courts and the LGSCO; legal aid is available; solicitors are available and there is no hindrance to court access' (*R (on the application of HL) v Secretary of State for Health and Social Care* [2023] EWHC866 (Admin) (para 155)).

These two perspectives represent, on the one hand, a bottom up perspective that people find it difficult to understand or challenge decisions in social care and, on the other, a legalistic view that redress mechanisms are available and therefore that there is no problem. In all four nations, the first point of redress for people with concerns about social care is the local authority (or joint local authority/health authority) internal complaints procedure. Dissatisfied complainants can then take further complaints to the relevant ombuds (Local Government and Social Care Ombudsman in England, Public Services Ombudsman for Wales, the Scottish Public Services Ombudsman and the Northern Ireland Public Services Ombudsman). Judicial review is also available if an action or inaction by a local authority may be unlawful or, for example, in breach of the Human Rights Act 1998. As the judge in the case quoted above noted, this does provide the potential for a legal remedy in certain circumstances but the cost and complexity of such legal action are prohibitive and inaccessible for most people, without expert advice.

Some might argue that the availability of a non-legalistic complaints procedure makes it easier for those who wish to raise concerns about social care provision. However, it is not necessarily a simple as this. When I carried out research on social care complaints in the early 2000s, the only redress mechanism for social care in all parts of the UK was the internal local authority complaints procedure. I questioned at the time whether this was the most appropriate mechanism for disputes about social care (Gulland 2007). I concluded that there were a number of problems with using a complaints procedure for disputes, particularly where the dispute concerned allocation of resources or decisions about funding. Internal complaints procedures also suffered from a perceived lack of independence (Gulland 2009). An additional problem with a complaints procedure was that people were often reluctant to make a complaint as the idea of complaining had negative connotations and implied wrongdoing by an individual, when the complainant wanted to challenge a decision or a policy. Complainants also found that the focus on informality in complaints procedures sometimes meant that their concerns were not taken seriously (Gulland 2011). Expert advice and advocacy could help a person to frame their dispute in legal terms, particularly if they wished to challenge a decision about lack of services, inadequate services or about charges for services. This could change their 'complaint' into something that looked more like an appeal.

Since I carried out that research, there has been some movement in redress mechanisms in all four nations, but in England, Wales, Scotland

and Northern Ireland, the main route is still the internal complaints procedure. Reviews of social care redress have continually suggested that appeals procedures might be a more effective form of redress for social care decision making. The Care Act 2014 provides for an appeals procedure in England but this has not yet been implemented. Some local authorities do have 'appeals procedures', separate from complaints procedures but these are not mandatory (Equality and Human Rights Commission 2021: 7). The Public Services Reform (Scotland) Act 2010 introduced standardised complaints procedures and reporting requirements in Scotland but, so far, there have been no moves to introduce appeals. Proposals for a new National Care Service in Scotland include a proposal to 'reform and strengthen complaints and redress processes' (Scottish Government 2022) although no further details are available at the time of writing. A recent proposal for change to social care provision in Northern Ireland did not mention redress mechanisms, although it did propose rights to information and independent advocacy (Department of Health 2022). In Wales, the main avenue of redress is also through the complaints procedure. However, there is a specific option of a 'review' where the dispute concerns charging arrangements. The guidance on reviews suggests that this is a more appropriate approach than a complaint

> Instead, it is to establish a consistent review process for such decisions so that where a person wishes a determination in relation to charging, or the level of a charge, reviewed, they will be able to ask an authority to do this in a relatively straightforward way and in doing so, potentially obviate the need for a person to make a formal complaint to the authority (Welsh Government 2023, s1.2)

Here, the Welsh Government guidance does not explain why a review is more appropriate but the implication is that a review will enable a reconsideration of the decision without the association of blame that might come with a complaint. This guidance relates specifically to charging arrangements where the issues at stake may appear to be more 'factual' than those relating to assessment of need, where interpersonal relationships may be more important. Of course, the current system of internal complaints in the other jurisdictions and right of complaint to an ombuds is based on principles of administrative law and does not assume an allegation of blame. However, this is not necessarily clear to individuals who are unhappy with a decision (or lack of a decision) when it comes to their immediate needs for social care services.

The claimant in the judicial review case noted at the start of this section challenged the legality of the lack of appeals in social care in England. In this case, the claimant argued, amongst other things, that the current system of complaints about social care was not compliant with Article 8 of the

European Convention on Human Rights (right to private and family life). However, the court found that the current arrangements were sufficient. This decision confirmed the legality of the Department of Health and Social Care's decision to postpone the introduction of an appeals procedure in social care in England although it does seem rather optimistic regarding the ease of access. Inquiries into social care continually find that people find it difficult to challenge decisions (or non-decisions) about social care, there is a lack information about their rights and that there is a shortage of advice (House of Lords 2022, Equality and Human Rights Commission 2021, Feeley 2021, Braye and Preston-Shoot 2020). Research into access to justice in the current economic climate, given cuts to legal aid and insufficient provision of advice agencies, would also question the claim that 'there is no hindrance to court access' (Mullen 2016; Robins and Newman 2021).

The Care Act 2014 in England, proposals for reform in Scotland and the implementation of financial reviews in Wales suggest that moving to an appeals procedure has been recognised as more effective form of redress than complaints procedures for social care decision making and financial matters but has not yet been fully implemented in any part of the UK.

In a recent chapter, Adler (2022) compares two mechanisms for achieving administrative justice: tribunals and ombuds,[1] arguing that they have two different purposes. Tribunals are primarily intended to review or substitute an original decision. Ombuds services on the other hand are primarily concerned with improving services at a collective level by providing recommendations for service improvements, as well as providing an apology or compensation for an individual complainant (Adler 2022: 631). There have been considerable developments in ombuds services in the last twenty years, with ombuds in all four nations taking on new responsibilities and taking more active roles in investigating complaints and providing advice to local authorities regarding their own internal complaints procedures (Gill and Kirkham 2020; Thomas 2023). This does provide an opportunity for an independent review of the complaint although limited by the fact that few dissatisfied social care users will take their grievances this far and constrained by the powers of the relevant ombuds. I will return to some recent ombuds decisions below.

If someone has a concern about the quality of services, their first contact for raising a concern is with the service provider, followed by contacting the appropriate regulatory body. Service providers are (mostly) regulated by the regulators in each of the four nations (Care Quality Commission in England,

[1] The use of the term 'ombuds' has recently replaced the more familiar 'ombudsman' in order to maintain gender neutrality. On the other hand, many of the ombuds institutions retain the term 'ombudsman'.

the Care Inspectorate in Wales, the Care Inspectorate in Scotland and the Regulation and Quality Improvement Authority in Northern Ireland). These bodies have a responsibility for the maintenance of standards and have powers to inspect, make recommendations for change and ultimately to close down unsatisfactory services. Despite these complex regulatory powers, shocking examples of abuse and poor quality care continue to beset social care services (Meenan 2016; Series 2022; Needham and Hall 2023). There is some overlap between responsibilities of regulators and of local authorities as local authorities retain responsibility for ensuring that human rights are upheld in any services where the local authority has commissioned the service. For example, if someone lives in accommodation provided by a private or third sector organisation but the local authority has commissioned and funded that service, the local authority retains a responsibility to uphold the resident's human rights. An example of this is provided in a recent Local Government and Social Care Ombudsman report relating to a person with a learning disability, where the Ombudsman found that excessive use of sleeping tablets in a care home impacted the resident's human rights. Although the care service was provided by an independent body, the local authority had failed in its responsibility to safeguard residents and to monitor the services which it commissioned (Local Government and Social Care Ombudsman, 2022: 10).

Inquiries into redress and complaints in social care continually emphasise the need for good information and advice to enable people to realise their rights in relation to social care. In England, Wales and Scotland, legislation relating to adult social care requires statutory bodies to provide information and advice and advocacy in relation to social care. In Northern Ireland, improved information and advice is proposed as an integral part of any change to adult social care (Department of Health 2022). However, people in need of social care services are often those with the most challenges in securing this advice and advocacy (Beresford and Slasberg 2023, House of Lords 2022). There are also concerns about independence and potential conflicts of interest if such advice and advocacy is not independent of the local authority or the service provider.

Human Rights

One of the key changes in social care culture and provision since the early 2000s is the rise of human rights as a concern in social care provision. The Human Rights Act 1998 incorporated the European Convention on

Human Rights into UK law. Other human rights provisions which are relevant to social care include the United Nations Convention on the Rights of Persons with Disabilities (UNCRPD), the United Nations Principles for Older Persons (UNPOP), the United Nations Convention on the Elimination of All Forms of Discrimination against Women (CEDAW) and the United Nations Convention on the Rights of the Child (UNCRC) (in relation to disabled children and to young carers). These latter provisions are not binding but have had important cultural effects on legislation and policy making in relation to social care.

Cultural change from these human rights instruments has also led to explicit reference to human rights principles in social care legislation, particularly in Scotland. The proposals for a National Care Service in Scotland take this further, by claiming that the service 'is essential to the realisation of human rights' (National Care Service (Scotland) Bill 2022, S1 (a)(i)). In Wales, the Social Services and Well-being Act 2014 also promotes wellbeing, independent living and participation at the heart of social care provision. However, as with services in Scotland, it has been criticised for being mostly rhetoric: 'in practice, social care is not yet enabling people to live the lives of their choice and is sometimes very far from doing so' (Tarrant 2021: 10).

In other parts of the UK, the emphasis on Human Rights is less explicit. The Care Act 2014 in England changed the language of social care from 'assessing need' to 'enabling rights'. The practical effect of this cultural change has been to frame social care policies in terms of user 'choice' or voice, with an emphasis on choice in how care is provided, for example, through personalised budgets or self-directed support (Needham and Hall 2023: 39). In Northern Ireland, a paper on social care reform in 2017 emphasised personalisation, wellbeing and the value of social care and is under consultation for implementation (Department of Health 2022). This report defines social care as 'to improve and, where appropriate, to protect people's social well-being by empowering and strengthening the capacity of individuals, families and communities to bring about positive changes' (p. 9). The more recent consultation proposes that any reform should lead to 'A human rights based system of service provision' (p. 15).

This change of focus is also reflected in disputes, particularly once complaints reach the ombuds stage. Whilst the main focus of ombuds services is administration (or maladministration), a recent report by the English Local Government and Social Care Ombudsman argues that 'Our findings and recommendations increasingly refer to legislation like the Human Rights Act and Equality Act' (Local Government and Social Care Ombudsman 2022: 5). It goes on to say that complaints procedures should include attention to human rights and that 'we do not expect members of the public to frame their complaints in the language of human rights' and that it is the duty of local authorities to recognise where there has been a potential breach and to assist the public in making rights-based complaints (Local Government and Social Care Ombudsman 2022: 19). Although complaining to an ombuds can therefore enable a person to raise human rights concerns, principles of administrative justice have focused on decision making, information provision and legality but have been unable to address the question of resources at the heart of most disputes about assessment and provision of social care.

For example, Braye and Preston Shoot argue that ombuds cases, before and after the implementation of the Care Act 2014 in England, show that the Act did not confer new rights to services and that disputes focused on issues of illegality or maladministration. Examples have included failure to provide effective information or reasons for decisions, or occasionally, failure to provide an effective assessment (2020: 3). Problems in implementing the principles of the Act have also been compounded by constraints on staff time, staff vacancies and that the need to devote 'time to complex cases frequently collides with organisation systems that have to prioritise management of workload demand' (p. 3). This point has been confirmed by Thomas who argues that 'put together, the LGSCO's service improvement recommendations are aimed at bureaucratising councils by imposing order and managerial oversight upon how they administer and deliver services' (Thomas 2023). We can also see examples of this in Scottish ombuds decisions which have also found examples of poor communication and failures to assess needs adequately but that failures to provide services because of resources or local authority priorities did not constitute maladministration (https://www.spso.org.uk/decision-reports/2022/october/decision-report-202003481-202003481). (https://www.spso.org.uk/decision-reports/2020/november/decision-report-201901360-201901360).

Case law on human rights in social care has identified key areas of risk to human rights, for example, in relation to the European Convention of Human Rights: Article 1 (right to life), Article 3 (dignity), Article 5 (liberty and security) and Article 8 (respect for private and family life) (Braye and Preston-Shoot 2020; Scottish Human Rights Commission 2020; Smith 2018). However, legal action has been less successful in asserting rights to resources, as cases have consistently upheld the findings in *R v Gloucestershire County Council, ex party Barry* [1997] UKHL 58 and *McDonald v the United Kingdom* [2014] ECHR141, which permit local authorities to take account of resources in making decisions about allocation of resources.

Policies on social care in the UK claim in some areas to be driven by human rights thinking, particularly in Scotland at a policy level, but also in recent challenges through the courts and in some ombuds decisions. However, the rhetoric of human rights contrasts strongly with the problems arising from constraints on resources. In the end, most social care disputes *are* about resources, whether about access to additional hours or to service provision or about the quality of care, which could often, although not always, be resolved by improved staffing, staff conditions, staff training or monitoring. Recent trends towards recognising social care within a human rights framework provide a potential for more legalised decision making. Whilst there have been moves towards introducing more individualised appeals or reviews within social care, there has been very little change in practice, mainly because of the underlying problem of resources.

Austerity

Several recent reports have described social care in the four nations of the UK as 'in crisis' (Braye and Preston-Shoot 2020; Needham and Hall 2023; Competitions and Market Authority 2017; House of Lords 2022). Needham and Hall note that the pressures on social care have occurred across the four nations of the UK but that some pressures are more acute in England because of funding cuts (p. 22). Whilst life expectancy has been falling in deprived areas (Loopstra et al. 2016), 'healthy life expectancy' has also been falling, leading to larger numbers of older people in deprived areas with more health issues, leading to a need for social care services (Office of National Statistics 2022). Lack of suitable care services has also led to more older people in deprived areas using crisis NHS services such as Accident and Emergency services (Age UK 2023). Austerity has had particularly harsh effects on disabled people. Stuckler et al. (2017) have argued that 'there is clear evidence that austerity is regressive, thus widening socio-economic inequalities'. In the case of people who may seek social care services, this includes severe cutbacks in disability benefits. In her book on austerity and disability, Frances Ryan vividly portrays the realities of people struggling on low incomes, the effects of social security cuts and inadequate social care services (Ryan 2019). The Covid-19 pandemic both revealed and exacerbated existing health inequalities (Bambra et al. 2021). The Care Quality Commission has shown that access to social care is structurally unequal with those from deprived areas and those with complex needs and from minority ethnic backgrounds finding access to care more difficult, which, it argues, is in breach of the Equality Act

2010. People with learning disabilities and autism have particular challenges in accessing suitable care 'despite multiple reviews and reports over decades' (Care Quality Commission 2022). These bleak statistics show how the overall context of austerity is having a direct effect on the health, wellbeing and longevity of people who may been in need of social care.

These reports point to a range of reasons for the crises in social care, including the pressure on staffing brought about by Brexit, the general ageing of the population and the additional pressures created by the Covid-19 pandemic. However, at least some of the crisis can be laid directly at the door of austerity measures, both in relation to cuts to local authority spending and in cuts to wider welfare measures such as social security and increasing health inequalities. In the face of these extreme pressures, it becomes difficult to imagine how people can access services or how justice might be achieved through changes to decision making and dispute mechanisms. However, it is still helpful to consider whether decision-making can be assessed from the perspective of fairness.

Administrative Justice and Participation

Most decision making in adult social care is made on the front line by social work professionals who bring professional social work values and expertise to their work. A key element of professionalism in social work is a commitment to human rights. The British Association of Social Workers states that 'Human Rights are at the centre of every-day social work practice' (BASW 2019: 5). The BASW guidance on human rights argues that social work as a human rights profession 'means that engaging with questions of human rights extends beyond the application of specific laws to a more holistic human rights orientation' (2019: 5). In this sense, the social work profession positions itself as a professional workforce which works to its own ethical and moral codes which go beyond strictly legal requirements to comply with legislation such as the Human Rights Act. Braye and Preston-Shoot have been particularly vocal regarding the relationship between professional social work values and adherence to the rule of law. 'Neither the law nor social work values, alone, will enable practitioners to decide what they ought to do' (Braye and Preston-Shoot 2016: 7) and that 'an exclusively legalistic model, where the law is elevated to become the main form of admissible knowledge, is inadequate for the complexities social workers face' (p. 8). Ife et al. (2022) make the explicit point that the role of social workers is to expand understanding of human rights by asking the question 'what human rights are at risk?' (p. 176).

It is interesting to note that one recommendation of the recent review of social care in Scotland was that social workers 'should be focused on realising those [human] rights rather than being hampered in the first instance by considerations of eligibility and cost' (Feeley 2021: 14). This social work profession perspective shows a clear conflict between 'professional' values where social work professionals need adequate time to carry out assessments effectively and the bureaucratic requirements of local authorities whose focus is more on efficient management of resources within organisations. Social work professional values also include participation and co-production with the people who use services, as a basic human rights principle, although the history of social care decision making in the UK shows that this has rarely been possible, given the cultural and financial constraints within which social workers operate (Beresford and Slasberg 2023; Manthorpe 2020).

Disability activists have stressed the importance of enabling people to make their own decisions about social care, based on the principles in the UNCRPD (Witcher 2015; Beresford and Slasberg 2023). Although the UK is a signatory to this Convention, the Convention has not been incorporated into law in the UK although there are plans by the Scottish Government to include the Convention in a Human Rights Bill for Scotland (Scottish Government 2023). Amongst other things, the UNCRPD provides for a right to independent living, described as the 'equal right of all persons with disabilities to live in the community with choices equal to others' (UNCRPD, article 19). Beresford and Slasberg argue that a complete rethinking of social care provision in the UK, in line with this principle, would lead to a transformation from a welfare-based to a rights-based system (Beresford and Slasberg 2023). The difference this would make from an administrative justice perspective would be that the principle of decision making by welfare professionals would be transferred to a participatory process where people in need of support would be equal partners in those decisions. They argue that this requires domestic legislation to provide for 'a legal right' for people to have their needs for independent living assessed and costed without regard to resources and a corresponding legal obligation on governments to set budgets based on those needs.

The Feeley report in Scotland in part reflects these demands, with its appeal to 'shift the paradigm' from managing need to enabling rights (Feeley 2021). The Scottish Government's intention to implement the findings of the report by establishing a National Care Service, although repeating these principles, has not included a right to services or a commitment to fully funding such services (Scottish Government 2022). Indeed, it has been criticised for failing to address this fundamental problem (Beresford and Slasberg 2023: 151).

Beresford and Slasberg also argue that there should be 'a review and appeals process independent' of the body responsible for decision making (2023: 129). It is interesting to reflect on how this might work in practice if the decision making process itself is participatory. A respondent to a recent inquiry into complaints regarding self-directed support in Scotland suggested that there was a 'perception due to the participatory ambition of the [Social Care (Self-directed Support) Scotland Act 2013] that some mechanism for [formal redress] was thought to be unnecessary' (University of Strathclyde and In Control Scotland 2022: 17). This insight is also recognised by Needham and Hall who argue that social care provision in the four nations of the UK can be considered in relation to two paradigms: 'standardisation' and 'differentiated care', where standardisation tends to focus on 'clearly defined and enforceable rights and duties' whilst differentiated care is based on a model of 'negotiation between stakeholders' (Needham and Hall 2023: 165). In this negotiatory model, rights take a back seat. Evidence from this can be found in the introduction of personalisation and direct payments in social care, where decisions about services may be in the control of the service user or negotiated between service users and assessors but where budgets are decided at local authority level. However, this has led to a bureaucratisation of decision-making about resources, cutting out the service user from the key aspects of decision-making (Pearson and Ridley 2017).

Improved review or appeals procedures might be helpful in enabling people to challenge decisions about eligibility or resources but are less helpful where people are themselves 'purchasers' of social care services. Given the move towards outsourcing provision of care to the private market, 'purchasers' are able to use their consumer power to choose their preferred options for care and to 'exit' by choosing another provider if the first one does not meet their needs. Some users of social care services are direct purchasers of services, either because they are 'self-funding' (because they do not qualify for means-tested state funding) or because they are using a personal budget, funded by the state. Even at this extreme end of social care funding, it is very difficult for people to use their consumer power in this way, because of limitations in the supply of care, because people often do not understand or have sufficient information about care and funding options, because people make decisions about care options at points of extreme crisis (for example, on discharge from hospital or sudden changes in their health or personal circumstances), have health issues or impairments such as dementia which make decision making difficult and because dispute mechanisms are not easy to navigate (Baxter et al. 2021; Competitions and Market Authority 2017). The Competitions and Market Authority report from 2017 points to areas of private law, where people living in care homes may have consumer rights to protection or redress but these are also difficult for people to understand or pursue. Where the local authority has been involved in the assessment, funding or purchasing of private services, there remains a duty to comply with the Human Rights Act 1998, which places a duty of care on local authorities (Local Government and Social Care Ombudsman 2022: 10). Despite the strong move to marketisation in social care across all four nations, the market is rarely a mechanism for ensuring fairness in the context of extreme inequality.

Conclusion

Despite some key policy statements about social care which change the focus from 'meeting needs' to 'enabling wellbeing', there is only some evidence of much practical change in enabling access to social care services across the four nations in the last twenty years. There is much promising rhetoric but resource constraints continue to underlie most decision-making about social care services. In this chapter, I have considered whether there would be value in looking more closely at human rights considerations which might enable the potential for participation and co-production in social care decision making. Social work professional values point to the importance of human rights thinking in assessments for social care, whilst disability activists have called for participation and co-production as the most important values. Much social care decision making happens when people are at their most vulnerable and where outcomes can make life-changing differences to people's health and wellbeing. For others, social care provision is a long-term feature of their struggle to participate fully in society. There is potential here for radical reconsideration of how social care works. Although some of the rhetoric in Scotland has embraced these ideas, there is little sign of sufficient funding being in place to enable meaningful implementation in the near future.

In the meantime, underlying everything is a landscape of austerity, poverty and intense deprivation and inequality for those most vulnerable in our communities. I have argued elsewhere that looking beyond the concerns of administrative justice and including a social justice perspective can help us to put procedural concerns in context (Gulland 2022). This leaves us with question of whether greater procedural fairness, either in decision-making or in redress, would really make a difference regarding fair access to social care. Reviews of redress in social care continually recommend more formal appeal or review procedures in place of complaints procedures. These would certainly enable a clearer focus on individual redress and might avoid some of the problems that beset complaints procedures, for example, by requiring clarity about when decisions have or have not been made and might enable a clearer focus on the rights of appellants to challenge decisions. So long as there is no specific right to services, it is difficult to imagine how a rights-based appeal process would work in practice. However, the principle of a right to challenge a decision may enable people to recognise their right to participate in the process. A participatory human rights approach may help to recognise people's rights to dignity and humanity.

References

Adler, M. (2006). Tribunal Reform, Proportionate Dispute Resolution and the Pursuit of Administrative Justice. *Modern Law Review, 69*, 958–985.

Adler, M. (2008). The Idea of Proportionality in Dispute Resolution. *Journal of Social Welfare and Family Law, 30*, 309–321.

Adler, M. (2010). Understanding and Analysing Administrative Justice. In M. Adler (ed.), *Administrative Justice in Context*. London: Hart.

Adler, M. (2022). The Future of Administrative Justice. In M. Hertogh et al. (eds.), *The Oxford Handbook of Administrative Justice*. Oxford University Press.

Adler, M., and Gulland, J. (2003). *Tribunal Users' Experiences, Perceptions and Expectations: a literature review*. London: Council on Tribunals.

Age UK. (2023). *The State of Health and Care of Older People in England 2023*. Available at: https://www.ageuk.org.uk/globalassets/age-uk/documents/reports-and-publications/reports-and-briefings/health--wellbeing/age_uk_briefing_state_of_health_and_care_of_older_people_july2023.pdf.

Bambra, C., Lynch, J., and Smith, K. E. (2021). *The Unequal Pandemic: COVID-19 and Health Inequalities*. Bristol: Policy Press (Policy Press Shorts Insights).

Baxter, K., Wilberforce, M., and Birks, Y. (2021). What Skills Do Older Self-Funders in England Need to Arrange and Manage Social Care? Findings from a Scoping Review of the Literature. *The British Journal of Social Work, 51*(7), 2703–2721.

Beresford, P., and Slasberg, C. (2023). *The Future of Social Care: From Problem to Rights-Based Sustainable Solution*. Cheltenham, UK: Edward Elgar Publishing.

Braye, S., and Preston-Shoot, M. (2016). *Practising Social Work Law*. 4th edition. London: Macmillan Education/Palgrave (Practical social work).

Braye, Suzy, and Preston-Shoot, M. (2020). Introduction: The Care Act 2014—Outcomes in Context. In S. Braye and M. Preston-Shoot (eds.), *The Care Act 2014: Wellbeing in Practice*. London: Sage.

British Association of Social Workers. (2019). *Social Work and Human Rights: A Practice Guide*. Available at: https://www.basw.co.uk/resources/social-work-and-human-rights-practice-guide.

Care Quality Commission. (2022). *State of Care 2021/22*. Available at: https://www.cqc.org.uk/publication/state-care-202122.

Competitions and Market Authority. (2017). *Care Homes Market Study: Summary of Final Report*. Available at: https://www.gov.uk/government/publications/care-homes-market-study-summary-of-final-report/care-homes-market-study-summary-of-final-report.

Department of Health. (2022). *Reform of Adult Social Care Northern Ireland Consultation Document*. Available at: https://www.health-ni.gov.uk/consultations/consultation-reform-adult-social-care.

Equality and Human Rights Commission. (2021). *Inquiry Into Challenging Social Care Decisions*. Available at: https://www.equalityhumanrights.com/en/inquiries-andinvestigations/inquiry-challenging-decisions-about-adult-social-care.

Feeley, D. (2021). *Independent Review of Adult Social Care in Scotland*. Available at: https://www.gov.scot/publications/independent-review-adult-social-care-scotland/pages/0/.

Gill, C., and Kirkham, R. (2020). Introduction. In R. Kirkham and C. Gill (eds.), *A Manifesto for Ombudsman Reform*, pp. 1–11. Cham: Springer International Publishing.

Gulland, J. (2007). *Complaining, Appealing or Just Getting it Sorted Out: Complaints Procedures for Community Care Service Users*. PhD Thesis: University of Edinburgh.

Gulland, J. (2009). Independence in Complaints Procedures: Lessons from Community Care. *Journal of Social Welfare and Family Law, 31*, 59–72.

Gulland, J. (2011). Taking Complaints Seriously: The Role of Informality in Complaints About Public Services. *Social Policy and Society, 10*(4), 483–494.

Gulland, J. (2022). Social Justice and Administrative Justice. In M. Hertogh, R. Kirkham, R. Thomas, and J. Tomlinson (Eds.), *The Oxford Handbook of Administrative Justice*. Oxford University Press.

Hertogh, M., Kirkham, R., Thomas, R., and Tomlinson, J. (Eds.). (2022). *The Oxford Handbook of Administrative Justice*. Oxford University Press.

House of Lords Adult Social Care Committee. (2022). *A "Gloriously Ordinary Life": Spotlight on Adult Social Care*. HL Paper 99. House of Lords. https://publications.parliament.uk/pa/ld5803/ldselect/ldadultsoc/99/9902.htm.

Ife, J., Soldatić, K., and Briskman, L. (2022). *Human Rights and Social Work: Towards Rights-Based Practice*. 4th edn. Cambridge: Cambridge University Press.

Local Government and Social Care Ombudsman. (2022). *Equal Justice: Learning Lessons from Complaints About People's Human Rights*. Available at: https://www.lgo.org.uk/assets/attach/6342/FR-Human-rights-autumn-2022-v1.4.pdf.

Loopstra, R., et al. (2016). Austerity and Old-Age Mortality in England: A Longitudinal Cross-Local Area Analysis, 2007–2013. *Journal of the Royal Society of Medicine, 109*(3), 109–116.

Manthorpe, J. (2020). Social Work and the Care Act 2014. In S. Braye, M. Preston-Shoot (eds.), *The Care Act 2014: Wellbeing in Practice*. Sage.
Mashaw, J. (1983). *Bureaucratic Justice: Managing Social Security Disability Claims.* New Haven: Yale University Press.
Meenan, H. (2016). The Residential Care of Older People in England and the Special Relevance of Dignity and Human Rights. In H. Meenan, N. Rees, and I. Doron (eds.), *Towards Human Rights in Residential Care for Older Persons: International Perspectives.* Routledge.
Mullen, T. (2016). Access to Justice in Administrative Law and Administrative Justice. In E. Palmer, et al. (eds.), *Access to Justice: Beyond the Policies and Politics of Austerity*. Oxford: Hart Publishing.
Needham, C., and Hall, P. (2023). *Social Care in the UK's Four Nations: Between Two Paradigms.* Bristol University Press.
Office of National Statistics. (2022). *Health State Life Expectancies by National Deprivation Deciles, England: 2018 to 2020.* Available at: https://www.ons.gov.uk/peoplepopulationandcommunity/healthandsocialcare/healthinequalities/bulletins/healthstatelifeexpectanciesbyindexofmultipledeprivationimd/2018to2020#main-points.
Pearson, C., and Ridley, J. (2017). Is Personalization the Right Plan at the Wrong Time? Re-thinking Cash-for-Care in an Age of Austerity. *Social Policy & Administration, 51*(7), 1042–1059.
Pearson, C., Watson, N., and Manji, K. (2018). Changing the Culture of Social Care in Scotland: Has a Shift to Personalization Brought About Transformative Change? *Social Policy & Administration, 52*(3), 662–676.
Robins, J., and Newman, D. (2021). *Justice in a Time of Austerity: Stories from a System in Crisis.* Bristol University Press.
Ryan, F. (2019). *Crippled: Austerity and the Demonization of Disabled People*. Verso.
Scottish Government. (2022). *National Care service: Statement of Benefits.* Available at: https://www.gov.scot/publications/national-care-service-statement-benefits.
Scottish Human Rights Commission. (2020). *COVID-19, Social Care and Human Rights: Impact Monitoring Report*. Available at: https://www.scottishhumanrights.com/media/2102/covid-19-social-care-monitoring-report-vfinal.pdf.
Series, L. (2022). *Deprivation of Liberty in the Shadows of the Institution.* Bristol: Policy Press.
Smith, S. (2018). *Human Rights and Social Care : Putting Rights into Practice.* Dunedin Academic Press.
Stuckler, D., et al. (2017). Austerity and Health: The Impact in the UK and Europe. *European Journal of Public Health, 27*(suppl_4), 18–21.
Stewart, A. (2017). Carers as Legal Subjects. In R. Harding, R. Fletcher, and C. Beasley (eds.) *Revaluing Care in Theory, Law and Policy: Cycles and Connections.* Abingdon: Routledge.
Tarrant, A. (2020). Personal Budgets in Adult Social Care: The Fact and the Fiction of the Care Act 2014. *Journal of Social Welfare and Family Law, 42*(3), 281–298.

Tarrant, A. (2021). *Adult Social Care Reform in Wales*. Wales Governance Centre. Available at: https://www.cardiff.ac.uk/__data/assets/pdf_file/0006/2569623/Tarrant-2021-Social-Care-Reform-in-Wales-Final.pdf.

Thomas, R. (2023). The English Local Government and Social Care Ombudsman: Systemic Administrative Justice and Bureaucratisation (Part II). *Public Law* (July), 424–447.

University of Strathclyde and In Control Scotland. (2022). *Accountability and the Implementation of Self-Directed Support: Complaints, Redress, and Human Rights Principles in Practice*. https://www.in-controlscotland.org/_files/ugd/fd9368_d8612fbdd5ce4486b71c2fde0110d89a.pdf.

Welsh Government. (2023). *Social Services and Well-Being (Wales) Act 2014 Part 4 and 5 Code of Practice (Charging and Financial Assessment)*. Available at: https://www.gov.wales/sites/default/files/publications/2023-04/parts-4-and-5-code-of-practice-april-2023.pdf.

Witcher, S. (2015). *Inclusive Equality: A Vision for Social Justice*. Bristol: Policy Press.

11

Afterwords to Socio-Legal Generation: Essays in Honour of Michael Adler

Jonathan Simon

Perhaps not surprisingly, the chapters in this volume devoted to the socio-legal contributions of Professor (emeritus) Michael ("Mike") Adler, are a lot like Mike himself: immediately engaging, unassuming, richly theoretical in imagination without (much) use of jargon, strikingly well informed on the details of politics, policy, and law, concerned with compelling issues like social welfare, prisons, and due process, and grounded in history, both of the past and the present. While reading them together could never be as fun as a long conversation with Mike during a rambling walk through his beloved Edinburgh, the collective effect of so many superb scholars whose work has been touched by Mike's is to find oneself on a very informed walk through Mike's major contributions including his expansion and re-reading of Jerry Mashaw's typology of forms of administrative justice, his work on law and discretion, his pioneering effort to bring ideas of administrative justice into dialog with prison studies, and his remarkably early and prescient interest in the effects of computerization of benefits administration on benefit uptake and procedural fairness.

In a volume that explicitly locates itself not just in Mike's work but in a generation that introduced socio-legal studies to the UK, and where so many of the contributors trained with as graduate students or collaborated with

J. Simon (✉)
Lance Robbins Professor of Criminal Justice, UC Berkeley School of Law, Berkeley, CA, USA
e-mail: jssimon@berkeley.edu

S. Cowan and S. Halliday (eds.), *Socio-Legal Generation*, Palgrave Socio-Legal Studies,
https://doi.org/10.1007/978-3-031-67244-6_11

Mike or recognized their research destiny in one of his many cross disciplinary conferences and edited volumes, I am naturally left thinking about what one might call Adlerian imperatives of socio-legal research; in short, *Mike as model*.

Readers can add their own after reading this volume, but my short list includes, in no particular order of importance or even stage of research:

- Always be considering administration because gatekeepers and decision-makers always lie between law and society, between law on the books and the law in action. While not every socio-legal scholar sets out to study the administrative state as it is conventionally conceived, to the extent that they are capturing the way law touches everyday life they will be encountering administrative decision-making.
- Because of the inevitability of administration in law there can never be only one mode or measure of administrative justice. Whether six, four, or three, we have to recognize that different ideas of justice follow from different sources of legitimation. Furthermore we have to consider administrative justice as it is to be evaluated both internally and externally.
- Whether you call it discourse, values or narratives, the words administrators use to describe what they do and why they do it, matters. Whether we as researchers regard it as a form of false consciousness or symbolic compliance, the terms in which decision-makers think and talk about their decisions are a kind of sociological event all its own.
- Socio-legal work should be grounded in historical understanding. Social policies aimed at the poor in the Anglophone world have evolved continuously since at least the sixteenth century and the institutions we study are always undergoing processes of dynamic change which ironically we can best capture if we come at them from a knowledge of how things were and might have been different.
- Get close to your subject. Walk in their shoes if possible and always take their values and their experiences seriously and generously.
- Never assume that law is its own power, but rather examine carefully the forms of power that are brought to bear to make law work (whether computer programs or human rights treaties).

This book also names a "socio-legal generation" and reminds us that the best social science is not value neutral but value sensitive. In its deepest sociological sense, generation is not just birth cohort (although that's inevitably relevant), but also a collective set of meanings and beliefs shaped by exposure to a distinctive historical conjecture (in the Stuart Hall, Antonio Gramsci sense of a particular political and social context). Born during or just after World War II and raised in societies coming to grips with the magnitude of the Nazi and Soviet crimes against humanity and the legacies of colonialism, the socio-legal generation came to the subjects of law and justice with a deep awareness of the burdens of history and the hubris of government.

Like others in this generation, Mike's interest in administrative justice went along with a deep awareness of the deficits in contemporary societies of racial and social justice. In Mike's case this took an activist turn that led him to the American South at the peak of the civil rights movement in Mississippi and into organizing at University to turn public opinion against apartheid in South Africa (Mulcahy this volume). In this respect Mike and his generational colleagues stand in stark contrast to the first generation of American Legal Realists and other Progressives whose appealing anti-formalism in law went along with a presumption of White supremacy and sometimes a comfort with authoritarian forms of administration in the name of efficient government.

This generation also experienced the promise of the postwar democracies to create more truly egalitarian societies and world order. In the UK this took the form of historic welfare institutions and human rights treaties (in stark contrast to the US, see Kagan this volume), both of which have been under sustained attack in recent years. During Mike's decades of studying social benefit administration in the UK, social policy shifted from trying to increase the public's use of benefits to increasing the stigma associated with benefits and the use of sanctions to take them from those who do not meet idealized criteria of desert; but its residual commitment to income, equality, and integration has made it possible for Mike to remain a critic through governments moving steadily deeper into the politics of austerity. One of the contributions of great students of the administrative state like Adler, Jerry Mashaw, and Philip Selznick, is a reminder how the administrative state with its path dependence can protect the gains of social justice won by the social justice movements of the past.

This is perhaps most salient as a new generation begins to assume power both academically and politically. Michael Adler represents, in my view, the very best that the long Baby Boom generation had to offer in social values and social analyses. In the global North, including Adler's post-war England, Boomers inherited a bold experiment in creating mixed economies aimed at achieving social integration and democratic engagement through an expanded welfare state. Mike in his research charted the potential and pitfalls of this new governmentality, especially in terms of its relation to equality, dignity, and due process. They (and I'm a trailing edge part of this generation too) also witnessed the rise of a neo-conservative, neo-liberal counter offensive favoring markets, responsibilization, and punitive responses to less than perfect behavior. Mike also followed this arc and his powerful work on benefits sanctions remains one of the defining characterizations of this post-welfare moment (along with my colleague Loic Wacquant's discussion of prisons and workfare (Wacquant, 2014: 238-256).

This book and its opportunities to revisit the major debates around administrative governance that Adler's career tracks come at an opportune time as we see a broad retreat of the neoliberal political economy consensus about trade and welfare in favor of both right- and left-wing agendas of reconstruction. Many of the institutions that Mike studied, including prisons and benefit sanctioning systems, along with related forms of administrative power like the immigration and asylum systems, are the very heart of contemporary political and policy debate. As welfare and authoritarian interventions both become more plausible across the globe, the fundamental questions that gave rise to the modern socio-legal movement since the 1960s have become new again. What forms of inequality are being recast and reproduced even as governments claim to shift their attention away from elites? How can the possibilities of justice latent in the classical model of legal due process be realized in a world of increasing administrative power?

Reference

Wacquant, Loïc. (2014). Crafting the Neoliberal State: Workfare and Prisonfare in the Bureaucratic Field. In *Bourdieu's Theory of Social Fields*, pp. 238–256. Routledge.

SPRINGER NATURE

GPSR Compliance

The European Union's (EU) General Product Safety Regulation (GPSR) is a set of rules that requires consumer products to be safe and our obligations to ensure this.

If you have any concerns about our products, you can contact us on ProductSafety@springernature.com

In case Publisher is established outside the EU, the EU authorized representative is:

Springer Nature Customer Service Center GmbH
Europaplatz 3
69115 Heidelberg, Germany

The manufacturer's authorised representative in the EU is Springer
Nature Customer Service Centre GmbH, Europaplatz 3, 69115 Heidelberg,
Germany. If you have any concerns regarding our products, please
contact ProductSafety@springernature.com

Printed and bound by CPI Group (UK) Ltd, Croydon, CR0 4YY
01/10/2026
02225903-0019